Social History in Perspective

General Editor: Jeremy Black

Social History in Perspective is a series of in-depth studies of the many topics in social, cultural and religious history for students. They also give the student clear surveys of the subject and present the most recent research in an accessible way.

PUBLISHED

John Belchem *Popular Radicalism in Nineteenth-Century Britain*
Sue Bruley *Women in Britain since 1900*
Simon Dentith *Society and Cultural Forms in Nineteenth-Century England*
Joyce M. Ellis *The Georgian Town, 1680–1840*
Peter Fleming *Family and Household in Medieval England*
Harry Goulbourne *Race Relations in Britain since 1945*
Tim Hitchcock *English Sexualities, 1700–1800*
Sybil M. Jack *Towns in Tudor and Stuart Britain*
Helen M. Jewell *Education in Early Modern England*
Alan Kidd *State, Society and the Poor in Nineteenth-Century England*
Arthur J. McIvor *A History of Work in Britain, 1880–1950*
Hugh McLeod *Religion and Society in England, 1850–1914*
Donald M. MacRaild *Irish Migrants in Modern Britain, 1750–1922*
Donald M. MacRaild and David E. Martin *Labour in British Society, 1830–1914*
Christopher Marsh *Popular Religion in the Sixteenth Century*
Michael A. Mullett *Catholics in Britain and Ireland, 1558–1829*
R. Malcolm Smuts *Culture and Power in England, 1585–1685*
John Spurr *English Puritanism, 1603–1689*
W. B. Stephens *Education in Britain, 1750–1914*
Heather Swanson *Medieval British Towns*
David Taylor *Crime, Policing and Punishment in England, 1750–1914*
N. L. Tranter *British Population in the Twentieth Century*
Ian D. Whyte *Migration and Society in Britain, 1550–1830*
Ian D. Whyte *Scotland's Society and Economy in Transition, c.1500–c.1760*

Please note that a sister series, *British History in Perspective,* is available which covers all the key topics in British political history.

Social History in Perspective
Series Standing Order
ISBN 0–333–71694–9 hardcover
ISBN 0–333–69336–1 paperback
(outside North America only)

You can receive future titles in this series as they are published by placing a standing order. Please contact your bookseller or, in case of difficulty, write to us at the address below with your name and address, the title of the series and the ISBN quoted above.

Customer Services Department, Macmillan Distribution Ltd
Houndmills, Basingstoke, Hampshire RG21 6XS, England

THE GEORGIAN TOWN
1680–1840

Joyce M. Ellis

palgrave

First published 2001 by
PALGRAVE
Houndmills, Basingstoke, Hampshire RG21 6XS and
175 Fifth Avenue, New York, N.Y. 10010
Companies and representatives throughout the world

PALGRAVE is the new global academic imprint of
St. Martin's Press LLC Scholarly and Reference Division and
Palgrave Publishers Ltd (formerly Macmillan Press Ltd).

ISBN 0–333–71134–3 hardback
ISBN 0–333–71135–1 paperback

This book is printed on paper suitable for recycling and made from fully managed and sustained forest sources.

A catalogue record for this book is available from the British Library.

Library of Congress Cataloging-in-Publication Data
Ellis, Joyce M.
    The Georgian town, 1680–1840 / Joyce M. Ellis.
        p.   cm. — (Social history in perspective)
    Includes bibliographical references and index.
    ISBN 0–333–71134–3
    1. Cities and towns—Great Britain—History.   2. Urbanization—
    Great Britain—History.   I. Title.   II. Social history in perspective
    (Houndmills, Basingstoke, England)

    HT133 .E45 2000
    307.76′0942—dc21   00–062615

10   9   8   7   6   5   4   3   2   1
10   09   08   07   06   05   04   03   02   01

Printed in China

CONTENTS

LIST OF TABLES

Acknowledgements

In a study of this kind it is not possible to acknowledge all the secondary authorities adequately and I must therefore apologize to all those historians whose work I have apparently overlooked or misrepresented. Thanks are due to the other contributors to the second volume of the *Cambridge Urban History of Britain* for advice, information and constructive criticism during our collaboration and to successive generations of students for forcing me to clarify my ideas. Jeremy Black has been a positive editorial force, while the Arts and Humanities Research Board deserves my gratitude for supporting the period of research leave which gave me time to complete the book. Most of all I would like to thank my family for many forms of help and encouragement.

Nottingham   J. M. E.

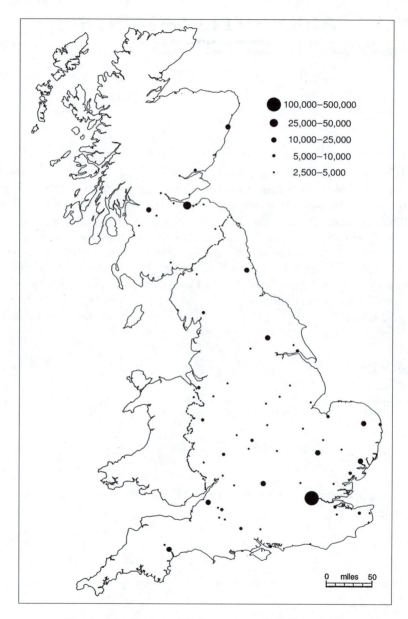

Map 1   Distribution of the larger towns in Britain *c*.1670

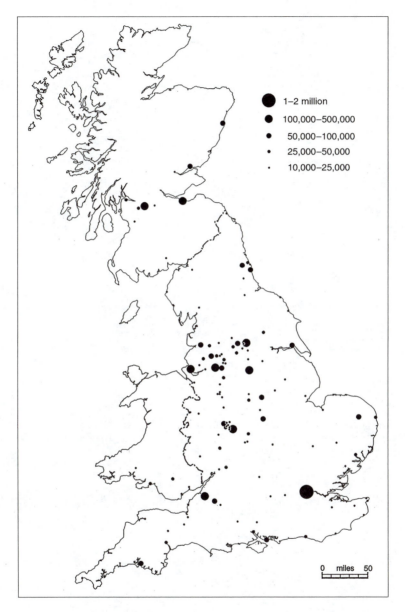

Map 2   Distribution of the larger towns in Britain in 1841

INTRODUCTION

Now I pray you, what is a commercial nation, but a collection of commercial towns?

George Chalmers (1794)[1]

When Celia Fiennes began her travels through her native land in the 1680s, domestic tourism was still in its infancy: as a result, she complained, the English were in effect 'strangers to themselves', ignorant of their own country and suffering from 'the evil itch of overvaluing foreign parts'.[2] Contemporary perceptions of Britain's relative wealth and status certainly lagged some way behind the decisive upturn in activity that took place in the 1670s and 1680s, decades which are now recognized as crucial to the gradual process of economic and social transformation that prepared the way for the industrial revolution. Foreign visitors to Britain, in particular, rarely strayed outside London and when they did visit provincial towns their impressions were rarely favourable. From a European perspective, Britain's urban system was still that of a peripheral economy, the 'paltry' size of all the towns outside London inviting comparisons with the countries of Scandinavia and central Europe rather than with the developed, highly urbanized, economies of France, Italy and the Netherlands.[3]

Over the next hundred years, in contrast, as the pace of change increased and the trickle of foreign visitors and domestic tourists became a flood, comparisons with continental Europe tended to become steadily more favourable. To judge France by its country towns, in the opinion of Joshua Gilpin, 'one would suppose this to be the thirteenth not the eighteenth century': their defensive walls, dark, gloomy streets, and feudal dependence on the aristocracy were contrasted with the open, paved and lighted streets of their British counterparts, streets that were lined with neat, trim shops and with the simple but substantial homes of prosperous and independent citizens. Urbanization indeed lay at the

1

heart of this new vision of Britain as an active, enterprising and socially well-balanced nation. Many contemporaries identified the fast-growing towns as the source of 'every improvement, comfort and even elegance' subsequently diffused throughout the land by the 'commercial industry' of their inhabitants.[4] Recent research has tended to confirm this analysis and it is now widely recognized that the rapid growth and remarkable vitality of British towns in this period played a central role in the development of a more modern economy and society. It is also recognized that the expansive element in urban society, the new social attitudes and cultural values that were helping to change patterns of consumer demand, to mobilise capital resources and to generate novel industrial processes and products, were not confined to the great capital cities of London and Edinburgh, nor even to the specialist ports, resorts and manufacturing towns whose growth attracted so much attention from contemporary observers. On the contrary, it is now clear that the smaller market towns and historic county centres, once dismissed as standing outside the mainstream of eighteenth-century development, actually shared in the general urban and economic expansion, acquiring specialist marketing, manufacturing, leisure and other functions. As such, they served as a vital interface between national urban developments and the large majority of the population still living in the countryside.

Defining the Topic: Time, Place and Context

The aim of the present volume is to present a wide-ranging, coherent survey of the main structures and functions of eighteenth-century towns, of the principal phases of their development and of their impact on ordinary people both inside and outside their boundaries. Nearly two decades have passed since the publication of Penelope Corfield's pioneering and influential survey of the development of the eighteenth-century town, decades which have witnessed a notable upsurge in enthusiasm for research in urban history.[5] The 1990s, in particular, have seen a growing volume of research, much of it focused not so much on broad general interpretations as on more specialized studies of specific periods, themes and individual communities.[6] Meanwhile a whole range of new questions and ideas has engaged a new generation of historians, relating in particular to the way urban communities perceived and presented themselves and to the place occupied by the female majority of urban residents within these communities. The effects of rapid urban growth on villages and the attitude of recent immigrants to the social and cultural influence of urban society have also excited the interest of researchers, many of whom no longer feel confined to traditional topics based on direct and relatively unambiguous documentary evidence. This has opened up the field considerably, although not always uncontroversially. Scholars seeking to examine the ways in which different sections of town society understood and used their physical environment to support inherently ideological concepts of consciousness and identity, for instance, face considerable difficulties in evolving a methodology sufficiently sensitive to answer their questions but sufficiently rigorous to withstand academic scrutiny. Similar problems confront the growing number of historians who recognize the need to undertake comparative research, particularly in a European context, but who are also painfully aware of the difficulties involved in developing compatible and reliable systems of classification.[7]

Both the chronology and the coverage of this introductory survey need some explanation, since neither fits precisely into a conventional historical framework. The first point to make is that neither 1680 nor 1840 marked a decisive, clear-cut watershed in urban development. As with so many other themes in social history, historians working on towns tend to think in terms of fairly broad time-spans and are only too well aware that both the causes and the consequences of change usually work themselves out very slowly over long periods of time. Choosing to focus on the so-called 'long' eighteenth century, from the later Stuart era to the dawn of the Victorian age, rather than on the period 1700 to 1800, seems fully justified in these terms. Some of the most significant social, cultural and economic changes that shaped the Georgian town – among them the expansion of both foreign trade and domestic industry, the development of a consumer market, the rise of the press and the growth of urban sociability – rested on well-established foundations: many can be dated back in England to the Stuart Restoration of 1660 or even earlier.[8] However, there was undoubtedly an accelerating pace of change from the later decades of the seventeenth century, initiating a period of sudden and sometimes dramatic change in the urban system not only in England, but also in Scotland and even, to a lesser extent, in Wales. It also seems logical to extend this new frame of analysis into the early decades of the nineteenth century, a period of urban history which has until recently been sparsely researched, but which is now widely accepted as a transitional phase with significant linkages back into the eighteenth century. The municipal and parliamentary innovations of the

1830s, for instance, which swept away many of the administrative and political institutions of the traditional urban system, represented the culmination of a protracted campaign for 'reform' dating back to the 1780s. Victoria's accession to the throne in June 1837 seems, therefore, to mark the end of the Georgian era in an urban, as well as a political, context.

The decision to attempt a social history of the *British* rather than simply the *English* town clearly poses both conceptual and practical challenges. In practical terms, for instance, Welsh towns have been poorly covered in the secondary literature, partly as a result of acute problems of primary documentation which themselves add to the difficulties of interpretation. It is also undeniable that those towns which have been researched display a number of distinctive economic, cultural and demographic characteristics which set them apart from towns of similar size and functions across the English border.[9] Scottish towns were, of course, even more distinctive: legal, administrative and ecclesiastical differences persisted long after the union of the crowns in 1603 and the departure of the Scottish parliament from Edinburgh in 1707. The chronology of Scottish urban development in the later seventeenth century was also noticeably different from that in Restoration England, while Welsh towns did not experience the sustained growth commonplace in both English and Scottish centres after 1700 until quite late in the century. However, the research which is currently transforming our knowledge of Scottish towns suggests that their cultural and economic development increasingly converged with that of England, a process that was encouraged by the growing influence exerted by London over Edinburgh society.[10] Including Wales and Scotland, therefore, reflects a real need to understand the origins of the integrated urban system of the nineteenth century.

The Wider Context

It also reflects the growing recognition by urban historians of the value of a comparative dimension to their interpretation of change over time. Britain may have been an island, but it was very far from being isolated from the world beyond the seas. The expansion of trade in this period clearly linked the inhabitants of British towns into a world-wide economic system. Changing fashions among these affluent but fickle consumers dictated the patterns, styles and even the names of the fabrics produced by textile manufacturers in Chennai (Madras) and Norwich alike: by 1711 it had become a commonplace that 'The single Dress of a Woman of Quality is often the Product of an hundred Climates', while Defoe claimed that 'most of [the manufactures] of foreign countries, are to be found... in the remotest corner of the whole island of *Britain*, and are to be bought, as it were, at everybody's door'.[11] The Atlantic economy which nurtured the west-coast ports of Bristol, Glasgow, Liverpool and Whitehaven, as well as the spa towns of Bath and Cheltenham, had a social as well as an economic dimension. The arrival of a West Indian heiress, 'about seventeen, half mulatto, chilly and tender', in Jane Austen's *Sanditon* (1817) certainly attracted a great deal of attention from the other residents, but only because it represented a rare and notable success for this struggling resort: 'West-injines', North Americans and East Indian 'nabobs' were familiar figures in Georgian urban society.[12] The west-coast ports also had strong commercial and cultural links with their counterparts in Ireland, as did many of the towns of west Wales, where poor land communications put a premium on sea routes across to the ports of Cork, Waterford and Wexford, as well as to Dublin and Belfast. The rapid development of eighteenth-century Dublin into a major colonial capital increased the strength of these ties, to the extent that the gentry of Anglesey and Gwynedd may well have regarded Dublin rather than London as their primary social and cultural centre. The connections of east-coast ports such as Hull, 'The Dublin of England' in the eyes of one enthusiastic visitor, not unnaturally looked more towards the North Sea and the Baltic, although it should be noted that one of Hull's greatest commercial firms, Joseph Pease & Son, had close family connections with Ireland as well as with Rotterdam.[13]

   This wider European, as well as imperial, context needs to be borne in mind when studying the Georgian town precisely because it was in this period that the experience of Britain started to diverge from that of the continental countries with which its towns had previously been compared. Rather than being on the periphery of European development, the accelerating pace of urbanization had by the later eighteenth century placed Britain at the epicentre, a phenomenon which Adam Smith addressed directly in Book III of *An Inquiry into the Nature and Causes of the Wealth of Nations*, first published in 1776. Smith attributed Britain's steady accretion of economic and political power largely to the simultaneous triumph of the market economy, which he implicitly equated with 'civilization'.[14] This equation of 'the modes of civil life' with activity and industry was not confined to works of political and economic theory: William Hutton, the first historian of Birmingham, was equally convinced that soundly based urban growth was synonymous with national prosperity. Hutton, however, took the connection between 'civic' and 'civilization' one step further, arguing that 'urban' also implied 'urbane': 'Civility and humanity are ever the companions of trade; . . . a barbarous and commercial people, is a contradiction'.[15]

Conclusion

As later chapters will demonstrate, there were always dissenting voices raised in opposition to this chorus of praise, voices that grew more vociferous as the pace of urban growth speeded up in the last quarter of the eighteenth century. Economic and demographic expansion posed new administrative and environmental challenges, while the onward march of market forces in some cases strained the bonds which had bound together traditional civic communities. Decades of crisis and upheaval, the 1780s and 1820s, in particular, fostered growing political and cultural polarization, so that by the early nineteenth century class divisions had assumed a growing importance in urban society. The 'new Babylons', as Corfield has pointed out, evoked sharply contradictory responses: the challenging, dynamic, competitive world of the fast-growing towns, which held out the prospect of unprecedented success, could also inspire equally well-founded fears of unprecedented failure.[16]

On the other hand, focusing on the 'long' eighteenth century helps both to keep these challenges in proportion and to emphasize the relative ease with which British towns accommodated a period of such rapid and dramatic change. New social groups, new agencies and structures, new types of urban community, were all absorbed into an established framework of civic culture that was arguably growing stronger and more influential in 1840 than it had been in 1680. Indeed the basic resilience and durability of British urban life, despite the dramatic physical transformation of the urban environment, the seismic shifts in traditional social and economic structures, and the explosive potential of the notoriously volatile urban population at times of tension and distress, has been emphasized by many historians working in the field over the past few decades. The flexibility of urban society, combined with the underlying stability of key aspects of urban life, played a major role in ensuring a peaceful, as well as prosperous, transition from the Georgian town to the Victorian city.

1

THE URBAN PROSPECT

Methought a City to my Eyes appear'd,
Where Towers and Temples, high their Summits rear'd.
Where honest Industry bore up her Head,
And Arts and Sciences, around her spread; . . . .

Anon (1741)[1]

England, Scotland and Wales were not urban nations in the closing
years of the seventeenth century. Although it is impossible to claim total
accuracy for the figures, it is clear that 67 to 70 per cent of the population of England, 75 to 78 per cent of the population of Scotland and 85
to 87 per cent of the population of Wales lived in the country, typically
in farmsteads or small village settlements containing no more than a few
hundred people. The urban inhabitants of Britain therefore constituted
a minority, well short of 2 million people in all, of a total population of
around 6.3 million.[2] This is in stark contrast with the urban-dominated
society of today and it was not in fact until 1911 that the proportions of
town and country dwellers were to be reversed.

Town and Country

Basically, the unequal division reflected the nature of the contemporary
economy and society. In 1680, and indeed throughout the eighteenth
century, the rural population was overwhelmingly dependent on
agriculture for its livelihood. Since agricultural productivity, although
steadily improving, was very low by modern standards, it was impossible
for the country to sustain a large urban population. The majority of

7

farms were small and most agricultural workers lived on the borders of subsistence, thereby limiting the demand of the bulk of the population for the goods and services which towns could provide. This necessary preoccupation with the basics of life is emphasized by estimates that, when prices were high, as much as 80 per cent of the average budget was devoted to basic foodstuffs, mostly bread, while fuel took up nearly half of the remainder. It was therefore a frugal society in which new goods were comparatively rare, with much being made over and mended. Much of the 'industrial' production that did take place was still carried out within the home for domestic consumption.[3]

The scope for urban expansion in such an economic environment was clearly limited. However, scattered among the fields, villages and streams was a network of towns, each a densely clustered settlement clearly distinguished from the surrounding countryside. Most of these towns had medieval origins and at first sight still appeared to present a medieval profile to the outside world. The many early eighteenth-century prints of urban 'prospects' looked across acres of open country-side towards towns that were still dominated by a skyline of 'Towers and Temples'. Except in the sophistication of their execution, they appear indistinguishable from the images of two centuries before, sketched by Tudor heralds or described by antiquarians like Camden and Leland.[4] In some cases the persistence of the traditional urban world was still more marked. A few of the old-established cities still retained their defensive walls and gates, although many urban fortifications – those of Gloucester and Northampton, for example – had been demolished in the aftermath of the Civil Wars of the 1640s. Some walled cities, includ-ing Norwich, Exeter and York, even maintained the tradition of closing their gates on Sundays and at night; Newcastle upon Tyne shut them when threatened by the Jacobites without or striking keelmen within. Newcastle was also, like Bath, Canterbury, Exeter and Chichester, among those that still lay mostly within the line of their walls.

Both walled and unwalled towns, even many of the larger ones, were still overwhelmingly rural in character and appearance.[5] Urban growth in modern times has resulted in an untidy sprawl of development across the surrounding countryside, whereas Georgian towns on the whole remained astonishingly compact, accommodating their growing popu-lations by increasing the density of settlement, rather than by extending its area. Not a single new street was built in Leeds, for example, between 1634 and 1767, although the population more than trebled between those years. This intensification of settlement had undoubted drawbacks for the congested town centres, but it also meant that the whole of the urban population lived within walking distance of the surrounding countryside and could enjoy their own urban prospects across the tranquil rural landscape. Nottingham in the late seventeenth century was encircled by 1500 acres of open fields and crocus meadows; the road into town from Trent Bridge was said to be the finest approach in England. A few minutes' brisk uphill walk in Newcastle brought you from the densely populated, smoky riverside to the open spaces of the Town Moor or the pleasant lanes leading to small villages well supplied with welcoming inns. Even in the sprawling giant of London, it was still possible in the early years of the century to shoot woodcock within a few hundred yards of smart West-End squares, to walk in the hayfields on the Whit Sunday holiday, and to catch sturgeon in the river at Stepney. To some extent, therefore, the urban population could enjoy both town and country.

It should not be imagined, however, that the rural world stopped at the outskirts of most Georgian towns. On the contrary, the country penetrated into the heart of the urban landscape. Milkmaids, hay-wagons, farm-carts, chickens, stray pigs, flocks of sheep and herds of cattle were an everyday sight in most city streets. One-half of the area within the walled part of Leicester in the late seventeenth century was not built over at all but was laid out in gardens and orchards or left as open wasteland, while Nottingham's reputation as a 'garden city' is amply borne out by the work of contemporary artists like Siberechts and Kip. Norwich had long been famous as a city of flowers, gardens and orchards; Thomas Fuller characterized it in 1662 as 'either a city in an orchard, or an orchard in a city, so equally are houses and trees blended in it'.[6] Two years earlier, Aberdeen had been described in very similar terms as 'planted with all sorts of trees . . . so that the quhole toune . . . looks as if it stood in a garding or little wood'.[7] Even smoky Newcastle retained a pleasantly rural area within its northern walls, dotted with the houses of gentlemen living in the midst of fields and gardens. As the century progressed these open spaces in the larger towns tended to disappear under intensified settlement, but many smaller communities retained this semi-rural environment. A fire in Shrewsbury's Abbey Foregate in 1774, for instance, destroyed 16 barns, 15 stables and several haystacks as well as 47 houses and four shops. Haymaking was still taking place in the orchards of Bury St Edmunds in the early years of the nineteenth century.

Yet the traditional appearance of the Georgian town and the survival of substantial rural elements in its landscape should not obscure the important changes that were already under way as the eighteenth century opened and which were to have a major impact on its development. The timeless image presented by the prospects was already being eroded by significant details; the windmills, the laden barges and carts, the rope-walks outside Newcastle and the lengths of cloth stretched out on sturdy tenterhooks outside Colchester, even the civic promenade on the southern outskirts of Preston, all hinted at the shape of things to come. The walls of the traditional town were now crumbling and were regarded as at best a recreational amenity, at worst an intolerable obstacle to traffic. The urban world was changing and as it changed it was growing in influence. In part this reflected a simple expansion of the urban network, as established towns increased their activity and their populations and as new towns grew up to share in their prosperity. Town-dwellers were therefore a growing minority, increasing not only in absolute numbers but also in proportionate terms. At the same time, the towns were beginning to exert a much greater influence over the surrounding countryside and the rural population. As agriculture slowly improved and trade increased, ever greater numbers of people came into contact with urban life, albeit briefly, as they went in search of employment, entertainment or simply to sell their produce at a weekly market. Modern studies of migration all emphasize the mobility of the rural population, indicating that very few of the men and women living in the countryside in 1680 can have passed their lives without some experience of the urban world. Most would have ventured no further than their local market town but some gained a much wider experience of urban life; indeed Anthony Wrigley has estimated that as many as one in six of the adult population of England had lived in London at some point in their lives.[8]

The Urban Hierarchy c.1700

London's general impact and relative importance within the country had long been proverbial; a matter of mingled wonder, pride and anxiety. Nourished by its seemingly inexhaustible supply of migrants, the capital towered over the rest of the urban network as it did over every sphere of national life. To say that it was the largest town in Britain in no way adequately reflects its pre-eminence. After two centuries of almost unbroken growth, by 1700 the number of the capital's inhabitants had risen to about 575,000, representing 11 per cent of the total population of England and Wales, compared with an estimated 55,000 in 1520. Modern estimates suggest that it had recently overtaken Paris in the European rankings, becoming one of the largest cities in the world – only Constantinople, Beijing and possibly Edo (Tokyo) still surpassed London.[9] It had become a giant conurbation with key political, social and cultural significance as well as economic importance. And the physical evidence of its triumphal progress was there for all to see. From the Restoration onwards, London had begun to expand rapidly in all directions, engulfing the villages on the periphery of the capital. By 1700, the cities of London and Westminster had coalesced and were no longer separate communities. Anxieties about the speed of metropolitan expansion had been expressed throughout the seventeenth century; now the political arithmeticians were beginning to wonder whether 'this monstrous city' would swallow the nation's entire population and wealth into its ever-expanding jaws.[10] On the other hand, the vigour of the capital's development aroused awe and admiration and it naturally set the standard by which all other urban communities were judged. A comparison with London was the highest form of praise that contemporary travellers could bestow on a provincial town. Celia Fiennes, for example, found echoes of London in towns as different as Exeter and Liverpool, exclaiming that the latter was 'London in miniature as much as ever I saw any thing'.[11]

London was, by any standards, a giant. If, however, one moves out of the capital the urban scene changes drastically in scale and becomes much more uncertain. At one level, England appears to have been very well endowed with towns; informed contemporaries certainly thought theirs was a relatively urbanized society (see Table 1.1). On the basis of their calculations it would seem that, despite its predominantly rural character, in the closing decades of the seventeenth century Britain contained around 1000 communities that could be called towns, the majority of them in England. John Adams, for example, in his *Index villaris or, An alphabetical table of all the cities, market towns, parishes, villages and private seats, in England and Wales* (1680), compiled a list of 788 separate cities and towns excluding London and Westminster. A decade or so later, Gregory King, the pioneer of social statistics, made a series of calculations which assumed the existence of between 795 and 846 towns. As this range of estimates indicates, King was working with imprecise information and was further hampered by the lack of any simple definition of what constituted a town at the time. Both he and Adams were clearly uncertain about the precise dividing line between town and village, and

Table 1.1   Distribution of the urban population in Georgian Britain

Town size	Number of towns			% of urban population		
	17th century	1801	1841	17th century	1801	1841
Over 100,000	1	1	9	21	22	37
50,000–99,000	1	7	16	3	12	10
10,000–49,000	9	50	95	8	20	14
5,000–9,999	16	58	156	7	9	17
2,500–4,999	51	212	392	11	16	14
1,000–2,499	277	471	374	27	17	7
<1,000	650	237	113	23	4	1
Total	1005	1036	1155	100	100	100

Source: J. Langton, 'Urban growth and economic change from the seventeenth century to 1841', in *CUHB*, pp. 463, 471.

many historians would question their inclusion of communities with as few as 500 inhabitants or 150 houses among the ranks of English towns; excluding them would reduce the number of 'towns' in 1700 by several hundreds.[12]

Doubts have therefore been cast on the urban status of the innumerable small settlements which lay on the disputed frontier between town and country life. Any rigorous definition based mainly on population size would certainly exclude the hundreds of 'towns', such as tiny Beaminster in Dorset with barely 500 inhabitants, which had populations below 1000 in the closing years of the seventeenth century, and might well call into question all those communities with between 500 and 2500 inhabitants. But are historians entitled to apply such a rigid test of status when it is quite clear that urban identity was not merely a matter of numbers? Even the smallest settlements in these categories seem to have been set apart from the surrounding villages by distinctive patterns of employment and activity; they were in the countryside but not part of it. Relatively few of the inhabitants of these small market towns would have been actively involved in farming; thus only a handful of the tradesmen living in Petworth, Sussex, in the later seventeenth and early eighteenth centuries farmed land, while most of their counterparts in neighbouring villages combined their trade with smallholding. Trade was these towns' lifeblood and the basis of their existence.[13] All of them functioned as local markets, serving a hinterland of between three and six miles in radius and enjoying sudden upward fluctuations of population on market days. Some small towns, for example Market Weighton in the

East Riding or Farnham in Surrey, had an importance as markets out of all proportion to their size; Defoe was informed that 'on a market-day eleven hundred teams of horse, all drawing waggons, or carts, loaden with wheat' had been counted in Farnham, which had a resident population of no more than 1500.[14] The services provided in such small towns were significantly different from those of the largest villages; somewhere like Tonbridge in Kent with a population of only 600 in the 1660s might not have had a wide range of specialized trades but often acted as a base for a handful of professional men serving the population for miles around. In such ways the smallest of towns could act as a pivot and focus for life over quite a wide area of countryside. There seems little point, therefore, in worrying too much about a rigid cut-off point between town and village. In practice, contemporaries were confident that they could identify a town when they saw one and they adopted a flexible, commonsense definition: a town was a settlement which looked like a town and in which the majority of the inhabitants behaved like townspeople – that is, they did not earn their living directly from working on the land.

On the other hand, adopting a more conservative 'threshold' figure of 2500 inhabitants can prove useful in providing some comparative information about the scale and pattern of urban growth over a period of time. Such a strict definition leaves us with just under 80 British towns, though in this context Wales can be effectively excluded from the picture. Given its many acres of barren, mountainous countryside, it is not surprising that there were few substantial towns beyond the fringes of north Wales, the Vale of Glamorgan and the English border. The largest urban populations were probably those of Carmarthen, Brecon, Wrexham and Haverfordwest, each with no more than 3000 inhabitants in the early years of the century; English travellers commented with some surprise that the latter, 'a large, populous and Trading town', was 'a better town than we expected to find, in this remote Angle of Britain'.[15]

Scotland, too, was a predominantly rural society and thus relatively poorly endowed with towns as the eighteenth century opened; it suffered, in particular, from a distinctive lack of middle-ranking inland towns. It is not easy to be definite about the state of Scottish urban development but it is apparent that many of its historic burghs were struggling to sustain both their wealth and their relative importance in the aftermath of a prolonged period of urban instability and decay. Although a handful of well-established centres retained a significant influence over their localities, Glasgow and Edinburgh were the only cities which were actually expanding in 1700.[16] Edinburgh, which remained 'the metropolis of this ancient kingdom', even after the Act of Union in 1707 had removed the Scottish Parliament to Westminster, dominated the Scottish hierarchy, just as London dominated England but not to such a great degree. Despite its relatively modest size – its 50,000 inhabitants made up only 5 per cent of Scotland's population in 1700 – it was easily the richest town in the country and far more prosperous than its relative size would suggest.[17]

London's dominance over England's provincial towns, even the largest ones, is perfectly clear from any representation of the urban network. Gregory King's calculations in the late seventeenth century, revised slightly to excise the very smallest settlements, suggest that the urban population of England and Wales in 1700 was just over 1 million, around 22 or 23 per cent of the national total. Given that London's population was over half a million at this date, this would mean that the capital alone contained half the urban population of the country. Compared with London, all other English towns were pitifully small. There were only half a dozen provincial towns with over 10,000 inhabitants, and London was fully 20 times as large as the leading English provincial city in terms of population. This was an astonishing imbalance by continental standards; in France, for example, there was not only a large group of towns with more than 20,000 inhabitants but also at least five provincial cities, Lyons, Marseilles, Rouen, Bordeaux and Nantes, had populations over 40,000.[18]

Nevertheless, as Appendix 1 demonstrates, Britain's larger provincial centres were substantial and dynamic communities in their own right, recognized by contemporaries as 'great towns' in terms of both population size and status within the urban hierarchy.[19] Although the population estimates given by different historians can vary considerably, it is unquestionable that the towns at the very top of the provincial rankings included Norwich, Bristol, Glasgow and Newcastle upon Tyne. Below them came Exeter, Aberdeen and York. Just as London towered over these leading provincial cities, so they, in turn, dominated the lesser centres in their regional hinterlands. Bristol, for example, characterized by Minchinton as the 'metropolis of the west', was the social and economic focal point of not just the west country but also much of south Wales.[20] Newcastle functioned in a similar manner as 'the great Emporium of all the Northern Parts of England, and of a good share of Scotland'.[21] It is noticeable, however, that only York among this small group of leading provincial cities relied almost exclusively for its prosperity on its role as a regional centre; the key to success usually lay in combining regional primacy with a solid place in the national economy. Thus Bristol, Glasgow, Newcastle, Exeter and Aberdeen all owed much of their prosperity and population to coastal and foreign trade, while both Exeter and Norwich were important centres of the textile industry.

Beneath these eight major cities, there came just under 30 large towns ranging in population from 5000 to 10,000, a group so heterogeneous in character, function and heritage that they fall into no obvious category. It is not even possible to say that they all acted as centres for an established hinterland. In fact, among this mixture of historic, traditional towns and enterprising upstarts, only about half were regional or county centres and only two of these, Chester and Bury St Edmunds, relied principally on this role for their prosperity. All the others, from Ipswich and Worcester to Leicester and Perth, derived substantial benefits from other forms of activity, usually industrial. Shrewsbury, for instance, not only dominated a huge hinterland stretching through central Wales to the west coast, but also controlled the marketing and finishing of north Wales's woollen industry; Defoe reported that although 'they all speak English in the town...on a market day you would think you were in Wales'.[22] Meanwhile, Oxford and Cambridge drew healthy incomes for their resident populations from supplying the universities.

The other towns at this level of the urban hierarchy, those which were not traditional county centres, lacked even this degree of coherence. Some were 'new' towns, while others looked back on centuries of prosperity. Their populations earned their living in a number of different fields. Nine of them relied almost solely on industry, whether based in the town itself or in the surrounding countryside: Colchester, Coventry, Leeds, Manchester and Tiverton all depended on textiles, Birmingham on metalworking, Chatham, Portsmouth and Plymouth on shipbuilding and dockyard work. There were also four major ports, Great Yarmouth, Hull, Liverpool and Sunderland, which all specialized in the movement of bulky raw materials. Sunderland, for example, was expanding rapidly through the coastal trade in coal, but its local influence was constrained by economic rivalry with nearby Newcastle and administrative and social rivalry with the smaller county town of Durham.

The bottom tier of substantial urban communities was made up of about 50 somewhat more modest towns with between 2500 and 5000 inhabitants, ranging from larger market towns, such as Leominster and Uttoxeter, to smaller county centres, such as Ayr, Gloucester and

Hereford. It included a few ports, like Boston and Southampton, and some small manufacturing towns, like Walsall in the Black Country, but basically the majority of communities of this size, though often possessing minor industries, were substantial commercial centres, whose hinterlands often included several smaller towns.[23] They therefore fulfilled a dual role, providing local markets and services for their immediate locality while also supplying this wider region with more specialized commercial, administrative and social services. The wholesalers of towns like Lichfield, Preston or Durham supplied the shops of smaller towns and villages; their lawyers and clerks served the assizes, the cathedrals and the county gentry; and their social facilities helped to attract those gentry into the town in the first place. Typical of this category was Warwick, a prosperous county centre in a fertile agricultural region, with about 3300 inhabitants; evidence indicates that by the 1690s it had attracted some of the local gentry into residence and, as might be expected, could offer them the services of a few specialized crafts and trades, such as a watchmaker, a bookseller and a goldsmith, not often found in the smaller market towns. The contrast between the small population and modest prosperity of Warwick, on the one hand, and the vast resources of London on the other could hardly be greater. Population alone is perhaps a crude measure but in this case it is hard to question the significance of the differences in scale which it reveals; as the new century opened, the capital was some 170 times bigger in terms of population than the county town.

Changes in the Urban System

Even so, puny though the majority of English towns were at this time, it is important to realize that many of them were expanding, and some were expanding with extraordinary rapidity. Here, then, is another significant contrast, one which represented a dramatic improvement on the uncertain developments of previous centuries, stretching back into the middle ages and the onset of the Black Death in the mid-fourteenth century. Some historians would claim that this catastrophe ushered in a protracted period of economic difficulty as the population of England was dramatically diminished by a century of plague, so that by the late fifteenth century empty and crumbling buildings were a common sight in many towns. They argue that the towns were losing both their economic impetus, as trade declined and more and more industry migrated into the countryside, and their cultural role, as the Reformation attacked both religious and civic ritual. Even when the national population began to expand again in the sixteenth and early seventeenth centuries, the increase brought more problems than prosperity to the beleaguered provincial towns, which could not support the influx of migrants looking for work. Only London prospered, gathering in the country's surplus population to fuel its headlong expansion and reinforce its already dominant position in the urban hierarchy. By the middle of the seventeenth century, if this interpretation is to be accepted, the slow decay of the medieval urban world was only just reaching its conclusion, leaving urban civilization a pale shadow of its rich and varied past.

It has to be said that this thesis, identifying an extended period of crisis and decay which reached its nadir in the sixteenth and early seventeenth centuries, has not attracted universal support.[24] On the contrary, the timing, extent and even the very existence of such a 'crisis' have been hotly disputed over the last few decades; rival schools of thought argue that the crisis occurred at an earlier date and was over by the mid-sixteenth century – or, indeed, question the whole notion of a general urban crisis. The fate of the town in the three centuries before 1660 has thus become an academic minefield into which unwary travellers stray at their peril. But two common assumptions underlie most of the discussions, however technical or controversial these might be: that most towns suffered some problems of adjustment in the wake of population change; and that a new phase in their development began in the second half of the seventeenth century.

At the time of the Restoration, despite the physical destruction and economic dislocation of the Civil War, any signs of crisis in England's towns were few and far between. All the evidence suggests that the century after 1660 marked the beginning of a period of urban revival and accelerating change, a veritable 'urban renaissance', with the onset of a cumulative and long-term process of growth.[25] This was the more remarkable as the country's overall population increase was decidedly sluggish. Modern estimates suggest that the national population grew only slightly between the 1650s and 1700 and may even have suffered periods of absolute decline, while the urban population was experiencing definite expansion. It has to be emphasized, once again, that all such population estimates are extremely approximate, given that there was no national census until 1801. However, it seems unquestionable that in the later seventeenth century England was experiencing some degree of urbanization, in sharp contrast with the experience of continental Europe, where the urban system was entering a period of stagnation or even outright decay, which was to last until the 1750s.[26]

What is more significant, however, is the evidence that urbanization was not confined to London, as it had been so often in the past; instead, a broadly based pattern of growth became apparent from about the 1670s, pointing the way towards the 'more complex and polycentric urban society' identified by Penelope Corfield.[27] Indeed some provincial centres were even showing faster growth rates than London, although of course they needed to recruit much smaller numbers of people to achieve a high rate of growth than did the already enormous capital city. Many of the larger towns were particularly buoyant, as they exploited the gains to be made from expanding foreign trade and increased specialization, which minimized competition between them. These two factors together account for much of the success experienced in this sector, but an important secondary role was played by the development of many towns as centres of aristocratic residence and entertainment. It was noticeable in Nottingham, for instance, that 'many people of good quality from several parts, make choice of habitations here where they find good accommodation, which must be no small advantage to the place'; one aristocratic visitor in the 1680s was so impressed that he praised it in lyrical terms as 'Paradise restored, for here you find large streets, fair built houses, fine women, and many coaches rattling about, and their shops full of merchantable goods'.[28]

However, not every town was equally fortunate and it cannot be assumed that expansion was taking place everywhere or that it was proceeding at the same pace. Many established Scottish towns, with the notable exceptions of Edinburgh and Glasgow, were actually losing ground in the late seventeenth century under the cumulative weight of war, epidemic and famine; the population of Aberdeen, for instance, fell by over 20 per cent between 1695 and 1700 as a result of the famines of the later 1690s.[29]

In England, in contrast, many historians have argued that growth was effectively confined to the larger centres while the smaller towns marked time, at best advancing very slowly and at worst settling into gentle decay. The issue is by no means clear, not least because of the elusiveness of concrete evidence about the smaller market towns in a period when there were distinct local and regional variations in the pace of both growth and decay. However, recent research has challenged conventional assumptions of long-term decline and suggested that many smaller centres in both England and Scotland experienced a revival in their fortunes in the last decades of the century.[30]

If so, they were sharing in something much more significant than a simple rise in the percentage of the population living in towns; the shape of the urban world was also involved. From the middle ages onwards the urban scene in England had been dominated by southern towns; in the early seventeenth century only Newcastle and York among the northern cities could be regarded as substantial communities. By 1700, however, there were signs that this was changing and that the general expansion of the late seventeenth century had been accompanied by changes in the distribution of the urban population across the country. The south was still a long way from losing its primacy; the continued urban strength of East Anglia was still apparent and the Norwich–Great Yarmouth axis represented the largest urban complex outside London. However, the pattern of distribution that had been familiar for centuries was slowly giving way to one that was to characterize the English landscape to 1914 and beyond. By 1700, the midland and northern towns had begun to climb the urban rankings and, as they grew, they began to forge ahead of some long-established centres, upsetting the neat traditional hierarchy; producing in fact the sort of vigorous but incoherent pattern already noted in the middle-rank towns. The explosive growth of Liverpool, Manchester and Birmingham, as well as the rise of Glasgow on the west coast of Scotland, confirmed that a new phase of urban history had begun.

Images of the Urban World

The new expansiveness and vitality of the urban world in the closing decades of the seventeenth century was accompanied by significant changes in the definition and perception of the town. It has already been noted that contemporaries were uncertain about the theoretical dividing line between town and village, a confusion that was reflected in the language. Originally the word 'town' (derived from the Old English 'tun', an enclosed place or piece of land) was applied to any collection of houses enclosed by a wall or hedge, indeed to any clustered or nucleated settlement, however small. This indiscriminate usage was still current in the sixteenth century, but the term was beginning to acquire a more precise and specific meaning, implying a community with certain independent rights and privileges in its local government. By the later seventeenth and earlier eighteenth centuries, as the urban population started to expand, the modern emphasis was emerging; 'town' was becoming an increasingly specialized term for a large settlement, defined as the antithesis of the smaller 'village'.[31] Though the dividing line in particular cases remained unclear, the gradual acceptance of this dichotomy between town and village was a significant change in contemporary perceptions.

This shift in the definition of the town coincided with the spread of a new awareness and appreciation of urban forms. Improved surveying methods established new standards in mapping, supplying accurate horizontal plans of the growing towns to complement the striking vertical images provided by urban views or prospects.[32] The year 1680 marked the beginning of a golden age for the prospect as increasing public demand transformed a trade previously dominated by foreign artists and by views of London. Native artists and provincial towns now played a far greater part in the business; the most successful and prolific publishers of printed prospects, Samuel and Nathaniel Buck, succeeded in depicting nearly 80 different towns in the years between 1721 and 1753. The buoyant demand for these works was one sign of growing local patriotism among the residents of provincial towns, but it also represented an increased sensitivity to the visual impact of the urban landscape. Celia Fiennes already expected major towns to present an impressive visual image to an approaching traveller and expressed disappointment with those that did not. As the eighteenth century progressed, critical attention shifted from the distant prospect, from the town as an ornament in the wider landscape, to the quality of the townscape itself. Streets and buildings alike were expected to present sophisticated residents and visitors with aesthetically satisfying vistas and spectacles; in essence, to provide suitable scenery for playing out the drama of urban life. This expectation lay behind much of eighteenth-century town planning, from the grand schemes of Bath and Edinburgh to much more humble projects; when the little town of Tremadoc, Gwynedd, was planned in 1805, for instance, the visual impact of every house and tree was carefully weighed in the effort to create 'urbanity' at the smallest possible cost.

This preoccupation with the image which a town presented to the world was reflected not only in art and planning, but also in a flood of literature dedicated to the glorification of the urban world.[33] It could be argued that this represents nothing more than the general increase in the activity of the press in the eighteenth century, but the character of the literature produced in praise of the town does appear significant. Poetry and prose alike reflected a strong belief in the town's role as a civilizing agency, spreading not only useful knowledge but also 'urbane' values among the rude countrymen. Urban growth and rising confidence seem to have given particular stimulus to the writing of town histories, which appeared in ever-increasing numbers as the century proceeded. The amateur historians, often themselves professional men or tradesmen, offered the growing urban middle classes, perhaps even some skilled workers, a vision of the past in which the spotlight fell on urban, rather than aristocratic success. Moreover, they reinforced local pride by applauding the giant strides in wealth and culture made in modern times as well as by chronicling the distant, preferably Roman, origins of the provincial towns, emphasizing their key role in the vanguard of progress. The vigour and self-confidence of this new urban world found one of its most eloquent exponents in William Hutton, who proclaimed in ringing tones that 'When the word *Birmingham* occurs, a superb picture instantly expands in the mind, which is best explained by the other words grand, populous, extensive, active, commercial and humane.'[34] Exposure to its stimulating atmosphere was credited with startling conversions from indolence to industry and enterprise; who could doubt that further progress and further glories lay ahead?

Hutton emphasized the economic, social and cultural impact of his dynamic community on residents and visitors alike, but it should be remembered that urban expansion had equally dramatic effects on the towns' visual impact. As the pace of urban growth accelerated in the later seventeenth century, the landscape of many British towns began a slow evolution which was to change them out of all recognition. In some rapidly expanding towns, whole new streets and squares were built on the periphery of the increasingly crowded centres. The sheer size of the largest towns and the speed with which they devoured the surrounding fields began to attract the same reactions of mingled awe and alarm which had accompanied London's runaway growth during the sixteenth and seventeenth centuries. But this new phase of urban expansion offered much more than a simple change of scale; it presaged a transformation of the physical environment which was particularly striking in the more prestigious residential and commercial areas. Spurred on by their new wealth, their new status, above all by their new sensitivity to the quality of the landscape, the upper levels of urban society began to remodel their surroundings to exacting new standards.[35] This was achieved partly by the widespread use of more expensive, more durable building materials, replacing the traditional wood, plaster, mud and thatch with the urban permanence of brick, stone and tile, and in the process beginning to erase some of the regional characteristics that had resulted from the use of local materials.

The new urban fabric was much less prone to disastrous fires, which was one very cogent reason for the adoption of these new methods of construction.[36] However, the eclipse of the traditional vernacular landscape owed much more to general changes in taste than to fire regulations. Brick, stone and tile triumphed because they suited a type and style of architecture that was becoming increasingly popular in the later seventeenth century and held almost unchallenged sway for most of the Georgian era. The fashion for classical architecture and design swept all before it, transforming domestic building and with it whole residential districts. Solid, dignified, adaptable to every situation and almost every pocket, the Georgian town house penetrated to every corner of the land, displacing local vernacular styles with a new nationwide standard that stressed symmetry and classical simplicity.[37] Nor was the impact of the classical style confined to private building. In complete contrast with the modest public initiatives of the sixteenth and early seventeenth centuries, there was now enthusiasm for civic improvement on an often ambitious scale. The demand for an aesthetically satisfying visual environment and for higher standards of comfort and convenience came together to promote a wide range of initiatives; new or remodelled churches, town halls, market buildings, custom houses, schools, freshly paved or widened streets, all contributed to the gradual evolution of the Georgian urban landscape. In some towns, particularly those visited by disaster or experiencing rapid economic growth, the landscape was transformed practically overnight. Northampton in 1675 and Warwick in 1694, like Blandford in 1731, sprang from the ashes of their great conflagrations almost totally remodelled in the latest style and were regarded by contemporaries as shining examples of modern planning and design. Along with the more spectacular developments taking place in the west end of London, in Bath, Bristol and Edinburgh, they set the standards for other towns to copy.

Ambitious townscaping and major rebuilding projects were not, however, the most typical patterns of development. In most towns classicism arrived piecemeal, unplanned and unheralded, transforming the landscape through decades of small personal decisions rather than through sweeping changes. It was a matter of building one or two new houses, refronting others, adding a fashionable doorcase or Venetian window, cutting back timber jetties or concealing gables behind a parapet roof; squares, circuses and fashionable terraces were the exception rather than the rule. Even in Bath the transformation took years to complete, as the upper town slowly expanded and older buildings in the historic centre were gradually refaced. By the end of the century, the unspectacular process that characterized most redevelopment had indeed produced an urban landscape radically different from that of 1680, and it is that mature Georgian landscape which is reflected in the many paintings and engravings surviving from the later years of the period. In the absence of similar representations of the early eighteenth-century town, it is all too easy to project the elegant classicism of the early 1800s back into a very different world.

A more realistic prospect of the urban landscape at the beginning of the Georgian age can only be obtained by looking beyond these later images to the earlier stages of the transformation. By the closing years of the seventeenth century, 'this Dance of building new Fronts' had progressed to the extent that many towns had begun to 'put on quite a new Face'.[38] However, the scramble to keep up with the twists and turns of fashionable architecture and design was still in its very early stages and the traditional urban fabric was largely intact. Towns outside the stone belt were still dominated by timber-framed houses with thatched roofs and casement windows with leaded lights; in 1698 Fiennes reported that 'there are no good buildings [in Norwich] the town being old timber and plaister-work'.[39] These tall buildings, packed tight together along winding streets, leaned towards each other over the congested traffic, blocking out the light and dripping inexorably on pedestrians' heads whenever it rained; nothing could have been further from the eighteenth-century passion for order, comfort and convenience. It was particularly frustrating that established medieval street plans offered so little opportunity for the cohesive facades, broad thoroughfares and open prospects demanded by contemporary taste. Yet the process of change was painfully slow and was hedged about with powerful constraints. It was limited by the existing topography, which posed a range of obstacles from those, like marshy ground, which could be overcome at considerable expense, to others which were beyond the reach of contemporary technology. It also faced the problems raised by existing patterns of landownership, which had defeated attempts to remodel London after the Great Fire and proved almost equally obstructive elsewhere.

Supplies of local capital to finance redevelopment were also crucial. On a national scale the availability of capital counted as a stimulant rather than a constraint; the abundance of capital generated in eighteenth-century England and the relative shortage of alternative outlets meant that investment in urban development was comparatively attractive. Local shortages, however, particularly in towns which were not sufficiently prosperous to accumulate large stocks of surplus capital, could well inhibit not only new building, but even the remodelling of existing structures. The smaller, less successful towns therefore retained much more from the past, proving fairly resistant to the tide of fashion that swept all before it elsewhere.[40] Thus, in some parts of the country, local building styles resisted the onslaught of the national trend towards classicism, a resistance that was stiffened by the continuing use of local building materials and traditional colour schemes. Before the coming of cheap bulk transport, builders relied on stone from nearby quarries and bricks baked from local clays, while the 'common colours' used in the bulk of exterior paintwork were made up from locally available pigments.[41] The bricks used to construct the houses of Georgian Chichester were as different from those of Birmingham as they both were from the limestones of Stamford or the granite of Aberdeen, and each lent individuality to the changing urban landscape of these very different towns.

The survival of local identity, despite the almost universal adoption of classical standards in all aspects of the built environment, emphasizes that it is misleading to look for one archetypical 'Georgian town'. Even in 1680 there was clearly an immense range of size and experience in the urban world, each environment generating its own characteristic visual image; a local market town and a major conurbation might have had some things in common but also many significant points of difference. With the proliferation of specialized functions that accelerated as the century progressed, the sea ports, canal ports, dockyards, manufacturing towns, university towns, road towns, inland spas and seaside resorts became, if anything, more distinct. The initial impact of urban development and the transformation of the urban landscape that accompanied it was thus to differentiate Georgian towns rather than to standardize them.

2

URBAN GROWTH

The richest crop for any field,
Is a crop of bricks for it to yield,
The richest crop that it can grow,
Is a crop of houses in a row.

Anon[1]

As the Georgian age unfolded, the cumulative and long-term process of urban growth which had begun in the later seventeenth century gathered strength. Rapid urbanization still lay in the future, but even in the early years of the eighteenth century there were few towns that did not experience significant population growth, while several were expanding at a spectacular rate. By the time of the 1801 census, Britain had developed into one of the most densely populated countries in the world, with many more urban residents living in a greater number of larger towns (see Table 2.1).

All the available evidence suggests that urban population growth outstripped growth in the population as a whole, so that in the later

Table 2.1 Percentage of population living in British towns, 1650–1800*

	1650	1700	1750	1800
England and Wales	8.8	13.3	16.7	20.3
Scotland	3.5	5.3	9.2	17.3
Europe	*8.3*	*9.2*	*9.5*	*10.0*

* Estimates based on the population of towns with 10,000 or more inhabitants.

Source: J. de Vries, *European Urbanization, 1500–1800* (1984), p. 39.

eighteenth century nearly one in three English people were living in towns, compared with fewer than one in seven in 1700. The remarkable rate of this acceleration stands out more clearly when set against the experience of other European countries (see Table 2.2). Indeed, Anthony Wrigley has calculated that between 1750 and 1800 about 70 per cent of all the urban growth in Europe as a whole was taking place in England, at a time when the urban population of the Netherlands was actually falling.[2]

Table 2.2 Urban population percentages by nation, 1700–1850[*]

	1700	*1750*	*1800*	*1850*
Europe	*11–14*	*11–13*	*11–13*	*19*
Belgium	26–35	18–23	18–22	34
England	13–16	17–19	22–24	45
France	11–15	12–16	11–13	19
Germany	8–11	8–10	8–10	15
Italy	14–19	15–20	16–20	(23)
Netherlands	38–49	33–41	34–39	39
Portugal	18–23	13–15	14–17	(16)
Spain	12–17	12–18	12–19	(18)
Switzerland	6–8	6–9	6–8	(12)

[*] Estimates based on the population of towns with 5,000 or more inhabitants.

Source: P. Bairoch, *Cities and Economic Development: from the Dawn of History to the Present*, trans. C. Braider (Chicago, 1988), pp. 215, 221.

Over the next 40 years, as the rate of growth in Scotland rose to meet that of England and even Wales began to catch up, the urban population doubled again. By 1841, therefore, the urban minority, now approaching 51 per cent of the total British population, had assumed substantial proportions.[3]

Quantifying Change

The impact of the expanding towns was even greater than the census figures suggest; indeed, many contemporaries, impressed by the evidence of urban growth and identifying it as a sign of Britain's rising status as an imperial power, found the relatively modest results of the 1801 census difficult to reconcile with their own perceptions of the scale and accelerating pace of expansion. This apparent contradiction can perhaps be explained by the fact that contemporaries based their impressions on a variety of qualitative as well as quantitative indicators, taking into account a town's relative social and cultural standing, as well as the nature and vitality of its economic activity, its comparative wealth, and the extent of its influence over neighbouring communities. Above all, perhaps, their sense of wonder at the pace and scale of change was based on the rapid expansion of the built-up area of the faster-growing towns; William Hutton, for instance, declared in 1783 that 'The Traveller who visits [Birmingham] once in six Months, supposes himself acquainted with her; but he may chance to find a Street of Houses in the Autumn, where he saw his Horse eat Grass in the Spring'.[4] The crude measures of population totals and growth rates, on which historians are forced to rely as the best available evidence for significant urban development, are an inadequate proxy for these myriad, subtle indicators.

Moreover, despite the successful research activity into English population history that has taken place over the last few decades, there are still major gaps in our knowledge of urban populations before the 1801 census, while comparable figures for Scotland and Wales are even thinner on the ground. All population evidence from pre-census times is difficult to work with, but the problems posed by urban settlements are particularly acute. Uncertainty about the lower threshold of population necessary to qualify places as 'towns' does not help, nor does local patriotism, which in several cases produced inflated and potentially misleading estimates. Defoe, for example, thought that London's population in the early 1720s was already 1.5 million, rather than the 600,000 which modern estimates suggest as a more realistic figure; although Defoe's impression that London's growth was accelerating between 1700 and 1720 was probably correct, 1.5 million was not reached until the 1820s.[5] Several energetic and enterprising provincial towns also greeted the results of the 1801 census with dismay and disbelief. The response in Newcastle upon Tyne, for instance, was 'universal surprise' and its outraged citizens virtually demanded a recount. Since they were absolutely convinced that the town 'has not only maintained its rank, but even risen in the scale of national importance', the official figure of 28,294, indicating that the town had slipped well down the urban hierarchy, coming to rest at the same level as Nottingham and not far above Sunderland, was simply unacceptable.[6]

The problem for the historian is that in some cases injured local pride reflected the realities of urban life far better than the apparently clear-cut evidence of a census based on administrative divisions. Figures for Newcastle were returned separately from those of its Gateshead suburb on the opposite bank of the Tyne, just as Plymouth was artificially separated from Devonport, while many fast-growing towns had the fringes of their built-up areas credited to neighbouring parishes. At the other end of the scale, smaller towns embedded in large rural parishes often had their 'urban' populations inflated by the inclusion of the inhabitants of nearby villages.[7]

Despite these formidable problems, painstaking labour has succeeded in arriving at working estimates for the populations of Britain's towns in the years between 1680 and 1841, and it is unlikely that subsequent research will discover major inaccuracies in the urban rankings produced on this basis. Historians can therefore be reasonably confident about the relative performance of Georgian towns in terms of population growth; they are also able to use this hard-won knowledge to go one step further and investigate the origins of these expanding urban populations.

Population Growth: Migration

Despite the fact that the evidence available to those few demographers who have attempted to work on the population history of British towns in this period is both limited and, in many respects, far from conclusive, it is possible to draw some tentative conclusions.[8] Where urban growth was occurring, it was by a combination of two demographic processes: natural increase among established residents and a persistent flow of migrants from the countryside. However, there is no doubt that the level of population growth experienced by Britain's towns in the eighteenth and early nineteenth centuries was heavily reliant on migration. Even settlements that were not expanding dramatically saw a constant turnover of population as a steady stream of immigrants flowed in to replace those who had moved on, moved back or fallen prey to the notoriously high urban death rates. The larger and more rapidly growing the town, the greater its proportion of recruits from the countryside; Hutton estimated, for example, that at least half of Birmingham's inhabitants over the age of 10 were immigrants, while it was claimed in the 1750s that fully two-thirds of London's adult residents had been born outside the capital. Certainly, of the 3240 adults examined in the Westminster General Dispensary in 1781, only 25 per cent had been born in London, although this may well be an unrepresentative sample of the capital's population as a whole.

This heavy dependence on in-migration was by no means unpreced-ented. Towns had for centuries been net consumers rather than produ-cers of population and indeed Souden estimated that half to two-thirds of the inhabitants of English provincial towns in the later seventeenth century were migrants.[9] However, in contrast with the experience of the sixteenth and seventeenth centuries, most newcomers to the Georgian town had travelled relatively short distances. The growing number of expanding provincial towns made it unnecessary for would-be migrants to move very far afield, which explains why the migration fields of apprentices in both England and Scotland contracted sharply during the eighteenth century. Towns therefore drew many of their recruits from smaller settlements within their own immediate orbit, usually within ten or twenty miles; this was as true for rising manufacturing centres such as Sheffield as for more stable county towns like Dumfries. In general, the larger the town, the stronger its powers of attraction, but there was still an unmistakable regional bias to migration patterns.[10]

As the pace of urbanization increased in the later years of the century, so too did the rate of immigration, particularly into London and the rapidly growing port and industrial cities. Even in Nottingham, where natural increase made a significant contribution to growth from the mid-1740s, migration was responsible for nearly 60 per cent of the rise in population between 1780 and 1801 as the local framework-knitting industry expanded and turned the previous trickle of just under 200 in-migrants a year into a flood. In Liverpool, between 70 and 80 per cent of an estimated population increase of 20,000–22,000 in the 1790s can be attributed to immigration, which also accounted for just over 60 per cent of Scotland's total urban growth in the first half of the nineteenth century.

Immigration on this scale obviously raises the question of what drew so many people into the towns, despite the evident dangers that were inseparable from living and working in such an environment. London in particular had a well-established reputation as a demographic sink, and contemporaries were acutely conscious of what Sharpe has termed 'the massive penalty of urban living'. In the opinion of Dr Thomas Short, for instance, urban life necessarily entailed 'a Variety of avoidable and inavoidable Causes . . . , to impair Health, and often shorten Life in all Ages and Sexes'; he blamed not only the fetid air and poor ventilation inseparable from high population densities in the close-packed towns, but also the temptations posed by 'Intemperance, Intriguing, Night-revelling, Luxury, Excess, or other Vices', as opposed to 'the truest and most innocent natural Pleasures' of rural life.[11]

In the circumstances, traditional explanations of urban growth tended to focus on 'push' factors, such as the enclosure movement and the decline of rural industry, which were thought to have driven reluctant migrants into the towns. Female migrants, in particular, may well have been influenced by the restricted work opportunities and low wages available to women in the countryside. Hundreds of thousands of young women certainly moved into the larger towns in this period, producing what one demographer has called 'a remarkable predominance of women', in contrast with the more balanced or emphatically male-dominated populations of smaller country towns and villages and of the heavy industrial areas. By the 1690s the sex ratio (the number of males per 100 females) in larger English towns had already fallen to an average of 83.4, while in Edinburgh the ratio was as low as 76.[12] This female bias in urban populations continued unabated well into the next century; indeed the 1801 census revealed that Oxford was the only substantial town in England and Wales not to house a majority of women.

It would be a mistake, however, to see the bulk of immigrants, male or female, as reluctant recruits to urban life; much more characteristic was Hutton's comment that, in fuelling Birmingham's rapid growth from the 1660s, 'numbers of people crouded upon each other, as into a Paradise'.[13] Unlikely as that might seem in the case of Birmingham, Georgian towns still held out the vision of excitement and opportunity that had proved an irresistible attraction since the days of Dick Whittington. Young people poured into the expanding urban centres in search of the many economic advantages of town life, from education and training for a brighter future to the more immediate gains to be made from higher wages and a buoyant market for casual labour. Defoe assumed as a matter of course that the rural population, both male and female, would be quick to move into the town in response to a rise in the demand for labour, and gave a graphic account of the local impact of a boom in the demand for East Anglian cloth in 1712–13:

> The poor farmers could get no Dairy-Maids; the Wenches told them in so many words, they would not go to [farm] Service for Twelve-pence a Week, when they could get nine Shillings a Week *at their own Hands*, as they called it; so they all run away to . . . *Colchester*, and other Manufacturing Towns of *Essex* and *Sussex*.[14]

Williamson describes the rate of immigration into English cities during the industrial revolution as 'really quite spectacular' in comparison with that of developing countries in the 1960s and 1970s; while the enormous bias in urban populations towards young adults, which declined after 1841, is unmatched in today's Third World. This young-adult bias, moreover, tended to be even more pronounced for female than for male migrants, contributing to the historic predominance of women in the Georgian town.[15]

Employment opportunities in the vibrant economies of Georgian towns were therefore powerful magnets attracting young people away from their farms and villages, and they also played a part in determining the migrants' destinations. Not all towns offered the same economic opportunities at the same time, and consequently not all towns grew at the same rate; the scale and direction of population movements were both closely linked with the waxing and waning of particular urban economies.

Population Growth: Natural Increase

Urban demographic growth was not solely attributable to immigration, however, and by the late eighteenth century natural population increase may have begun to contribute more significantly. It had always played an important part in the expansion of smaller country towns, where the hazards of urban life were less extreme and the cocktail of epidemic and endemic diseases that debilitated the inhabitants of the cities proved less noxious. Now it began to affect the larger towns as well; in Exeter, Nottingham and Leeds, for example, the parish records of the later eighteenth century show baptism figures edging above the heavy annual toll of burials and the proportion of growth derived from immigration declined.[16] Even in London, the tide seems to have turned from natural decline to Victorian growth after a period of particularly high mortality in the period 1700–75 (see Table 2.3).

The causes of this unprecedented surplus of births over deaths are a matter of debate. Given that the larger towns almost certainly continued to deserve their lethal reputation as reservoirs of disease, with renewed epidemics of typhus compounding the impact of Asiatic cholera after its arrival in Sunderland in September 1831, conventional explanations among English demographic historians tended to focus on increased fertility. Improved employment and housing opportunities, together with access to higher earnings, were assumed to have led not only to an increased number of marriages at younger ages among urban residents,

Table 2.3　Population movements in London, 1730–1830

	Crude birth rate (per 1,000)	Crude death rate (per 1,000)	Surplus/deficit (per 1,000 p.a.)	Estimated population per decade	Natural increase/ decrease
1730s	43.1	48.6	− 5.5	675,000	− 37,000
1740s	34.4	46.0	−11.6	675,000	− 78,000
1750s	40.5	44.8	− 4.3	675,000	− 29,000
1760s	36.5	42.2	− 5.7	740,000	− 42,000
1770s	40.2	42.1	− 1.9	811,000	− 15,000
1780s	37.4	36.0	+ 1.4	890,000	+ 12,000
1790s	37.4	34.6	+ 2.8	975,000	+ 27,000
1800s	33.1	33.2	− 0.1	1,162,000	− 1,000
1810s	34.0	28.9	+ 5.1	1,434,000	+ 73,000
1820s	32.2	26.7	+ 5.5	1,595,000	+ 88,000

Source:　L. Schwarz, 'London, 1700–1840', in *CUHB*, p. 651.

but also to a higher level of illegitimate births. The predominantly youthful migrants who made up such a large proportion of the urban population, young men and women at the height of their reproductive as well as their working capacities, would inevitably begin to make use of the social – and sexual – opportunities for which urban life was renowned.[17] As Defoe rather sourly noted, the influx of young migrants into the East Anglian cloth towns had precisely these consequences: 'the Ale-houses in the great Towns were throng'd with them, young Fellows and young Wenches together, till the Parishes began to take Cognizance of them upon another Account, too dark to talk of here', but clearly a rise in illegitimacy is implied.[18]

Recent research, however, has pointed to a remarkably celibate culture among all sections of the urban population, suggesting that the Georgian town did not in fact offer 'the superior degree of luxury and debauchery', which most contemporary commentators thought was 'usually and justly attributed to towns'.[19] In reality, towns in this period contained much higher proportions of widows, bachelors and spinsters than rural communities, while marriages between immigrants tended to take place at relatively late ages, so limiting their reproductive potential. It seems unlikely, therefore, that rising fertility alone can explain any natural increase taking place in the populations of British towns in the later eighteenth and early nineteenth centuries.

As a result, demographic historians have begun to look more closely at the complex interaction of fertility and mortality to explain the surplus of births over deaths experienced in many towns in this period, focusing in particular on the possibility that death rates among infants may have been falling. Even in London, where infant and child mortality was exceptionally high, due mainly to smallpox and gastric disease, family reconstitutions appear to indicate a significant reduction in infant mortality from the early eighteenth century, a reduction that continued until 1840. Given that infant deaths accounted for up to 50 per cent of all deaths recorded in Georgian towns, and that infant and child mortality were exceptionally high in all urban areas, the slight improvements noted in the survival chances of children under two years of age in most urban areas could well have had a major cumulative impact on their populations; a relative fall in infant mortality would entail an eventual rise in fertility, since these town-bred children would grow up to have a better chance of marrying, and would marry at a younger age, than recent migrants.[20] It was possible, therefore, despite the immense challenge posed by the well-known 'urban graveyard' effect, for towns with high mortality rates to achieve a surplus of births and thus make a positive contribution to their overall rate of population growth.

On the other hand, it should be recognized that these improved infant survival rates were both relative and highly sensitive to economic and environmental conditions. Whenever urban growth ran ahead of the capacity of the local infrastructure and population densities began to soar, as they did in Glasgow after 1831, then childhood deaths from typhus and diarrhoea rose with them. The rate of population growth in each individual town thus depended on a delicate balance between endogenous fertility and mortality rates, on the one hand, and the rate of immigration on the other. As a result, the demographic experience of neighbouring communities could diverge quite sharply, producing significant variations over time. Georgian Chester, for instance, compared very favourably with its faster-growing neighbours in north-west England in terms of its relatively low mortality rates, prompting contemporaries to praise its 'proportional healthiness'. On the other hand, Chester's birth rates were equally sluggish, indicating perhaps that its increasingly specialized role as a shopping and residential centre acted to curb fertility through restricting the employment and marriage prospects of its poorer inhabitants, 'among whom the greatest principles of increase and decrease are to be looked for'.[21] Since these same restrictions also served to discourage large-scale immigration, it is not surprising that Chester's population growth lagged well behind that of its neighbours, despite the fact that the rate of urbanization in the north-west out-stripped that of any other region in the years 1680–1840.

Urban Growth: Patterns of Development

With natural increase thus reinforcing the demographic effects of immigration, the process of urban development in Georgian Britain clearly turned upon the features of town life that made it attractive to ever-larger numbers of migrants. Urban growth therefore reflected rising urban wealth, which created the economic opportunities that provided the basic motivation for migration; and rising urban wealth in turn reflected the buoyancy of the national economy.

Many factors contributed to this ever-increasing national prosperity. Rising agricultural productivity and surpluses, with a growing trend towards regional specialization; the integration of these regions into a national market; expanding overseas and inland trade, the latter oper-ating through a progressively more sophisticated distribution system; an increasingly diversified industrial base; a peaceful political situation within Britain itself; all these came together to produce a buoyant home market. It is widely accepted that this 'consumer revolution' played a vital part in stimulating urban growth in eighteenth-century Britain.[22] The number of people whose income could stretch beyond the basic necessities of life grew enormously and so, consequently, did the market for consumer goods and services that the towns were best placed to supply, not only to their own residents, but also to a wider clientele in the surrounding countryside. In such an environment, most towns succeeded in generating and attracting sufficient new resources of capital and enterprise to fuel sustained and often dynamic expansion.

Urban growth was not, however, uniform. Indeed the eighteenth century was one of the most dynamic periods in British urban history, as the fortunes of individual towns fluctuated with the changing character of the national economy. Although the general trend was decidedly upwards, the process was highly selective; not all towns benefited from the expansion of consumer demand, and some enjoyed only short-term or intermittent success. As the long-sustained rise in real incomes, which had underpinned widespread urban growth in the later seventeenth and early eighteenth centuries, died away, many historic county towns and regional centres found that their rate of population growth began to fall well below the national average (see Table 2.4)

Table 2.4   Differential growth rates of leading British towns

	Cumulative % growth rate p.a. (17th century–1801)		Cumulative % growth rate p.a. (1801–41)
Highest			
Liverpool	3.13	Brighton	4.83
Manchester	2.69	Bradford	4.12
Paisley	2.48	Merthyr Tydfil	3.68
Sheffield	2.44	Preston	3.64
Birmingham	2.36	Liverpool	3.17
Oldham	2.08	Glasgow	3.10
Sunderland	2.08	Stockport	3.09
London	0.81	London	1.79
Edinburgh	0.44	Edinburgh	1.77
Lowest			
Canterbury	0.12	Portsmouth	1.18
York	0.12	Chester	1.16
Ipswich	0.10	Colchester	1.09
Salisbury	0.09	Salisbury	0.68
Oxford	0.04	Perth	0.55
Cambridge	−0.03	Shrewsbury	0.54

Source: See Appendix 1.

Although very few actually declined in size, their share of Britain's total population began to fall markedly so that they experienced the sort of relative 'failure' which had already afflicted York in the mid-seventeenth century. In the case of Norwich, England's second city in 1700, the 1801 census revealed that its population had actually fallen since 1775, while towns such as Cambridge, Canterbury and Salisbury discovered that they had sunk well down the provincial rankings. It is hardly surprising, therefore, that many provincial cities which had, as Anthony Wrigley puts it, 'for many centuries . . . exchanged places in the premier urban league', found the results hard to accept.[23]

In sharp contrast, towns such as Sheffield, Bath, Wolverhampton, Paisley, Bolton and Greenock, all of which gained promotion to this league in the course of the eighteenth century, had all profited from the new opportunities opened up by rising national prosperity. The most impressive growth rates of all tended, perhaps not surprisingly, to be found among towns which had made only modest progress by 1700. Liverpool's population in 1801, for instance, was 14 times greater than it had been a hundred years earlier, while the growth rates of Sheffield, Manchester and Bath did not lag far behind. As Appendix 1 demonstrates, these fast-growing towns all doubled or tripled in size between 1801 and 1841, confirming their new-found status in the upper ranks of the urban hierarchy. The 1841 census also confirmed the promotion of a new cohort of dynamic upstarts, towns such as Bradford, Brighton and Merthyr Tydfil; Brighton's population, for example, grew by an average of 14 per cent a year in these four decades and Bradford's by 10 per cent.

Contemporaries were undoubtedly impressed by the rapid growth of so many 'new' towns and by the relative eclipse of historic urban centres, so much so that explanations of the changing patterns of urban growth tended to suggest that such nominal 'villages' as Manchester, Bradford or Sheffield owed their success to the absence of traditional corporate restraints on free enterprise.[24] It would be a mistake, however, to exaggerate the influence of institutional arrangements on urban development in this period; neither Liverpool nor Glasgow, for instance, appears to have been handicapped by its corporate status. It should also be recognized that many of the so-called 'new towns' were in fact old-established urban communities which had already begun to experience rapid population growth in the later seventeenth century as their buoyant economies attracted large numbers of migrants. The mushroom growth of Merthyr Tydfil from a few scattered houses into the 'metropolis of ironmasters', as a result of the dramatic expansion of pig-iron production in South Wales in the 1790s, was a rare exception to this general rule; contemporaries were amazed by 'the triumph of fact over probability' represented by its meteoric rise.[25]

In other ways, however, Merthyr ran true to type; there, as elsewhere, the key to success seems to have been specialization of function and the exploitation of one of the many niches opened up by the rising pace of economic expansion in Britain as a whole. Industrial towns acquired a growing share of the manufacturing process, while continuing to service the rural industry of their hinterlands; ports handled growing quantities of agricultural produce, raw materials and manufactured goods for an expanding, world-wide network of customers and suppliers; while health and leisure resorts orientated themselves towards the lucrative task of catering for the increasingly sophisticated consumer economy. Although the growth of the resorts needs to be kept in proportion – between 1801 and 1841 the population of Manchester alone increased by more than the expansion of all the inland spas and seaside resorts put together – it is worth emphasizing the success of these archetypal products of the consumer revolution in an age more commonly associated with rapid industrialization.[26] The new wave of resorts promoted in the later eighteenth and early nineteenth centuries, just like the classic 'new towns' of the industrial revolution, evolved as a response to changing market conditions and in particular to the expansion and diversification of demand. These were precisely the conditions promoting change over the whole urban network between 1680 and 1840.

Regional Differentiation

Urban growth and the movement towards greater specialization of function that it entailed for towns throughout the emerging urban network, were accompanied by a clear trend towards the rationalization of functions amongst towns in particular regions, thus reducing potentially harmful competition. Regional identities had traditionally been very weakly defined in the British context and there were few clear-cut regional boundaries. Indeed it is hard to find contemporary references to regions, such as East Anglia or the West Midlands, before the end of the eighteenth century.[27]

However, the varying pace of growth and changing patterns of development at a local level both encouraged the emergence of integrated regional networks of towns, particularly in the north west of England, the western Scottish lowlands, Yorkshire and the West Midlands. In the West Riding of Yorkshire, for example, Leeds evolved into a specialist cloth-finishing centre, while Halifax and Bradford were best known for worsted weaving, Huddersfield for kerseys, Barnsley for wire making and later linen weaving, Sheffield for fine cutlery, and Pontefract for market gardening; all complemented by the spas at Knaresborough and Harrogate, and the smart residential town of Doncaster.

A similarly complex network was also developing in the West Midlands, where the growing influence of Birmingham was exercised in a climate of creative tension with that of the older county centres of Coventry, Warwick and Lichfield, as well as with the rising industrial towns of Wolverhampton and Walsall. Towards the end of the period this intricate local economy evolved even further, as investment from Birmingham and Warwick led to the unusually rapid growth of Leamington Spa from a village of 315 inhabitants at the time of the 1801 census to a town with a population of nearly 13,000 in 1841. Meanwhile, a number of small industrializing towns in the region began to concentrate on different types of metal products which were then sold through Birmingham; one or two places even became component towns, making parts to be assembled in Birmingham workshops.

Birmingham's emergence as the dynamic commercial and industrial capital of the West Midlands was mirrored by the rise of Glasgow, Leeds, Liverpool and Manchester within their own rapidly developing regions.[28] Each of these cities lay at the heart of a complex web of social and economic relationships, relationships that were continually strengthened by investment in transport improvements and in the professional and commercial services which integrated their fast-developing hinterlands ever more closely into their spheres of influence. The speed and scale of their growth aroused in contemporary observers a mixture of terror and excitement. Just as early modern London had been condemned as a parasite, devouring the nation's wealth and luring migrants to an early grave, so Manchester in the 1820s and 1830s was portrayed by its critics as a smoky, ravening monster, 'a diligent spider ... placed in the centre of the web', absorbing all the creative energies of the surrounding counties without giving anything in return.[29]

This was undoubtedly an exaggerated and unfair response to the rise of these great provincial cities; to some extent, of course, their regional predominance merely echoed the influence that had traditionally been exercised by historic centres such as Bristol, Newcastle, Exeter and York. Indeed Glasgow's steady rise up the Scottish urban hierarchy in the century before 1700 was due primarily to its well-established role as the market-place of the western lowlands, rather than to the expansion of new transatlantic trade routes, so that its economic and demographic success in the eighteenth century rested on entirely traditional foundations. On the other hand, contemporaries were probably right in identifying these 'new' regional centres as signs of a more profound urban transformation. It was not simply that they were significantly larger than their counterparts in 1700, nor even that they had evolved into much more diversified communities. By 1840 their apparently inexorable progress provided incontrovertible evidence that a new urban world had evolved, one in which the traditional county boundaries and structures had very little influence and in which successful cities reformulated their local spheres of influence on their own terms.

Easy access to river transport, for example, was no longer one of the most influential factors in urban growth. The key to success lay rather in the creation and attraction of new sources of wealth; if the potential for growth was there, investment in road or river improvement schemes, in

Table 2.5   Urban population growth: regional variations

Annual average % growth (17th century–1801)		*Annual average % growth (1801–41)*	
Highest			
North-west England	5.82	North-west England	5.44
Western Scottish lowlands	2.88	Western Scottish lowlands	5.29
Yorkshire	2.36	South Wales	5.11
West Midlands	2.28	Yorkshire	3.83
Northern England	2.10	West Midlands	3.13
England and Wales	1.52	Britain	2.92
Scotland	1.31		
London[a]	1.45	London	2.65
Lowest			
South-west peninsula	1.08	Outer south-east England[b]	2.15
English home counties	1.07	Southern Scotland	2.07
Rural Wales	1.04	South-west peninsula	1.98
Eastern Scottish lowlands	0.72	Inner south-west England[c]	1.92
East Anglia	0.58	East Anglia	1.74

[a] London figures calculated using the 1801 and 1841 boundaries, plus satellite towns at both dates.
[b] Bedfordshire, Berkshire, Buckinghamshire, Hampshire, Oxfordshire and Sussex.
[c] Dorset, Gloucestershire, Somerset, Wiltshire.

Source: J. Langton, 'Urban growth and economic change from the seventeenth century to 1841', in *CUHB*, p. 480.

canals, and eventually in railways, could overcome the deficiencies of the original site. Birmingham, for example, although remote from natural water transport, became the hub of the growing canal network in the later decades of the eighteenth century, establishing strong links with the expanding northern ports.[30] Access to the busy transport networks of Georgian Britain, and thus to the rapidly expanding home and overseas markets, was just as likely to be the consequence as the cause of urban prosperity.

Contemporaries were also well aware of an important geographical element to change, confirming the later seventeenth-century evidence of the growing significance of the industrial north and west and the relative eclipse of the southern and eastern regions of England which had been dominant throughout the medieval and early modern periods (see Table 2.5).

This shift in the urban world's centre of gravity reflected the changing conditions of Britain's economic life in the long eighteenth century.[31] Although the traditional urban system still exhibited considerable residual strength, the modest performance of towns outside the 'energy rich' economies of the coalfields merely highlighted the spectacular rise of the urban West Midlands, West Riding, central Lancashire and west central Scotland. At the close of the seventeenth century, London was 20 per cent bigger than all the towns of those regions put together; by 1841 they were 80 per cent bigger than the capital, whose inhabitants were actually outnumbered by the combined urban populations of Cheshire, Lancashire and the West Riding. Moreover, although the rate of urbanization undoubtedly increased after 1801, there is considerable evidence that the new regional patterns of urban growth had emerged long before the early nineteenth century; indeed, recent research suggests that they preceded, rather than followed, the classic period of the industrial revolution.[32]

Small Towns

The changing fortunes of Britain's great mass of smaller towns tend to be overlooked in this period of far-reaching change; the fate of these minor settlements seems trivial in comparison with the dramatic upheavals taking place in the upper reaches of the urban system. However, it is worth remembering that, in the later seventeenth century, at least half the urban population lived in towns with fewer than 2500 inhabitants. It is also clear that small market towns up and down the country continued to play a vital role well into the nineteenth century, bridging the gap between town and countryside and providing most British people with the first experience of urban society. Their relative vitality and prosperity, therefore, underpinned that of the urban system as a whole.

Earlier studies of eighteenth-century urban development tended, none the less, to assume that the majority of small towns failed to respond to the competitive pressures created by economic change and regional differentiation. Specialization and rationalization, it was argued, had a damaging effect on those minor towns which failed to find a particular manufacturing, marketing or other niche and were eclipsed by larger, more rapidly growing neighbours. The gradual provision of better transport and communications, in particular, would inevitably

divert trade to larger towns which could offer travellers, prosperous
farmers and wealthy consumers a range of comfortable inns, permanent
shops selling a wider choice of goods, and regular visits from substantial,
London-based salesmen.[33] Few market towns in Essex, for example, could
compete with Chelmsford, which in 1775 had over 40 shops, including
bookshops and coffee-houses, and no fewer than 48 inns; Chelmsford's
resident population at this date was slightly under 2800. As the scale and
pace of improvement increased, moreover, and a wider range of trades
and services spread out into the larger villages, even larger country
towns such as Chelmsford stagnated. By 1800 the number of inns in the
town had fallen to 31, while it cannot have enhanced the fortunes of
Lewes in Sussex, for instance, that the 75 families living in the nearby
village of East Hoathly were by the 1750s served by a well-stocked retail
shop, a butcher, a shoemaker, a chandler, a blacksmith, a carpenter, a
wheelwright, a weaver and a barber. A sizeable group of marginal
centres, like those at Harlow in Essex, Methvold in Norfolk and Kineton
in Warwickshire, had lost their markets altogether by 1800, contributing to a sharp contraction in the number of market towns in the country
as a whole in the last decades of the period. Minor towns in mid and
north Wales, such as Lampeter in Ceredigion and Caerwys in Flintshire,
were similarly vulnerable to de-urbanization; while several of the
smaller Scottish centres, particularly towns in the border counties such
as Coldingham and Coldstream, or Sanquhar in Dumfries and Galloway, failed to preserve their urban character into the early nineteenth
century.

Recent research has, however, offered a much more optimistic interpretation of the overall performance of small towns, suggesting that
their rate of expansion in the years between c.1670 and 1811 kept pace,
not only with the growth of the national population, but also with the
development of the provincial urban system as a whole. Indeed Peter
Clark is convinced that most small towns retained their importance in
Georgian society, growing in population and prosperity, becoming 'more
distinctively urban and urbane', despite increasing competition and
the inexorable decline of traditional open markets.[34] Even in the early
nineteenth century, when the viability of many minor centres came
under pressure, some country towns succeeded in weathering the storm,
sustaining their urban functions and status well into the Victorian age.

As in the case of their faster-growing and more dynamic neighbours,
the key to success for small towns was developing more specialized,
more sophisticated, economies. Many smaller centres benefited from

craft or industrial specialisms; Kettering, for instance, developed a prosperous worsted industry, while Dumbarton owed its rise to glass making and Holywell to local investment in brass, copper and cotton. In many cases, their activities complemented those of larger towns, so that their relationship was symbiotic rather than directly competitive. Small ports such as Aberystwyth, Hartlepool or Dunbar could thus make a comfortable living from the lively coastal trade in coal and agricultural produce, or even develop new export trades, alongside great commercial giants like Liverpool or Hull. Some coastal towns were able to develop an additional source of income as seaside resorts. Weymouth, for instance, was promoted by Ralph Allen as a summer resort with a season which complemented that of the dynamic inland spa of Bath, while Blackpool catered for industrialists, merchants and professional families from the burgeoning towns of north-western England. Stamford, Cowbridge, and Forfar, meanwhile, exemplified the type of inland 'resort' whose prosperous and gentrified landscape attracted both temporary visitors and permanent residents from among the enlarged urban and rural elites. Stamford was also one of many smaller towns which benefited from improved transport networks and the growing volume of inland trade, as well as a proliferation of new administrative functions.

Smaller towns once again followed the pattern of their larger neighbours in that there were clear regional differences in their rates of growth and relative success over the Georgian period as a whole. Once again it was the West Midlands, West Riding, central Lancashire and west central Scotland which saw the highest concentration of successful towns and the highest rates of small-town growth, while East Anglia, south-west England, north Wales and the Scottish borders lagged well behind.[35]

It should be recognized, however, that there were also considerable variations within regions, as small towns interacted with one another as well as with larger, more dynamic, centres. In Dorset, for example, Blandford Forum developed in the second half of the eighteenth century into an important inland communications centre, within easy travelling distance of the coastal towns of Poole, Melcombe Regis and Weymouth. An outer ring of relatively successful smaller centres, from Bridport to Shaftesbury, also benefited from the gradual improvement of transport and communications, each growing a little faster than the county population as a whole. Yet several other Dorset towns clearly failed to attract the same degree of custom and stagnated, among them the county town of Dorchester, which was handicapped by its poor rural hinterland and even lost its role as a gentry resort to fashionable Melcombe.[36] A similar story of conflicting fortunes could be repeated from every region in Georgian Britain.

The Capital Cities

What various transformations we remark,
From East Whitchapel to the West Hyde-park!
Men, women, children, houses, signs, and fashions,
State, stage, trade, taste, the humours and the passions;
Th'Exchange, 'Change alley, whereso'er you're ranging,
Court, city, country, all are chang'd or changing.

David Garrick (1777)[37]

The world of the capital cities of Scotland and England in the long eighteenth century seems on one level to be light years away from that of the great mass of small towns. However, the development of Edinburgh and London during this period was strongly influenced by the same dynamics of economic change and regional differentiation that were transforming the urban system as a whole. Their relatively slow expansion after the later seventeenth century epitomized the modest growth rates of smaller towns in the traditional urban heartlands of southern and eastern Britain. As a result, London's lead over its nearest provincial rivals declined dramatically; whereas in 1700 it had been 20 times as large as Norwich and 27 times as large as Bristol, by 1841 it was only six times larger than Manchester and seven times larger than Liverpool. Edinburgh was actually overtaken by Glasgow as Scotland's largest city in the early decades of the nineteenth century. In 1841 Glasgow, with over a quarter of a million inhabitants, accounted for 10 per cent of Scotland's total population, while Edinburgh and Leith together contained another 6 per cent.

However, the rapid expansion of these 'shock cities' should not obscure the continued importance of both these capitals. The fact that Edinburgh's legal, financial, educational and ecclesiastical systems retained their independence, even after the parliamentary union of the early eighteenth century, meant that Edinburgh continued to exercise considerable control over 'North British' affairs and made the city a magnet for salaried professionals. In social and cultural terms, too, Edinburgh functioned as a regional capital whose region embraced virtually the whole of Scotland. Students trained in the capital carried its influence far beyond its immediate hinterland, while its buoyant consumer industries and service sector made it 'the rendezvous of Politeness, the abode of Taste, and winter quarters of all our nobility who cannot afford to live in London', as well as catering for its resident population of wealthy merchants and professionals.[38] Meanwhile it continued to benefit from its traditional role as the major commercial and manufacturing centre of the fertile Lothians, exchanging agricultural goods for the products of its strong industrial base and conducting an extensive coastal and overseas trade through its satellite port of Leith. The stability and balance of its economy, despite the setback suffered by its relatively undercapitalized industrial sector in the 1825 recession, allowed it to sustain a doubling of its population in the first quarter of the nineteenth century.

It would be an even greater mistake to underestimate the continuing metropolitan vigour and distinctiveness of Georgian London, which emerged in the eighteenth century as the 'wonder city' of Europe and a major player on the world stage.[39] Whatever the changes in the British urban system in this period, no one could doubt London's continued primacy, a primacy that was unique among European capital cities. Although its growth had slowed considerably after the headlong expansion of the sixteenth and seventeenth centuries, its share of the total population of England and Wales remained at around 10 or 11 per cent until 1801 and grew steadily thereafter, reaching 14 per cent in 1851. In contrast, the population of Paris grew very little after 1700, rising from 510,000 to only 581,000 by 1800, while its share of the national population did not rise above 2.5 per cent.

London developed in this period from a national into an imperial capital, the focus of the political, administrative, military and financial activity of Britain's expanding overseas empire. This concentration of power naturally attracted a similar concentration of wealth. From the later seventeenth century, London became the hub of English aristocratic life, attracting the rich and well-born from all parts of the kingdom and at all times, but particularly during the months of the social season, from mid-autumn until the spring. To these fashionable inhabitants of Westminster and the West End, London was quite simply 'the town', a unique and sophisticated environment, qualitatively as well as quantitatively different from 'the country', a term which was understood to include even the greatest provincial cities. Characters in Farquhar's *The Recruiting Officer* (1707), for example, bewailed the dull conformity of the 'country town' of Shrewsbury, while even Norwich was described in 1686 as being 'remote from the centre of affairs and in a great deal of quiet'.[40]

London's sheer size and wealth, together with the nature of its market, ensured that it played a crucial role in stimulating the national economy and promoting social change; as the principal centre of consumption and innovation, it pioneered ideas and fashions which were to transform provincial life. It was also a major industrial city, supplementing the basic 'maintenance' industries that were common to all towns at this time with specialized finishing processes using materials that were often brought in from the industrializing regions or from Britain's overseas empire. It lay at the heart of England's internal transport and trading networks, but it was also one of the world's greatest international ports, continuing to dominate trade with mainland Europe, with India and with the Far East, long after the rise of the Atlantic trade increased the relative importance of Liverpool, Glasgow, Bristol and Whitehaven; Joseph Addison described it in 1711 as 'a kind of *Emporium* for the whole Earth'.[41] Contemporaries must have regarded Samuel Johnson's famous assertion that 'when a man is tired of London, he is tired of life; for there is in London all that life can afford', as little more than a neat restatement of the obvious.[42]

London's expanding population, moreover, was now spreading out over a much greater area of land, creating a much greater visual impact on residents and visitors alike. In the later seventeenth century, London's built-up area was still extraordinarily compact, stretching in a straggling mass of buildings along a relatively narrow strip of land on the north bank of the river Thames. By the 1760s, the pattern of settlement had not only thickened and solidified around this central core, but had also dispersed as far as Hyde Park in the west, Mile End in the east, and St Pancras in the north; meanwhile, Westminster and Blackfriars bridges were opening up south London to the developers. Thereafter, the 'palpable immensity' of this vast conurbation, the mass of humanity crowding its streets and the mass of merchant vessels crowding its river, not to mention the constant and tumultuous noise – 'a universal hubbub; a sort of uniform grinding and shaking' – consistently stunned new arrivals.[43]

What made Georgian London unique, however, was not simply its absolute size. The capital's powerful centralizing influence extended over the whole urban system in the eighteenth century, spreading out from its immediate hinterland in south-eastern England to embrace most of the other English regions, Wales and even Scotland. George Colman noted in 1761 that 'scarce half a century ago, . . . the inhabitants of the distinct counties were regarded as a species, almost as different from those of the metropolis, as the natives of the Cape of Good Hope'.[44] By the early years of the nineteenth century, in contrast, a Swiss-American visitor to Britain reported in amazement that 'nobody is provincial in this country'.[45] This decisive break with the patterns of the past owed a great deal to London's crucial role as the power-house of British economic and social development, a contribution that underpinned the dynamic expansion of new regional and cultural centres in the north and west. Indeed, Britain's remarkable success in generating and maintaining the momentum of urban growth may well have depended on a creative tension between metropolitan hegemony and regional diversity.

3

MAKING A LIVING

Full are thy towns with the sons of art;
And trade and joy, in every busy street,
Mingling are heard; . . .
James Thomson (1746)[1]

Whereas the Victorian city is conventionally associated with slums, sweatshops and factories, the Georgian town evokes images of leisure and luxury; it is identified in the popular imagination with Bath and Jane Austen, rather than with the darker urban world portrayed by Charles Dickens or Elizabeth Gaskell. This sharp dichotomy, however, overlooks the fact that 'work', in its broadest sense, had been an essential element of urban life ever since the initial separation between town and country, a separation which was described by Friedrich Engels as 'the first great division of labour in society'.[2] At this very basic level, therefore, the livelihood of the urban population depended ultimately on trade; on marketing and processing agricultural products, and exchanging them for consumer goods, skills, capital and services originating in the town itself.

The greater sophistication and specialization which characterized urban economies in Georgian Britain meant that many eighteenth-century towns had moved away from such an absolute dependence on local demand and were hooked into wider regional, national, or even international markets. Rapidly expanding urban populations had also begun to constitute substantial markets in their own right; it has been suggested, for instance, that London's population had grown so large by 1700 that, if every other sector of its complex and vigorous economy had failed, its inhabitants could have survived by taking in each other's washing. These changing market conditions had certainly encouraged

47

the development of specialist urban economies catering for the extremes of conspicuous consumption and of equally conspicuous production. However, the clear distinction drawn by contemporary observers between towns 'of mirth and gallantry', on the one hand, and those 'of Considerable Business and a flourishing Trade', on the other, can be misleading if it obscures the fact that the vast majority of the urban population had to work hard in order to maintain themselves and their families.[3] It was, after all, primarily the greater economic opportunities offered by urban areas that encouraged so many young men and women to migrate into the towns in this period.

Occupational Structures: Sources of Information

Discussing the precise nature of these opportunities in terms of urban occupational structures is, however, surprisingly difficult. In some respects, eighteenth-century towns appear to have been well served by written sources which, for various reasons, recorded the occupations of a wide range of their inhabitants. Historians can draw on parish registers and on a variety of legal, administrative, tax and electoral records (poll books), as well as on the registers of insurance companies and on commercially published town directories, the earliest of which appeared in London in 1732 and in Edinburgh in 1752. Unfortunately, each of these sources has its drawbacks: they are rarely comprehensive or continuous in their coverage, they suffer from inbuilt biases, and their information is all too often incompatible or contradictory. Directories, for instance, need to be read in the knowledge that they were intended to draw attention to 'the Names, Occupations, and Situation of the Warehouses, Offices, Shops, etc. of the People in Trade', rather than to provide a full census of the town's economic activity and employment structure.[4] James Sketchley's *Bristol Directory* (1775), for example, contains only 4200 names out of an estimated total population of 55,000. Those who were omitted or under-represented in these sources, even when they are carefully analysed and aggregated to provide the widest possible coverage of a particular town, clearly formed the bulk of urban workforce.

Uncovering the occupational patterns of these poorer, less prominent members of the community, especially women and children, but also including numerous part-time and unskilled male workers, involves a great deal of perseverance on the part of the historian in locating and interpreting a wide range of source material, some of it indirect and circumstantial. It also involves, for the most part, moving away from the 'scientific' authority conveyed by tables and statistics to building up a picture of people's employment based on detailed descriptions of their everyday experiences.[5] Multiple occupations, in particular, pose acute problems of classification. Samuel Green, listed as a 'victualler and cook' in the 1787 *Directory of Sheffield*, can be fitted fairly easily into a conventional occupational structure, but under what heading should researchers classify Samuel Goodlad, described in the same source as 'victualler and musician', or even Ann Parker, 'cutler and vigo button maker'? And was this Ann Parker, of Pea Croft, whose trademark identified her as a manufacturer of table knives and razors, identical with the Widow Parker, of White Cross, who was listed as a manufacturer of horn buttons?[6] If so, might this particular inconsistency in the directory indicate that Ann operated some of her business interests in her own right but others as the surrogate of her dead husband? Even allowing for the assumption that people actually did what they said they did, something which should never be taken for granted, the precise meaning of what they said often remains unclear.

Occupational Specialization

Historians, however, are used to working with incomplete and unsatisfactory data, so that it is possible to draw some reasonably firm conclusions about occupational structures in eighteenth-century towns. First and foremost, the sources appear to confirm Adam Smith's observation in *The Wealth of Nations* (1776), one of the most influential texts in modern economics, that the economic vigour and dynamism of the British economy was closely related to rising levels of economic specialization. Smith illustrated his analysis of the beneficial effects of this division of labour, by which tasks were broken down into their component parts, each process being carried out by a different specialist, using the example of the 'very trifling manufacture' of pin-making.[7] Maxine Berg's recent research into the metal trades in Birmingham demonstrates this process in action: her examination of 652 wills left by male and female metalworkers between 1776 and 1787 threw up no fewer than 165 different occupational designations. Indeed, a visitor to a Birmingham workshop in 1757 was amazed by 'the Multitude of Hands' involved in producing each individual gilt button, estimating that 'they go thro' 70 different Operations of 70 different Work-folks' before they left the premises.[8]

Of course, Birmingham's economy was in many ways unique and contemporaries were inclined to emphasize the exceptional nature of its business environment; the poet Robert Southey, for example, accepted without question that 'in no other age or country was there ever so astonishing a display of human ingenuity'.[9] On the other hand, similar patterns of specialization can be found elsewhere, as in the coachmaking trade in the West End of London, where occupational designations used in the Westminster poll book for 1784 go far beyond the simple 'coach and harness maker' that you might expect to find in a provincial town with a much smaller market for luxury goods, to include coach builder, coach carver, coach draughtsman, coach founder, coach frame maker, coach harness-maker, coach harness-plater, coach joiner, coach liner, coach livery lace-maker, coach-maker, coach painter, coach plater, coach smith, coach spring-maker, coach trimmer and coach wheelwright.[10]

As this indicates, specialization among the workforce was closely allied to specialization of function in the urban economy as a whole. It has already been established that the fastest-growing towns of Georgian Britain were successful precisely because they were closely associated with one or more specialist functions or trades, specialisms that were clearly reflected in their occupational structures. The degree of occupational concentration involved, however, varied considerably. In the 'immature' industrial centre of Merthyr Tydfil, for example, mining and ironworking dominated the local economy to such an extent that contemporaries doubted whether it actually deserved the title of 'town'; it lacked the amenities and broadly-based patterns of employment that were usually inseparable from urban status. On the other hand, it was by no means unusual to find as many as 40 to 50 per cent of the total workforce of an established manufacturing town employed in its staple industry. Late seventeenth-century Norwich, for instance, was so dominated by the textile industry that Defoe pictured a casual visitor wondering whether the town had been deserted, 'the inhabitants being all busie ... in their garrets at their looms, and in their combing-shops, so they call them, twisting mills, and other work-houses'.[11] In metalworking towns, such as Birmingham and Sheffield, where the smoke of the forges hung heavily in the air and the streets were alive with people carrying components from one workshop to another, the dependence of the local economy on its staple industry was more immediately apparent. Even in textile towns, however, it would have been difficult to ignore the dense concentration of drying frames that covered the surrounding fields, the fulling mills and dyehouses that lined urban rivers, and the increasingly impressive cloth halls built to house the vital wholesale markets which brought together merchants and producers from the whole industrial region.[12] From the 1790s, moreover, the introduction of steam-powered mills and gas-lighting gave the textile towns a visual drama that was all their own: a visitor approaching Leeds from the north at nightfall reported that 'we saw a multitude of fires issuing, no doubt from furnaces, and constellations of illuminated windows (manufactories) spread over the dark plain'.[13]

Other towns exhibited other specialisms, both industrial and commercial. Unsurprisingly, trade and transport occupied a high percentage of the population of port towns everywhere in Georgian Britain. Merchants, sailors, watermen and dock workers crowded the quaysides, while shipyards and ropeworks stretched along the adjacent shoreline, interspersed with the foundries that supplied metalwork for docks, cranes and quays, as well as for the ships themselves. Ports were instantly identifiable as major employers of labour, clustering tightly around the forest of masts that could be glimpsed between the warehouses that lined the waterfront, and reverberating with the noise of cargoes trundling through the narrow streets. 'The vast trade of Newcastle', one traveller commented in 1802, 'is visible on first entering it, from the bustle of its quays, and the animation of its streets'.[14] He estimated that 1547 keelmen and 9000 seamen were employed on the Tyne, in addition to those who made a living in the shipyards, docks, sail-cloth factories and roperies that were so closely connected with the port. A third of English seamen in 1808 worked from the port of London, where they congregated in the riverside suburbs of Wapping and Limehouse; a third of Scottish seamen sailed from the ports on the Clyde, principally Glasgow and Greenock.[15] Few commercial ports, however, could match the occupational concentrations found in the highly specialized dockyard suburbs of Portsmouth and Plymouth, where shipping trades could employ 73 per cent of the adult male workforce. Most port towns were also major manufacturing centres, heavily involved in energy-dependent, bulk industries such as glass making, pottery, sugar and tobacco refining, and brewing: indeed Henry Bourne's *History of Newcastle on Tyne* (1736) ranked brewers very highly among 'such as have their Living by Shipping'.[16] However, it was patently obvious to Bourne, as to all the other inhabitants of Newcastle, that their livelihood was basically dependent on the port's trading activities and that a long-term decline in coal shipments would have a disastrous effect on employment in every sector of the local economy.

It would be a mistake, however, to overlook the role played by occupational specialization in many other towns, even those without such an

overwhelming dependence on long-distance trade or large-scale industry. County towns were by definition local administrative centres and,
since many were also cathedral cities, their administrative functions were
enhanced by their role as diocesan centres; Canterbury's economy, for
example, was heavily influenced by the presence of so many 'Deans,
Prebends, Minor Canons, . . . and the Church militant upon earth'.[17] As
the legal capital of Scotland, Edinburgh was notoriously well supplied
with lawyers, as was the area around the Inns of Court in London, while
the activities of the duchy and county palatine courts in Preston meant
that attorneys, proctors and notaries formed a significant and influential
group within the town's occupational structure: indeed, in 1759 'the
business of the Law' was identified as 'the Staple trade of this place'.[18] In
each of these cases, the professional group involved was relatively small
in terms of the total population of the town. However, as with the health
and leisure services provided by spas and seaside resorts, this core activity
attracted many wealthy visitors, whose presence in turn stimulated the
development of an increasingly sophisticated consumer economy. Resort
towns and smart residential centres, such as Chester, Stamford or the
West End of London, certainly supported a lucrative tertiary sector
providing high-quality goods and services to their fashionable clientele.
However, there was also a demand for a much less skilled and specialized labour force at the other end of the spectrum. Portrait painters,
jewellers and fashionable milliners thus co-existed in these 'places of
great resort' with thousands of porters, building labourers, washer-
women and domestic servants. Indeed the census for Leamington Spa
in 1841 recorded domestic service as the occupation of no fewer than
43 per cent of the town's working population.[19]

Occupational Diversification

The importance of specialized occupational sectors in so many British
towns in this period should not, however, overshadow the continuing
importance of what might be called the fundamental bedrock of every
urban economy: the broadly based range of occupations that provided
its own inhabitants with the basic necessities of life, while also providing
a significant proportion of the goods and services required by its hinterland. In a society lacking the advantages of modern mass production,
simply feeding, clothing and housing the growing urban population was
bound to involve a relatively high proportion of that population. It

should also be recognized that most towns continued to act as focal points for the broader economic and social activity of the surrounding countryside, processing and distributing agricultural produce, operating as marketing centres, and supplying a wider variety of professional services and consumer goods than could be obtained in even the most substantial village.

The result was a correspondingly wide and increasingly varied occupational structure in Georgian towns, underpinning the daily existence of those whose livelihood depended primarily on the specialist economic roles of ports, manufacturing centres and service towns alike. It would be easy to underestimate the sheer number of people required to feed, clothe and house those employed in these more highly specialized sectors of the urban economy. As Appendix 2 demonstrates, certain rather basic occupations appear time and again amongst the leading trades recorded in urban directories: butchers, bakers, victuallers, innkeepers, tailors and shoemakers in particular. Admittedly, such directories, which reflected the professional and business community, rather than the occupational structure as a whole, may well have overstated the relative importance of these occupations in terms of overall employment in the town. It is unlikely, for example, that grocers, attorneys and peruke [wig] makers were major employers of labour, whereas a single Birmingham button maker could employ several hundred people.[20] However, it is worth noting that only about 25 per cent of Birmingham men who left wills during the eighteenth century worked in the metal trades, while sources such as directories and probate records were inherently unlikely to reflect the lower reaches of the service economy that flourished in the Georgian town. Norwich's 176 innkeepers, therefore, had a much greater chance of appearing in such sources than had the operators of the 450 taverns listed in 1753, while the self-employed craftsmen who dominated the building industry were even more likely to be overlooked. The more detailed and inclusive enumerations available for Scottish burghs in the later seventeenth century, on the other hand, confirm both the rich variety of occupations to be found in all major British towns and the relative importance of those in the basic victualling, clothing and building trades.[21]

It is generally accepted that this 'kaleidoscopic' sector of the urban economy continued to expand and to diversify well into the nineteenth century, as buoyant consumer demand encouraged the spread of new, specialized trades alongside the traditional staples. Indeed, Jon Stobart has recently suggested that by the 1790s the total number of luxury trades and services available to consumers in leading commercial and industrial centres such as Bristol, Liverpool and Manchester was actually larger than in most county and resort towns whose economies depended largely on this market for leisure and luxury; although the range of trades was as great in Bath as in Bristol, its overall luxury sector was much smaller.[22] Conversely, 'genteel' residential and resort towns often experienced a process of small-scale industrialization. Bath, for example, developed a thriving engineering industry, while in the 1830s, William Crosskill built up a major iron-works, employing around 800 workers, on the outskirts of the quiet minster town of Beverley.

These enterprising industrial ventures were not invariably successful: the spinning mills erected in Shrewsbury in the 1790s, for instance, did not have firm enough roots in the town's hinterland economy to survive beyond the 1830s. However, the breadth of occupational structures in Georgian towns was undoubtedly significant in providing an underlying stability to urban economies which were otherwise at the mercy of a rapidly changing business environment. If Newcastle's coal trade faltered, it was all too clear that 'there is not a Cobler that will not suffer greatly': in the short term at least, the impact on the local economy would be severe.[23] However, there was always the possibility of such broadly based economies successfully changing direction and harnessing new sources of growth if long-standing specialisms began to lose momentum. Thus in the course of the eighteenth century the port city of Chester and the manufacturing town of Colchester both survived temporary economic difficulties by capitalizing on the attractiveness of their new-found tranquillity to wealthy residents and visitors, while in the latter years of the period, Preston moved in the opposite direction, evolving into a busy, 'industrious' textile town. Flexibility was therefore the key to long-term prosperity for the urban community as a whole.

Occupational Versatility

Flexibility was also the key to the personal survival of the business elite in times of economic strain. James Oakes of Bury St Edmunds, for instance, who inherited one of the largest woollen yarn-making companies in Suffolk and ran it successfully for almost 30 years in the face of increasingly stiff competition from manufacturers in the West Riding, was able to 'reinvent' himself in 1794 as an equally successful country banker. Such radical changes of direction were made easier by the fact that few successful entrepreneurs had all their eggs in one basket. Most of them aimed to assemble a balanced portfolio of business interests, combined with a range of less volatile investments in land and securities that would enable them not only to ride out seasonal and cyclical downturns, but also to seize new opportunities when they arose. As William Cotesworth of Gateshead admitted with some pride in 1720, 'I dealt in Any thing I could gaine by', a strategy which underpinned the steady rise of his business fortunes from a suburban tallow chandler's workshop to the wealth and status arising from a substantial interest in Tyneside's coal and salt industries.[24] Oakes himself had dealt in coal and hops, as well as yarn, and had indeed been employing his spare capital to carry out many of the functions of a banker for some years before he finally sold off his interests in the yarn industry.

Similar transitions, albeit at a lower social and economic level, may well explain the numerous shifts in occupational designations found by researchers in towns all over Georgian Britain. Men and women shifted the emphasis of their activities as they responded to new opportunities in the rapidly changing urban economy, and when they did so they tended to change the way they classified themselves within the occupational structure. In Birmingham, for example, Samuel Bellamy described himself as an engraver and die-sinker when he took out a patent in 1777, but insured himself as a bucklemaker in 1787; while John Smith took out a patent as a jeweller in 1770, but in 1792 left a will which described him as a steel watch-chain maker and toymaker. In Shrewsbury, Richard Richards claimed to be a tailor when assessed for the poor rate for 1826, but four years later appears in the records as a tinplate worker. Indeed, given that Richards had also moved house in the interim, it would have been impossible to link these two records to the same individual had his name been less distinctive.[25]

Cases such as these suggest that the inhabitants of Georgian towns regarded their occupations as fluid and flexible rather than fixed for the whole of their working lives. Those men and women who had served an apprenticeship in a recognized craft or trading guild were certainly entitled to be known by that trade. Nevertheless, rather than living exclusively 'by my trade', most townspeople seemed ready to take on any potentially rewarding activity or employment within their reach. Many also had secondary or by-employments, rather than supporting themselves exclusively in the trade which provided their official occupational label.[26] There were very few formal obstacles to this occupational versatility in eighteenth-century towns, although some English corporations and Scottish burghs did attempt to maintain restrictions on men and women who tried to set up in business in an established trade or craft without serving a proper apprenticeship. Informal sanctions could also be invoked. William Hutton, for instance, who trained as a frame-work-knitter in Nottingham, was reported to the parish authorities as a potential drain on the poor rates when he first moved to Birmingham in 1750 and attempted to establish himself as a bookseller and printer, allegedly by rivals anxious to restrict competition in their trade.

The main barriers to entry into any occupation, however, were essen-tially practical ones. Without capital, credit and contacts, not to mention the necessary skills and aptitude, few people stood much chance of making a successful transition from one means of livelihood to another. In many cases, therefore, a change in occupational designation can be read as a sign of failure rather than of success. James Oakes recorded in his memorandum book the sad decline of a fellow yarnmaker, who was reduced by the collapse of the industry in Suffolk to selling tea and 'some little Grocery for the Country places round Bury': rather than accumu-lating assets during his years of prosperity, he had run up debts.[27] Sickness and old age could also take their toll, undermining the levels of strength and dexterity needed to operate successfully in a skilled occupation and causing downward shifts into menial labouring jobs. Robert Couper, for instance, who had worked for 24 years in Edinburgh as a shoemaker, was reported in 1745 to be 'now by reason of old age and other infirmity, especially his eyesight...rendered incapable to work in new work' and was confined as a result to basic cobbling, mend-ing and selling old shoes. William Glen, at the age of 68, was one step further along this downward slope when in 1762, after working for 34 years as a cobbler, he was admitted to the Cannongate workhouse.[28]

Relying on one individual occupation as a sole means of support was, therefore, a risky and uncertain long-term strategy; occupational plural-ism was a much more sensible response to the precarious livelihoods and irregular employment opportunities offered by the urban economy. The majority of townspeople worked in jobs which could be classified as casual labour and were badly affected by seasonal and cyclical fluctua-tions. The demand for labour fell off sharply in winter, when shorter hours of daylight and severe weather combined to slow down activity in many outdoor trades, while employment in the capital cities and in the resorts fluctuated according to the rhythms of the fashionable season. Most urban workers were therefore involved in what Olwen Hufton memorably described as 'an economy of expedients, multiplemakeshifts which together permitted some kinds of existence'.[29] The London widow who gave evidence that she maintained herself by knitting, sewing, nursing, and by recovering the debts that were owed to her, was clearly relatively affluent, since she had some capital to lend, but even so she was following a typical pattern. Most households in fact survived on a broadly based and flexible 'portfolio' of employments, mixing casual earnings with the receipts of more settled occupations. 'My husband is a brickmaker by trade', reported another Londoner, 'and in the summertime I assist in brickmaking and in winter I sell fish and fruite about the street.'[30] The many opportunities for casual employment presented by urban economies, for wives and older children as well as for their husbands, was undoubtedly one of the greatest incentives attracting migrant families into the towns.

Women's Work: Men's Work

Despite the predominance of women in urban populations throughout Georgian Britain, historians have rarely acknowledged the full extent of their contribution to the urban economy, concentrating their attention on the activities of 'the sons', rather than the daughters, 'of art'.[31] Women have traditionally been identified with consumption, rather than production, an identification which has recently been strengthened by claims that this period marked a crucial phase in the emergence of 'separate spheres' in gender roles, by which women were increasingly confined to the domestic world of the household and family life, leaving the public world of work to be dominated by men.[32]

In reality, of course, very few women could afford the luxury of confining their activities to the private sphere of domesticity: 'none but a Fool', wrote Eliza Haywood in 1743, 'will take a Wife whose bread must be earned solely by his Labour and who will contribute nothing towards it herself'.[33] However, many gender historians would argue that the spread of domestic ideology meant that working women were becoming increasingly marginalized within the urban economy, denied access to economic opportunities and resources, and confined to a fairly narrow range of occupations. If they were forced to leave their own homes in search of work, then ideally they should be employed in someone else's household, performing tasks that evoked the innate and immemorial feminine functions of caring for their husbands and children. Unfortunately, since most of the jobs defined as appropriate for women were thought to echo and fulfil their fundamental natures, it was assumed that performing these tasks did not involve any particular skill or merit: instinct and duty were all that was required. As a result of this inexorable logic, women were not merely denied the opportunity to compete for more desirable and lucrative forms of employment, but they were also extremely poorly paid in the restricted labour market which was all that was open to them. Furthermore, the overwhelming identification of women with low-skilled, low-paying and low-status work reinforced the desire of male workers to maintain these restrictions, since the intro-duction of female labour inevitably led to reduced earnings and, it was widely believed, declining standards of workmanship.[34]

These highly gendered attitudes, and the disadvantaged position which women occupied in the workplace as a result, are both indis-putable; women in Georgian Britain clearly did not participate in the urban economy on equal terms with men. Women's wages, graded by age, were lower than urban men's, they were effectively excluded from many trades and occupations, and their work was consistently under-valued. It would not be altogether surprising, therefore, if women from the wealthier sections of urban society chose to withdraw from active involvement in business as soon as their family circumstances allowed; as Amanda Vickery has pointed out, 'the belief that a heavy workload automatically translates into power and prestige is a curious one for women's historians to espouse'.[35]

It is abundantly clear, however, that economic activity had always been strongly gendered and there is remarkably little evidence that gender differences were increasing in this period. It is also important to recognize that urban women enjoyed several significant advantages over their rural contemporaries. Women's wages, for instance, might equal those of labouring men's in the countryside, while it could be argued that 'women's work' was considerably easier to find in towns than in the increasingly commercialized and specialized rural economy.[36] The proliferation of part-time and casual jobs that had resulted from rapid urban growth seems to have been concentrated in traditionally female areas of employment such as sewing, washing, scouring, nursing, dealing, helping out in shops, workshops and public houses, etc., while domestic service itself seems to have become increasingly feminized as the period progressed. Industrial and commercial expansion also created a multitude of new opportunities for women in trades and crafts which had not yet become 'coded' as male or which were simply expand-ing too fast to be subject to traditional restrictions. In the Birmingham hardware trades, for instance, women were active at all levels of the production process, working for high wages in the forges as well as operating as independent entrepreneurs, while the soaring demand for hand knitters and linen spinners in Aberdeen in the later eighteenth century largely freed them from their customary dependence on male weavers.

Another major advantage of urban life was the relatively sophisticated infrastructure of the town, a point that is echoed in Pamela Sharpe's work on Colchester. Working women, particularly those trying to survive on their own, depended on the availability of cheap rented accommodation in lodging houses and furnished rooms and on purchasing ready-made convenience foods from street vendors, bakeries, taverns and cook-shops. Essential domestic support was also more readily available in the town than in the countryside, thanks to the larger pool of women in a similar position, who could share both the costs of daily life and the household chores that would otherwise have restricted each individual's valuable working time. In Ludlow in 1729, for instance, Mary Southern was listed as the head of a household consisting of her sister and three other single women, all of them working in the glove trade; in 1741 Catherine Bowen, a tailor's widow, was sharing her house with no less than six other single women. These co-operative households meant that single women, too, could achieve a measure of dignity and independence in the tough urban environment. Indeed, many working women clearly took pride in the fact that they were able to maintain themselves 'at their own hands'. Looking back in 1758 on her working life as a milliner in Edinburgh, Cicely Murray wrote to her former partner that 'I am sartin never was too [two] more happy then we were ... I never think on the years we spent together but with regrate'.[37]

Such comments indicate that historians may be too ready to accept contemporary classifications of women's employment as unskilled extensions of traditional female roles, and thus to assume that working women failed to develop a strong sense of occupational identity. Elizabeth Sanderson is particularly critical of those who dismiss sewing as a menial 'feminine' occupation when discussing dressmaking or millinery, for instance, but readily accept it as a skill giving status and identity where male tailors or upholsterers are concerned. Women are not born with an instinctive gift for cooking, cleaning, sewing, spinning or shop-keeping; these are skills which have to be learned and which, in the context of the Georgian town, allowed the great majority of urban women to support themselves, and often their husbands and children as well. Indeed the sheer quality of female workmanship may lie behind the fact that women in the Birmingham hardware trades were paid at a much higher rate than can be explained by the straightfoward operations of supply and demand.[38]

It would also be a mistake to underestimate the impact on the urban economy of the many unpaid and quintessentially 'unskilled' functions which women performed within their own households. Even women in commercial and professional families, who might appear to have little direct role in income generation, in reality contributed sizeable capital sums to the family's income-producing assets in the form of their dowries, assets which were often held in their own names thereafter as a precaution against the risk of bankruptcy. They played an important role in maintaining trading networks, kept the household and workshop accounts, supervised living-in apprentices and employees, and were quite capable of running the business in their husbands' absence. It is also indisputable that, in every town in the country and at every social level, women bore the brunt of the daily grind of feeding, clothing and maintaining these households, taking decisions as consumers that are increasingly recognized as historically influential.[39] Recent research strongly suggests, therefore, that shopping was much more than a frivolous female pastime and that women's well-judged management of their 'house-business' could play a crucial role in determining their family's material well-being.

The Rewards of Labour

All these factors have to be taken into account by historians evaluating living standards in Georgian towns, in a series of calculations that are infinitely more complex than the traditional method of balancing a series of prices against a series of wage rates to plot real wage indices for a limited number of specific occupations.[40] Very few urban workers were in fact sole breadwinners, holding down a steady job in a recognized trade or craft and earning regular wages. In reality, most townspeople lived, not as individual economic units, but within family economies, to which every member of the household was expected to contribute and in which earnings, as well as expenses, were pooled. These 'earnings', moreover, rarely came in the form of a simple cash payment from a single employer. Instead, urban workers tended to draw their income from a number of sources, moving flexibly between wage labour, contract

labour and self-employment, and supplementing these earnings wherever possible with traditional perquisites and payments in kind. In any
case, the typical daily *wage rates* often quoted by contemporaries necessarily reveal very little about annual *incomes* in a world in which many
workers were paid 'by the piece' and in which casual and irregular
employment was the norm. Journeymen tailors in London, for instance,
were said to be out of work for three to four months a year, while
employers in many trades were only too ready to lay off outworkers and
contract labour during temporary depressions. 'As soon as the market
stops they stop', it was reported in 1719 of textile manufacturers in the
Spitalfields district of London. 'If they cannot sell their work they immediately knock off the looms and the journeymen as immediately starve,
and want work'.[41]

Even the Spitalfields weavers, however, whose wages and working
conditions became synonymous with the miseries of sweated labour in
the later years of the Georgian period, appear to have found their
situation reasonably tolerable until the 1760s. Generalizations based on
the experience of one group of workers within a single urban economy
are, of course, inherently unreliable, even in the case of a dominant
metropolitan economy such as London. There was no national market
for goods and services in Georgian Britain, so that urban incomes must
have reflected local variations in both prices and earnings; in the years
before 1750, for example, there appears to have been a significant gap
between the wage rates of building workers in the fast-growing ports of
Hull and Newcastle upon Tyne, on the one hand, and those prevailing
in Beverley and Durham, their much less dynamic neighbours, on the
other. These local differences suggest the existence of even steeper
gradients between the wage rates prevailing between the highly differ-
entiated regional networks outlined in chapter 2. Although there is
some evidence that the gap was probably narrowing in the later eighteenth century and at the beginning of the nineteenth, wages in Scotland
were substantially lower than those in England; even in Edinburgh and
Glasgow, they were perhaps only half the London rates, while they also
lagged well behind the wages paid in Lancashire. Arthur Young
marvelled in 1791 at the 'immense wages' paid to Birmingham metalworkers, adding that 'when it is considered that the whole family is sure
of constant steady employment; . . . I am inclined to think [the rewards
of] labour higher at Birmingham than in any place in Europe'.[42] He was
careful to note, too, that the cost of living in Birmingham was very little
higher than it was in Norwich, even though both wage rates and

employment opportunities in the East Anglian regional capital lagged far behind those prevailing in the West Midlands.

The conclusion reached by this well-informed contemporary commentator confirms the worm's-eye view of urban incomes, recorded in innumerable statements made by migrant workers to poor relief authorities in towns throughout Georgian Britain. Its stark bottom line was expressed by Thomas Kingsbury, a labourer who moved with his wife and six children to Bath in the 1790s from a small country town in southwest England: 'I Can Do Beeter with my familey her[e], Beter than I can Down in Devonsher'.[43] In general terms, moreover, it seems that family incomes were not only higher in eighteenth-century towns than in the countryside, but that they were also rising in the long term.

On the other hand, the long-term diffusion of prosperity within urban society was painfully slow, while relative inequalities of income became even more sharply pronounced as the period progressed. The rewards of labour were unevenly distributed across a wide spectrum of success and failure, reflecting deeply-seated assumptions about divisions of wealth, power and status as well as the basic economic laws of supply and demand. Those who did best in the competitive urban environment were, naturally enough, those who had inherited or accumulated sufficient capital to set themselves up in the most lucrative trades or professions. Peter Earle's analysis of the business life of London in the years between 1660 and 1730 left him in no doubt that 'in most cases those who ended up rich started off rich or at least pretty well off', a universal truth reflected in the contemporary maxim that 'He that is Born under a 3-penny planet will never be worth a Groat'.[44] Estimates of the personal wealth accumulated by these enterprising members of the 'middling sort' during their careers vary considerably according to the context in which they operated, but there is no doubt that many enjoyed substantial annual incomes, ranging from several thousand pounds a year in the case of the commercial elite of great port cities such as London, Bristol, Glasgow and Liverpool, to the more typical £150 to £200 a year that was sufficient to support an affluent urban lifestyle. Moreover, there are clear indications that both the number and the average size of such incomes was increasing as the period progressed and as new sources of wealth opened up to those best placed to exploit them. Merchant princes were now joined at the top of the financial tree by a more heterogeneous group that included manufacturers, professionals, wholesale and retail dealers, and even some of the new high-status craftsmen such as cabinet makers.

Even at lower income levels, townspeople who enjoyed any comparative advantage in the market-place, however slight, could deploy that advantage to good effect. Skilled workers in expanding industries, for example, could negotiate from a position of strength, extracting wage rates that averaged between 50 and 100 per cent higher than those of unskilled labourers and using them to buy long-term security through membership of friendly societies and trade associations. In many cases, employers had little option but to meet their workers' demands, however exorbitant. As the proprietors of a new glassworks in Dumbarton ruefully admitted in 1778, after their efforts to poach experienced glass-blowers from Newcastle upon Tyne had ended in the courts, 'It is the unavoidable misfortune of every infant manufactory to be obliged to take up with the very scum and outcasts of all other manufactories of the same kind in the kingdom'; the remuneration package they had offered included free fuel and accommodation, as well as a guaranteed wage of 20 shillings a week, 'whether the fires were in or out'.[45] Anyone who could work on their own premises or with their own tools also enjoyed a considerable advantage over their less fortunate neighbours. Even among casual street traders, those who owned their own baskets or barrows rather than renting them from a dealer would receive a significant boost to their incomes, while those who could also find the money to buy the goods they sold had at least one foot on the capitalist ladder.

In stark contrast, townspeople attempting to make a living in crafts, trades or professions which required little or no initial investment of capital or skill, had little bargaining power and their incomes suffered accordingly. Small shopkeepers, for example, often earned substantially less than skilled manual workers, while shoemaking and the needle trades were notoriously badly paid. 'Mere working tailors' in London, it was reported in 1747, 'are as numerous as Locusts, are out of Business about three to four Months in the Year, and generally are as poor as Rats'; the wages of a 'good Hand', when he could find work, were put at no more than 3 shillings a week.[46] Although money wages for semi-skilled and casual workers seem to have risen in most major British towns from the 1760s, increased earnings rarely exceeded parallel increases in the cost of living, while changing market conditions further weakened the position of many sections of the urban workforce. In Glasgow, for instance, despite the spectacular growth of the cotton industry after 1779, cutthroat competition among small employers combined with a flood of new labour into handloom weaving, severely depressing wages and leading to considerable unrest. A similar process in Bolton reduced male weavers' earnings from 25 shillings a week in 1800 to only 5 or 6 shillings by 1829, bringing them down close to the level of the casual labourers who scraped a precarious living on wages of sixpence or less a day. These men, women and children, with no regular income or job, with no specialist skills or talents to trade in the market-place and, all too often, with no family connections to support them in sickness or old age, were the most vulnerable and wretched members of the urban workforce.

When evaluating the rising material prosperity of the majority of the urban population, it is important to remember the extremes of poverty and insecurity endured by those at the very bottom of the social order. Though the urban economy held out the prospect of wealth and opportunity, it was a prospect that was darkened by the risks of debt, bankruptcy and destitution. There is also compelling evidence that inequalities of wealth were increasing along with the pace of economic change. In Liverpool, for instance, whereas the four wealthiest taxpayers in 1798–1802 declared taxable incomes averaging over £17,000 per annum, 86 per cent of the population fell below the minimum tax threshold of £60.[47] The fact that the top 5 per cent of urban households in the early nineteenth century seem to have accounted for 40 to 50 per cent of total income was bound to have implications for the development of social relations within the Georgian town.

4

URBAN SOCIETY

In no situations do men more certainly rise and sink in their relative
importance or non-importance in the scale of society, than when they are
constantly brought into contact with their equals, or their superiors . . . .

John Holland (1826)

The vitality of urban economies in Georgian Britain was clearly reflected
in the fluidity and flexibility of urban society. The urban environment
generated an almost palpable atmosphere of social mobility, as individuals
competed with one another to make a living in this rapidly changing
world. Thousands of individual dramas of success and failure were played
out in towns all over Britain, as men and women struggled to seize the
opportunities – and avoid the pitfalls – that seemed particularly characteristic of urban life. However, over and above these case studies of
personal achievement, or of disappointment and defeat, contemporaries
recognized that a fundamental transformation of social relationships and
experience was under way in the fastest growing urban and commercial
centres.

The geographical and social mobility associated with urban populations in this period, together with the structural changes in occupational relationships associated with the accelerating pace of innovation
and specialization, undermined both traditional models of the social
order and established patterns of behaviour. Many contemporary
observers regarded this transformation with unmixed delight, arguing
that the relative accessibility and diversity of urban society encouraged
wholesome feelings of 'good neighbourhood' and 'the reciprocal
duties of friendship', as well as fostering the enterprise and ambition
that were essential to maintain the momentum of Britain's economic

growth.[1] The upwardly-mobile William Hutton wholeheartedly endorsed this optimistic perspective in his autobiography, where he contrasted the hospitable welcome he received in Birmingham in 1741 with the reaction of Leicestershire villagers 29 years later: 'The inhabitants set their dogs at me merely because I was a stranger. Surrounded by impassable roads, no intercourse with man to humanize the mind, no commerce to smooth their rugged manners, they continue the boors of nature'.[2]

On the other hand, the widening gulf between rich and poor, in terms of both income and expectations, aroused fears that urban society was becoming so fragmented that it risked complete dissolution. If it was indeed true that 'One half of the world, knows not how the other half lives', as an anonymous author claimed in 1752, surely the moral ties that bound together this 'vast concourse of people', packed into the congested streets and alleyways of the growing towns, would gradually wither away?[3] How far could fluidity and flexibility be stretched, before they broke down into chronic instability? At what point did laudable ambition tip over into ruthless and selfish disregard for social justice and social cohesion? How compatible, in other words, were the values of 'civility', so strongly associated with urban life in the early years of the period, with the increasingly competitive, commercial world of the workshop and the market-place, a world in which 'the getting of Money, . . . whatever some Divines would teach to the contrary, . . . is the main business of the life of Man'?[4] Some of the issues raised by these complex and far-reaching questions will be examined in the next three chapters.

The Social Order

The commercialized, flexible social system that developed in the Georgian town had many far-reaching consequences, including a significant shift in the ways in which contemporaries conceptualized and described the social order itself. This did not involve a wholesale rejection of traditional principles of hierarchy and precedence. On the contrary, it has been argued that the concept of 'social space', which implies the separation of individuals by status, was one of the central defining characteristics of urban culture in this period.[5] Despite the pluralism and mobility that also characterized urban society, the inhabitants of eighteenth-century towns displayed a sensitivity to distinctions of rank and status that equalled their acute awareness of the very obvious inequalities of wealth that separated the social elite from the mass of labouring poor. Every public occasion was organized on the basis of strict rules of seniority and status; corporations and guilds, clubs and societies, fashionable assemblies and pious congregations, all marched, feasted, danced, drank and prayed in an order that embodied the traditional values of community life.

The key difference between these urban hierarchies and conventional models of the social order, in which there were 'fixed, invariable, external rules of distinction of rank' based on inherited status, was that they recognized the much greater possibilities of upward (and indeed downward) mobility that were available within the urban economy.[6] Georgian towns certainly did not offer their inhabitants anything approaching complete equality of opportunity; women's formal status, for example, was still essentially determined and defined by their subordination to a male head of household. Genuine 'rags to riches' stories were also surprisingly rare in this highly mobile age, since setting up in business or establishing a professional practice required considerable initial investment. Successful entrepreneurs were usually from the second or third generation of a prosperous family, establishing their own fortunes with the aid of the financial, social and cultural capital painfully scraped together by their predecessors. However, the very fact that such families *could* accumulate substantial fortunes through their own enterprise and abilities fatally undermined the credibility of social hierarchies based on immutable hereditary privilege. As Penelope Corfield has demonstrated, by the 1770s it had become commonplace to discuss the social order in terms of 'classes', rather than of fixed 'ranks' or 'stations', a linguistic and conceptual shift which reflected the social transformation that was gathering pace in towns all over Georgian Britain.[7]

The boundaries between these new social classes, however, are extremely difficult to define in anything except the most general terms. Classifications of status that moved beyond the rigid, formal distinctions conferred by birth and title, necessarily involved complex social negotiations, as individuals tried to locate both themselves and their fellow citizens within a shifting and ambiguous hierarchy of esteem. Into which class, for instance, should historians place Robert Peet of Newark, a 'labourer' whose probate inventory was valued in 1824 at £3000? How would his neighbours have balanced his evident material wealth against the social and cultural disadvantages implied by his manual occupation?

Much would depend, of course, on factors of which the historian is all too often unaware. The fine gradings of status within urban society were based on a multiplicity of factors, including gender, family background and connections, levels of education, social, political and religious affiliations, and personal conduct, as well as the size and principal source of each household's income.

In the comparatively small, stable communities that characterized many of Georgian Britain's slower growing towns, it seems likely that these multiple signals could be read with relative ease. Even in much larger towns, the surviving letters and diaries of permanent residents reveal an almost encyclopedic knowledge of the personal circumstances of everyone within the writers' circle of acquaintance. There were always uncertainties and ambiguities, however, and these would be felt most keenly in towns where a high proportion of the population came into daily contact with 'strangers', usually temporary visitors or newly arrived migrants. In these circumstances, snap judgements had to be made on the basis of clothing, accent and behaviour, indicators that could usually be relied on to distinguish the 'raggamuffins' and 'leather aprons' of the lower classes from their better-dressed superiors; judgements which were rarely foolproof when it came to discriminating between the finer gradations of the social order. The lively market in second-hand clothing, together with the increased availability of ready-made garments, meant that even those outside the social elite could cultivate a smart appearance, so that identifications based solely on dress and self-presentation could not be taken for granted. Indeed, foreign visitors to Britain frequently remarked on the high standards of neatness and cleanliness to be found even among the 'lowest class', although claims that 'hardly a beggar can be espied who doesn't wear a clean shirt under his tatters' seem to have been stretching credibility a little too far.[8]

These problems of social classification undoubtedly contributed to the 'degradation of gentility' which attracted so much attention from conservative writers. The inhabitants of Georgian towns came under increasing pressure to raise the general level of courtesy displayed in everyday life, especially by treating strangers with greater respect. As Londoners were reminded in 1780, the stresses and strains of living in the capital city would be intolerable unless its inhabitants accepted a few basic 'Rules for Behaviour for this populous City'.[9] Hard-headed business decisions were also implicated in these changes, since every stranger encountered in an urban shop, tavern or market-place was a potential customer, whose good will needed to be cultivated and whose pretensions to status had, therefore, to be accepted at face value. The result was a general levelling-up of civility, leading on occasions to the exaggerated and inflated courtesies deplored by contemporary critics. 'The title Madam is grown so common', satirists complained, that 'if you go into an eating house it must be "Madam" to the bar-keeper, and on Sundays, when chambermaids have got their best clothes on, the town is full of Madams'.[10]

As this indicates, however, navigating your way through the ambiguities of the urban social order still required subtle and careful judgements to be made, since overestimating the relative standing of a chance-met stranger could result in acute social embarrassment. At the same time that titles and forms of address were levelled up, therefore, many of the other outward signs of social subordination and deference were being levelled down. The elaborate rituals of traditional 'hat honour', which involved 'inferiors' showing their respect for their 'superiors' by removing their hats, were gradually attenuated to the point where a brief touch of the hat, or a slight inclination of the head, was considered sufficient acknowledgment between strangers. Deep bows and curtsies, or obsequious tugs of the forelock, were increasingly associated with a rustic lack of sophistication, or with a slavish subservience that was seen as foreign to British traditions of constitutional government. In 1738, for instance, Newcastle keelmen presented a petition to the corporation complaining that they were treated with 'a Barbarity abhorred by Jews, Turks and Infidals', and demanding that employers, as well as employees, in the coal trade should enter into a yearly bond specifying conditions of service.[11] When challenged to defend the radical wording of these demands, one of their spokesmen compared it directly with the language used by the social elite in their own political debates, locating himself firmly within this tradition.

The outspoken confidence of this Tyneside labourer exemplified the prevailing contemporary image of the urban working classes as quick-witted, independent-minded, and unimpressed by the respect that was supposedly due to those of superior status. Some contemporary employers found the 'insolence' and lack of deference displayed by domestic servants born and bred in an urban environment particularly unsettling; whatever incivilities they encountered on the busy streets, they wanted nothing more challenging than simplicity and submission within their own homes. 'We are obliged to take the lowest of the people', explained Soame Jenyns, 'and convert them by our own ingenuity into the genteel

personages we think proper should attend us', a strategy which inevitably encouraged servants to reject the servility and dependence that
were inseparable from their position.[12]

The corrosive effect of the urban environment on the basic principles
of subordination might also be reflected in the angry complaint by an
unemployed Macclesfield silkworker that 'we are so oppressed by one
beggar or another put over us to watch us, that one can't now-a-days
blow one's nose *like another gentleman!*' The fact that he had abandoned
the menial work assigned to him by the overseers of the poor in order
to go to the races with a friend undoubtedly added to the indignation
with which this story was reported in the local newspaper; this was
clearly someone with aspirations far above his proper station in life.[13]

Urban society in this period was therefore both ambivalent and
dynamic, driven forward by economic change and shaped by the many
frictions that were generated in the process. On the one hand, social
relationships were conditioned by an enduring attachment to the principles of hierarchy and an acute sensitivity to narrow distinctions of status.
On the other hand, the social rate of exchange within each individual
town was subject to continual renegotiation, as increased mobility
and rising levels of prosperity interacted with growing inequalities of
wealth to produce novel patterns of social difference.

These patterns also differed slightly, but significantly, in different
local contexts. National and regional variations, combined with the func-
tional and occupational diversity outlined in previous chapters, had a
profound influence on social development and experience within the
Georgian town. In Scotland, for example, tax records from the 1790s
demonstrate that the social structures of Edinburgh and of small county
towns such as Dumfries or Montrose were appreciably different from
those of busy commercial and industrial centres such as Glasgow, Aberdeen or Dundee. Contemporaries certainly took it for granted that you
could not expect to find much 'good Company' in such towns. Although
Birmingham's first historian took pride in the fact that 'Many fine
estates have been struck out of the anvil', he ruefully acknowledged that
'The smoke of Birmingham has been very propitious to their growth,
but not to their maturity. Gentlemen, as well as buttons, have been
stamped here; but, like them, when finished, are moved off'. The smart
'provincial metropolis' of Chester, in contrast, offered wealthy residents
'the pleasures of cultivated society on easy terms', while discreetly boast-
ing that its population contained a 'much less proportion of the lowest
class of poor than in manufacturing towns'.[14]

Social Structure and Experience

The social leadership of most Georgian towns remained in the hands of an upper class characterized by the ownership of substantial landed property. The titled and landowning families who maintained country houses in the vicinity continued to attend urban functions, to support urban charities, and to subsidize investment in the urban infrastructure. Lady Oxford, for instance, financed the building of Mansfield's new town hall in 1752, while the Duke of Northumberland led the subscription list for the new assembly rooms in Newcastle upon Tyne in 1774, contributing £400, whereas the majority of subscribers paid only £25. Provincial towns, in particular, judged the success of local social events in terms of the number and quality of the aristocratic names listed in newspaper reports, while the aristocrats themselves took care not to offend urban sensibilities by appearing too proud to mix with those of lesser rank.

However, these 'double-gilted gentry' shared their social eminence with a specifically urban elite, a resident upper class that included not only members of minor landowning families living in their town houses on a more or less permanent basis; but also an increasing number of affluent men and women whose wealth ultimately derived from active involvement in trade or the professions, but who were now enjoying a leisured retirement. The town of Cupar in Angus, for example, was said to be particularly attractive to 'Gentlemen of the military profession, having spent their youth in the service of their country . . . in the decline of life'.[15] Many of these 'town gentry' were in fact widowed or spinster gentle*women*; both Preston and the New Town at Edinburgh were notoriously full of 'old maids' whose families either could not or would not afford a dowry sufficient to secure a husband of suitable rank but who could find a comfortable niche in urban society. Their incomes, although often little more than a 'genteel competence', were sufficient to allow them entry into this leisured elite, especially since they were derived almost exclusively from passive investments in property and government securities.

The size of this leisured urban elite seems to have been fairly small, representing no more than 3 to 4 per cent of the population even in London, Edinburgh and the smarter county towns, although much higher concentrations could be found in specialist health and leisure resorts such as Bath, Brighton, Weymouth and Tenby. In the faster growing commercial centres, however, exclusive definitions of upper-class status were becoming increasingly problematic in the face of the rising wealth and leisured lifestyle enjoyed by the leading merchant and professional families. A strict interpretation of the conventions that governed the social hierarchy in this period would almost certainly have excluded them, since a significant proportion of their income was still derived from active involvement in commercial enterprise or professional practice. However, the vast fortunes accumulated by Hull's 'Baltic Barons', Glasgow's 'Tobacco Lords', Liverpool's 'West India Princes' and Leeds's 'Gentlemen Merchants', inevitably brought with them considerable social prestige. As Defoe pointed out, it was difficult on any objective grounds to exclude families which lived 'with the Splendor of the best Gentlemen, and ... the Luxury and Expence of a Count of the Empire', without making a significant dent in their capital.[16] They had often been educated at the same grammar or boarding schools as the offspring of the local gentry, they attended the same churches and assemblies, they belonged to the same book-clubs and antiquarian societies as well as to the same drinking and gaming clubs, they employed the same architects and painters, they visited the same health and leisure resorts, they sent their daughters to the same genteel boarding schools and their sons on the Grand Tour. Indeed, the whole urban elite appeared to share an active, competitive and commercial attitude to wealth. A Swiss visitor to London in 1727 clearly disapproved of the fact that 'as soon as you mention anyone to [English women] that they do not know, their first inquiry will be, "Is he rich?"'; while it was reported from Newcastle upon Tyne in 1758 that 'Every gentleman in the county, from the least to the greatest, is as solicitous in the pursuit of gain as a tradesman'.[17] The elevation of Robert Smith to the ranks of the peerage as Lord Carrington in 1796, while he was still an active partner in the Hull firm of Wilberforce and Smiths, emphasized the gradual erosion of any clear-cut distinction between a landed and a commercial elite, between 'true' and 'pseudo-gentry'.[18]

However, the opulent merchants, affluent bankers, eminent doctors and expensive lawyers who swelled the ranks of the urban elite also retained strong links with the broader ranks of the 'middling sort', the solid but not necessarily wealthy professionals, traders, shopkeepers and independent artisans who formed the backbone of the urban economy. While it is generally accepted that the middle class was growing in numbers, as well as significance, in towns all over Georgian Britain, it is difficult to define membership of that class except in the most general terms, in which case it would include everyone below the landed aristocracy but above the 'labouring poor'. In striving for greater precision, many historians follow the example of contemporary social observers such as Daniel Defoe and Joseph Massie, who tended to define the middling ranks of society in terms of their expenditure, whereas they classified those both above and below them in the social structure according to their incomes. According to Paul Langford, for example, 'In the last analysis the middle class ... was a class defined by material possessions', an analysis which seems to be supported by the sheer quantity and quality of consumer goods amassed by middle-income households as the urban economy expanded.[19] Whereas the vast majority of urban homes were very sparsely furnished in the later seventeenth century, a growing preoccupation with both domestic comfort and social display soon began to fill them with desirable possessions. The inventory of John Clay, for example, a Mansfield hatter and haberdasher who died in 1783, reveals an elaborately furnished house, complete with four-poster beds, crimson damask curtains, mahogany card- and tea-tables, carved mirror frames and decorative silverware.

It is generally agreed that this sort of comfortable middle-class lifestyle would require a minimum income of at least £50 a year in the early years of the period, together with several hundred pounds of accumulated savings, figures that should be adjusted sharply upwards from the 1790s to allow for inflation and wartime taxation. Calculations on this basis suggest that the middling sort made up around 20 per cent of the adult population of Georgian towns. In Scotland, for instance, it is estimated that they formed 10–15 per cent of the urban population in 1750, rising to 20–5 per cent in 1831, while comparable figures for London in 1798 suggest a range of between 17 and 20 per cent. Reassuringly, all these estimates seem remarkably close to those produced by historians who prefer to define the middle class in occupational terms, a decision justified by Shani D'Cruze on the grounds that they 'All organized their working and family lives around the small-producer household', an independent trading household in which wives and daughters played a significant role.[20]

These two qualifications for middle-class status, income and independence, distinguished the middling sort from the bulk of the urban population, the 70–5 per cent who were classified as the 'lower', 'industrious' or 'working' classes. However, here again, the boundaries were much less clear-cut in practice than they were in theory. In many ways, the gulf between the social status and experience of the commercial and professional elite, on the one hand, and that of the lower regions of the middle class, on the other, was much greater than the gap that separated the precarious existence of clerks, curates, petty shopkeepers and struggling artisans, from the relatively prosperous world of the best-paid skilled workers in expanding industries. While the latter were undoubtedly 'dependent' on their employers and relied on the market economy for the sale of their labour, it could be argued that many of their employers were becoming equally dependent on market forces, as were the dealers and service industries who relied on their purchasing power for their own prosperity. Industrial change, which steadily reduced the number of artisans who were genuinely self-employed, promoting instead the employment of waged labour under a skilled foreman, demonstrates that the impact of market forces in the Georgian town was not confined to the labouring poor.

The working class was itself at least as heterogeneous, as well as far more numerous, than the more prosperous and prestigious sections of urban society, as Defoe had recognized when he distinguished between 'The working Trades, who labour hard but feel no want', 'The Poor that fare hard', and 'The Miserable, that really pinch and suffer want'.[21] Those whom he described as the 'rich Poor' could enjoy a relatively high standard of living, sharing to a limited extent in the increased levels of comfort and security that characterized middle-class consumption in this period. Historians have demonstrated the emergence of a substantial new market among the urban workforce in the later seventeenth century for a whole range of consumer goods, from earthenware dishes and brass cooking pots, to knitted stockings and linen sheets. They may not have been able to afford the three complete outfits, along with the vast array of buckles, buttons, hats, wigs, ribbons, lace and other accessories that went with them, that were typical among Londoners of the middling sort in the early eighteenth century, but they could certainly possess a respectable suit of 'Sunday best' clothes, along with increasing quantities of simple shirts, shifts and underclothes. Their diet also increased in both quality and variety, as imported luxuries such as sugar, tea and dried fruit appeared in urban shops and market-places alongside domestically produced meat, butter and cheese. Tea drinking, for instance, which spread among the middling ranks of London society in the 1690s, had apparently become so commonplace by the 1740s that working-class women in Nottingham considered it an essential ingredient of 'a proper Breakfast', together with the luxury of hot, buttered, white bread.[22] By the 1820s, prosperous lace-hands in the Nottingham suburbs of New Radford and New Basford had furnished their substantial brick-built houses with an array of mahogany chests and tables, looking-glasses, framed engravings, and fringed dimity curtains, that rivalled the inventories left by middle-class householders fifty years earlier.

However, it would be misleading to concentrate on the experience of this affluent minority and to underestimate the precarious basis of their prosperity. While the laceworkers of Nottingham were exceptionally well paid in the trade boom of the middle 1820s, framework knitters in the same town were experiencing a painful and protracted slide into misery and depression, emphasizing both the diversity of working-class experience and their vulnerability to market forces. An occupational study of Bristol in the 1770s, for example, suggests that up to 65 per cent of the population could be classified as actually or potentially living in poverty; lacking the means to build up a significant cushion of savings, they could all too easily slide down the slippery slope into complete destitution. In a crisis, therefore, families reacted by cutting back drastically on their expenditure, trading down to cheaper lodgings and pawning their most desirable possessions, before finally stripping both their homes and their wardrobes down to the bare bones in a desperate effort to survive.

Since women's employment was so heavily concentrated in low-status and low-paid occupations, women featured disproportionately in the ranks of the urban poor and therefore suffered more than their fair share of distress. Domestic service certainly offered many single women a degree of protection from the most extreme vagaries of the urban labour market, but even servants were not immune to protracted periods of unemployment, which exhausted their savings and drove them onto the streets to make ends meet. Prostitution and pauperism alike emerged as major sources of public anxiety in London, Edinburgh and the great commercial cities of Georgian Britain in the later decades of the eighteenth century, as desperate women struggled to make a living within working-class communities often represented by outsiders as 'dirty Savages' or 'Brutes'. Certainly many of their inhabitants lived in conditions that could legitimately be described as brutalizing; the central districts of Glasgow, for example, were described in 1844 as 'an accumulated mass of squalid wretchedness ... probably unequalled in any other town in the British dominions'.[23] However, similar pockets of misery and squalor could be found in country towns all over Georgian Britain, albeit on a much smaller scale, often tucked away in courtyards and narrow alleyways behind the main streets. So many of Newark's poorest inhabitants were living 'herded together' in the town's Cross Gun Yard in the

1830s, for instance, that it was nicknamed Botany Bay. 'Like the [prison] colony over the sea' in Australia, recalled one local resident, 'it was used as a receptacle for the refuse of British humanity'; unsurprisingly, its inhabitants were periodically ravaged by memorable outbreaks of cholera, typhoid and smallpox. Their day-to-day experience of urban life must have been radically different from that of Newark's wealthy professionals, retailers and manufacturers, many of whom still lived where they worked or traded, within a few hundred yards of this 'human dustbin'.[24]

'Places of Great Resort'

The precarious livelihoods of their working-class residents did not, however, diminish the fascination which Georgian towns exercised over the inhabitants of the surrounding countryside. The vitality and diversity of urban society in this period made towns all over Britain into centres of sociability whose attractions were felt throughout their local spheres of influence. Although travelling dealers were increasingly penetrating country districts, and permanent shops were spreading into the villages, the sheer range and choice of merchandise to be found in urban markets continued to give them a significant edge as shopping centres. As a result, even the smallest market towns drew in hundreds of people on a regular basis, not simply to transact business, but also to meet friends and exchange gossip in the many inns, taverns and coffee houses that lined the main streets and clustered round the market-place. Contemporary letters and diaries record a high level of interaction between villagers and neighbouring small towns. Thomas Turner, for example, a shopkeeper in the Sussex village of East Hoathly, often made the short journey into nearby Lewes, on horseback or on foot, to buy stock, settle his debts, attend property sales, or visit a doctor, while the *Lewes Journal* was his main source of national and international news. He frequently 'had words' with his wife about her own determination to visit friends in the town, accusing her of subordinating 'Business and family advantage... to [her own] pride and pleasure', but then had to go into town himself to counteract the malicious gossip to which these quarrels gave rise.[25]

It is worth remembering, also, that religion remained a powerful force in Georgian Britain, and that religious events or organizations played an important role in consolidating the links between urban centres and their hinterlands. It is symptomatic of these close connections that Turner's first marriage had actually taken place at All Saints church in Lewes, while his duties as churchwarden in East Hoathly also drew him into the county town on a regular basis. The growth of dissenting congregations in the later eighteenth century accentuated these trends, drawing respectable country people into a vibrant evangelical nexus of prayer meetings, lectures, revival meetings, Sunday schools, missionary societies and Bible associations. It is not surprising, therefore, to find that church music festivals, lasting several days, became increasingly popular. The Three Choirs Meeting, founded in about 1718, which rotated between Gloucester, Hereford and Worcester, is an early and enduring example, but its lead was soon followed by provincial towns throughout Britain, each competing to organize the best attended and most profitable events. Choirs and music societies from parishes all over industrial Lancashire gathered together in Manchester in 1765, for instance, to take part in a grand performance of Handel's oratorio *Messiah*, an ambitious undertaking which inspired neighbouring Liverpool to stage a major northern music festival in the following year.[26]

Such festivals took their place among the many fairs, celebrations and commemorations that punctuated the urban year in county towns and larger regional centres. These public entertainments could attract thousands of visitors from the surrounding countryside, all eager to enjoy the sights and sounds of the 'big city' and to savour the unaccustomed excitement of being part of a crowd. Upwards of 10,000 people were reported to have attended Abingdon's annual hiring fair in October 1805, for example, vastly outnumbering the 4356 permanent inhabitants recorded in the 1801 census. Although the commercial significance of some traditional fairs declined considerably during the century, their overall popularity was maintained by their gradual transformation into 'toy' or 'pleasure' fairs, complete with travelling showmen, ballad-singers, card-sharpers and pickpockets. 'The Stupendous PELICAN of the WILDERNESS' was advertised as a forthcoming attraction at Gloucester's Barton fair in September 1794, together with an Asiatic panther, a sea lion, and '*two surprising Brothers*, Called THE ALBINOS: who ... are allowed by gentlemen of the first science to be the most curious phaenomena of nature's production'. In 1818, the attractions included a special guest appearance of 'TOBY, the SAPIENT PIG', who was allegedly 'Under the Patronage of the Royal Family and the First Nobility', but who could nevertheless be viewed by lesser mortals for the very modest sum of one shilling.[27]

At a much more elevated social level, fairs were sometimes associated with the annual influx of the landed gentry into county and regional centres, to attend short but glittering social 'seasons' that were timed to coincide with the arrival of the assize judges on their summer circuit or with a traditional local event such as St Dennis's Fair in Colchester. Such gatherings of the great, the good and the fashionable brought status as well as business to their host towns and were one of the main reasons why rival centres competed for the privilege of holding the assizes. Over the years these occasions had evolved an elaborate programme of events which mixed business with pleasure. Gentlemen sat on the county juries, met their lawyers and stewards, and attended political, administrative, economic and charitable meetings; they also mixed more informally with their peers at the race ground, the cockpit and the 'ordinaries' provided by the towns' leading inns, while occasionally taking the time to accompany their wives and daughters to the public breakfasts, balls, assemblies, plays, concerts that made these race or assize weeks so exhausting – but irresistible – for everyone involved. Even sober nonconformists such as Mary Robinson, the Dutch-born wife of a wealthy Hull merchant, seemed to enjoy playing an active role in the hectic social round, reporting with pride in July 1754 that 'thare was a deal of very good Company at hull in the Race weak & very brilent Assemblys'.[28]

By the middle of the eighteenth century, it is clear that most English regions had evolved a sophisticated calendar of social events and activities, many of which depended on the facilities and commercial infrastructure of the Georgian town for their continued success. At the highest social levels, the social elite moved in a regular pattern around the urban hierarchy, patronizing social events in nearby urban centres during the dreary winter months, when the roads were at their worst, travelling further afield to county and regional centres to attend quarter sessions, race and assize weeks, visiting local resorts in the summer, and paying occasional, lengthier visits to national centres, such as London or Bath, in the appropriate seasons. The mobility of this leisured population was such that the organizers of public entertainments had to reorganize their programmes to avoid 'interfering with Others in the Neighbourhood'; because, as the manager of the Mansfield assembly acknowledged in 1781, 'sometimes a Change would be very agreeable'.[29] However, the more plebeian, hard-working sections of the urban population were also mobile, visiting neighbouring towns for pleasure, and not simply to conduct business or search for work. As Peter Clark has pointed out, 'this increasingly interconnected urban world' was instrumental in pulling the whole urban system together.[30]

An Urban Renaissance?

According to an innovative and highly influential study by Peter Borsay, the increasingly sophisticated social and cultural environment of many English provincial towns in the later seventeenth and early eighteenth centuries played a vital part in stimulating a period of qualitative urbanization, an 'urban renaissance' that was in many ways as influential as the 'industrial revolution' that followed in its wake. The outward signs of this urban renewal were represented by the physical changes taking place in the urban landscape, which are discussed in chapter 5. However, they were also embodied in the proliferation of novel leisure activities, entertainments, organizations and amenities, mainly aimed at the wealthier sections of society, which transformed the social, cultural and intellectual life of the Georgian town.[31] By the early years of the nineteenth century, even a small county town like Brecon in mid Wales, which experienced very modest population growth over the century, rising from just under 1900 in 1679 to 2567 at the time of the 1801 census, had developed a more complex and distinctively urban way of life, one that involved a regular series of assemblies, concerts and private parties and an array of clubs and societies, as well as occasional theatrical performances in a permanent theatre, race meetings, and even a town hunt supported by subscriptions from local merchants and gentlemen.[32]

This flowering of urban culture was certainly encouraged by the patronage of local landowners; indeed many urban social events were timed to coincide with the full moon so that the carriages of the local gentry could pick their way safely through the dark and dangerous countryside on their way home. Competition between neighbouring towns to attract such welcome, wealthy visitors meant that civic authorities and private entrepreneurs were often prepared to invest heavily in enhancing 'the comforts and accommodations of life' in the urban environment, remodelling the leading inns or the town hall to create fashionable public rooms, and in many cases providing specialized leisure facilities such as assembly rooms and theatres. As Christopher Chalkin has demonstrated, in rapidly growing towns, where the need for greater specialized, purpose-built accommodation was most obvious, substantial investment was required. A new theatre in the fashionable resort town of Brighton, for instance, with seating for 1400 people, cost £12,000 in 1806.[33]

However, it would be a mistake to identify the new urban culture too closely with the landed gentry, since this would be to underestimate the enthusiasm with which the permanent residents of Georgian towns, both men and women, embraced its characteristic emphasis on civility and on the *public* forms of sociability. 'Civility' in this context implied far more than good manners, or even good breeding; it also indicated a wider cultural identification with the ideals of the English enlightenment. Sociability also had much broader implications than simple enjoyment, as Defoe recognized when he criticized 'that new-fashion'd way of conversing by assemblies'.[34] Assemblies were indeed one of the most characteristic institutions of the Georgian town. Unlike a private ball or party, where admission depends on a personal invitation, town assemblies were accessible to a much wider public for the price of a ticket or subscription, while the behaviour of 'the company' who came together in the assembly rooms to dance, converse and play cards was regulated by a code designed to mitigate the barriers of rank and status that divided them in their daily lives. Aristocratic visitors who showed themselves to be 'above their company', by insisting on the privileges of rank, were condemned as 'proud & Sulky'; like Jane Austen's fictional Mr Darcy, who 'was looked at with great admiration for about half the evening, till his manners gave a disgust which turned the tide of his popularity'.[35]

The expansion of leisure and luxury within Georgian towns clearly had a special significance for affluent women, whether occasional visitors or permanent residents. Whereas their lives in the countryside were increasingly circumscribed by conventional expectations of female fragility and propriety, towns were seen as 'female territory', where most women seem to have walked about freely, unveiled and for the most part unchaperoned, although they would not normally venture out after dark without some sort of escort. Even a pious country parson like John Penrose had no qualms about allowing his 20-year-old daughter to travel alone to an assembly in a sedan chair when visiting Bath in 1766. Betty Ramsden, the wife of a London schoolmaster, seems to have taken every available opportunity to go out on the town, usually by herself or in exclusively female company. Unlike Thomas Turner, her 'Good Man' did not appear to resent being left at home looking after their children, while she abandoned her domestic duties to visit the public pleasure gardens at Vauxhall and Ranelagh, attend assemblies, public trials and theatrical performances, or simply visit her friends to play cards and indulge in a cosy gossip.[36] The daughter of a Liverpool merchant packed an even more hectic social round into a 10-week visit to London in 1748, going out to one burlesque, two concerts, two ridottos, three oratorios, three routs, four dinners, eight plays and 21 teas, as well as making nine visits to Ranelagh and Vauxhall.

The sophisticated delights of London, Bath or Edinburgh were obviously exceptional. However, even in more modest towns such women had the opportunity to enjoy a much wider range of respectable occupations, amusements and companions than was available to them in the countryside. It was in this period, for instance, that recreational shopping – shopping as a major leisure activity – came of age, as fashionable shops were transformed into 'perfect gilded theatres', providing 'as agreeable an amusement as any lady can pass away three or four hours in'.[37] On the other hand, affluent women were very far from enjoying complete equality of opportunity within urban society, which was segregated by gender to an extent that surprised many foreign visitors. They were completely excluded from many public and private male functions, especially from the proliferating clubs and societies that were another of the characteristic institutions of Georgian society. It was noticeable that they were often left to their own devices even at ostensibly 'mixed' events such as assemblies while their menfolk, 'these lords of creation', retired to the card-room or hogged the conversation in the middle of the floor.[38] It is also clear that the social conventions that governed where it was acceptable for fashionable young women to walk unescorted were becoming much more restrictive in the later years of the period, ostensibly to protect them from contact with the squalor of the back streets and from the many prostitutes who haunted the fringes of fashionable society. In contrast, few areas of the town were completely closed to men from the upper ranks of urban society.

These qualifications on the relative freedom of urban women need to be set against Borsay's confident assertion that the urban renaissance had profound implications for the whole of urban society in every town in the land. Critics such as Angus McInnes, for instance, have argued that the new-style cultural and leisure activities diffused much too slowly and patchily to qualify as a 'renaissance', especially as their influence in smaller urban centres was largely confined to a narrow and inward-looking social elite.[39] Many smaller English towns in the North and Midlands certainly appear to have begun their 'renaissance' at exactly the point in the 1770s where Borsay stopped looking for it, while its impact in Scotland and Wales remained extremely limited until the early decades of the nineteenth century. Although Edinburgh rapidly became a major social centre, few provincial towns in Georgian Britain could sustain a vibrant culture of sociability for more than a short, hectic 'season'. Whereas a public rehearsal for Handel's *Music for the Royal Fireworks* in London in 1749 attracted an audience of over 12,000 people, and generated a three-hour traffic jam of carriages in the early hours of the morning, the genteel population of Canterbury surprised fashionable visitors by going quietly home to bed before ten o'clock at night. Indeed the wealthier residents of small county towns were often so starved of company that occasional visitors were greeted with positive rapture; in one such incident in 1785, a couple visiting relatives in Lincoln were welcomed by the city waits and by a full peal of the cathedral bells. As a result, although historians are generally agreed that urban culture changed considerably over this period, there is also a widespread recognition that the social and cultural world of many provincial towns could best be described as stuffy, shallow and sparse.

Popular Leisure

The day-to-day life of the hard-working mass of the urban population, those outside the restricted ranks of 'polite' society, was centred so strongly on making a living that little time could be given to formal social or cultural activities. Work was central to the experience of most of the lower middling ranks of society, as well as to the urban poor. Although some contemporaries were prepared to accept that 'relaxation must follow, as one period to another', abandoning the shop counter or the work-bench for any length of time during the long working day was simply impractical for men and women living so close to the margins of existence.[40] Those with valuable skills, whose jobs were both relatively secure and relatively highly paid, could perhaps have chosen to work for fewer hours when wages were high, translating their gains into increased leisure rather than into savings or consumer spending. Recurrent complaints by employers that 'these high wages occasioned much idleness and dissipation' among their workmen, who 'have been observed seldom to work on Mondays and Tuesdays but to spend most of their time at the ale-house or [playing] nine-pins', are often accepted at face value by otherwise sceptical historians, because the 'leisure preference' that they describe seems to represent a natural reaction to the grim realities of life in most Georgian towns.[41]

It is important, however, to treat such statements with caution, and to set them against other, apparently contradictory, claims that workers paid unusually high wages tended to 'waste' their earnings on luxury foodstuffs and high-status consumer goods. Both propositions seem to reflect the perennial anxieties of social conservatives, disconcerted by the potential impact of market forces on traditional values; they may have little relevance, therefore, to the actual behaviour of the urban workforce. Mark Harrison, for instance, has argued persuasively that a regular working week was characteristic of the urban environment in this period, certainly in the larger towns, with the vast majority of the working population being found at work between the hours of 6 a.m. and 6 p.m., from Tuesday to Saturday. Sundays were set aside for both religious observance and secular recreation, while some urban trades also incorporated 'Saint' Monday into their weekend holiday. However, many shops and businesses were also open on Mondays. Shorter working weeks were associated with periods of depression and short-time working rather than with higher rewards for labour.[42]

Long working days should not automatically be equated with the unrelenting intensity of effort that characterizes the modern workplace; indeed there is a great deal of evidence that urban workers paced themselves carefully and that the workplace was a significant source of companionship and sociability. Most organized leisure activities aimed at the working population, however, took place in the evenings (particularly on Saturdays), on Sundays and Mondays, or on traditional public holidays such as Shrove Tuesday, Easter or Whitsun. Although many of the traditional forms of popular leisure were based on rural models, notably the wakes holidays that were widespread in northern industrial towns, they began to develop in ways that were recognizably urban, a transformation that was already well under way in London in the early seventeenth century. As in the case of the urban renaissance, entrepreneurs responded to the growth of a market among the 'industrious classes' by promoting an increasing number and variety of commercialized leisure pursuits, ranging from theatrical performances, circuses and other shows, to cock-fighting, bull-baiting and horse-racing. Race week, for instance, seems to have loomed as large in the social calendar of the urban working classes as it did in that of the wealthy elite, with many urban workers following the example of the young William Hutton and taking time off to attend the races.[43]

It has to be recognized, however, that most accounts of urban popular culture in this period are actually about *men's* culture, and that women from the lower ranks of urban society had even less leisure time, and many fewer opportunities to enjoy it, than their husbands, fathers and brothers. It is noticeable, for instance, that factory owners in 1816 complained that their young male workforce got into mischief in their free time, while the girls 'have to nurse their younger brothers and sisters, or they work at home . . . to assist their mothers in sewing and housework'. The boys, in contrast, were said to 'have nothing to do'.[44] Most married women clearly spent the major part of their 'free' time either working in their own households or in the company of other women. However, married couples seem to have gone out together to public houses from time to time, while tradesmen's daughters and female servants were alleged to mix with prostitutes at pub dances and theatres in early nineteenth-century London. The blurring of any dividing line between respectable and 'fallen' women that this implied may have aroused concern among contemporary moralists, but it also indicated that women were not necessarily excluded from the second most important focus of male sociability, the public house.

Pubs were certainly integral to most men's working and non-working lives, providing warmth, light and entertainment, as well as a wide range of services and useful contacts.[45] Above all, perhaps, public houses provided the venue for the monthly or fortnightly meetings of an aston-ishing number and variety of clubs, societies and institutions, from book clubs, friendly societies and trade associations at one end of the scale, to sporting, gardening and raffish drinking clubs at the other. It was estim-ated in 1750 that as many as 20,000 men met every night in London in some sort of club, while the House of Commons was informed in 1812 that there were hardly any industrial workers in Birmingham who were not members of at least one society. Paisley textile workers, for instance, developed a fiercely competitive culture devoted to propagating florists' pinks, while those in the Lancashire cotton towns specialized in cultivat-ing bigger and better varieties of gooseberry. Large prizes, and even more substantial side-bets, rewarded successful competitors, and it was this focus on gambling, in addition to the drinking and smoking that seemed to be an inseparable element of club meetings, that seemed to mark them as an exclusively male environment. Few women, in any case, could have afforded the time and the regular subscriptions that male clubability required.

Poverty was also a major constraint on the leisure activities of the bulk of the urban poor, who could not afford to pay for commercial enter-tainments or to keep up with the payments that ensured continued membership of clubs and societies. However, in Georgian towns the public street was as much a centre for leisure and recreation as it was for business. Musicians, singers, jugglers, gamblers, freak and side shows, puppeteers and theatre companies alike operated in the open air or from temporary booths, attracting spectators who themselves attracted the much less welcome attentions of bands of pickpockets. Public holidays and traditional festivals were also celebrated in the streets, often by traditional rituals such as the 'whipping toms' of Newark; each Shrove Tuesday two or three blindfolded men, armed with cartwhips and preceded by a warning bell, proceeded through the streets flogging any-one who strayed into their path. Even newly-coined festivals such as Birmingham's Chapel Wake, invented in 1750 by an enterprising pub-lican to encourage trade, involved street activities, in this case racing horses through the town centre. After 1787, churches and chapels also provided havens of sociability through the Sunday school movement, which was open to young adults as well as to children, and which signific-antly expanded its recreational activities in the early decades of the nineteenth century. The Methodists, in particular, organized an impress-ive array of social and religious events, from prayer meetings and charity sermons to concerts, tea parties, love-feasts and annual treats.[46] The popular appeal of these church-based social and cultural events should not be entirely discounted by cynical historians. People went to chapel to make friends and find sweethearts, as well as to find God, while it is worth remembering that psalms and hymns were sung in Birmingham public houses when the licensing authorities banned dramatic performances in these embryonic music halls.

Such organized events, numerous as they were, were still outnum-bered by the countless improvised games and spontaneous amusements that flourished in the streets. Children up and down the land blocked gateways and narrow alleys as they crouched over marbles, dice and jacks; skipping and round games spilled over into the roadways; and gangs of young men playing football habitually jostled pedestrians, dis-rupted the traffic and smashed adjacent windows. As the day drew to a close, however, more peaceful pursuits held sway. Poorer townspeople brought chairs and benches out into the street on summer evenings to sit and gossip with their friends and to watch the world go by. Many outdoor activities, both individual and collective, were available free of charge since, for much of the eighteenth century, the urban population had access to public areas that were traditionally associated with games and festivals. It was also accepted that they could make use of the farmland that still lay close to the town centre, even in fast-growing cities such as Manchester and Glasgow, provided that they did no damage to standing crops. An open space of several hundred acres outside Coventry, for instance, was crowded on summer evenings with hundreds of men playing quoits, cricket, tennis and other ball games. Summer was also, understandably, the most popular time for swimming in local rivers and, later in the period, in the new canals. It was reported in 1833 that the rivers in Sheffield were 'crowded with bathers, although the water is often shallow, muddy, dirty and sometimes even offensive, the situations exposed . . . ; and the banks dusty, without grass and without trees'.[47]

The gradual degradation of the urban landscape, indicated in this vivid eye-witness testimony, was accompanied by mounting commercial pressures upon the open spaces that had traditionally been used to accommodate popular recreations. Residential development, of course, played a major part in whittling away public facilities, while farmers became much less tolerant of urban workers using their land as playing fields in their few leisure hours. The formation in 1826 of the Manchester Society for the Preservation of Ancient Footpaths indicates the growing public alarm provoked by this loss of public access to the countryside and by the resentment with which the working class greeted 'being expelled from field to field, and being deprived of all play-spaces'. Dr J. P. Kay was undoubtedly overstating his case when he claimed that 'the entire labouring population of Manchester is without any season of recreation and is ignorant of all amusements'.[48] Although working-class leisure clearly suffered during the worst years of the 1790s or the 1830s, for example, when time as well as money was in very short supply, 'recreation' and 'amusements' were cherished in times of slump as well as times of prosperity. With the return of prosperity, popular pastimes and holidays re-established themselves in an extravagant outburst of joy and relief. Nevertheless, the increasing pressures which urban development exerted on popular leisure certainly appeared to threaten the poorest inhabitants of Georgian towns with a form of social exclusion. Since they had neither the time nor the purchasing power to share in the cultural or material benefits of the 'urban renaissance', they risked being pushed even further to the margins of civic life.

5

LANDSCAPE AND ENVIRONMENT

There *shall broad streets their stately walls extend,*
The circus widen, and the crescent bend; . . .
Embellished villas crown the landscape-scene,
Farms wave with gold, and orchards blush between.
                              Erasmus Darwin (1789)

Darwin's shining vision of the future development of Sydney, written to
celebrate the successful landing of the First Fleet in 1788, pictured an
ideal city, where the best of town and country could co-exist beside the
'glittering streams' of the harbour.[1] In the enthusiasm of the moment,
the inglorious mission of the convict ships was overlooked. So was the
awkward reality of urban growth back in Britain, where economic and
demographic expansion all too often meant narrow streets, close-packed
tenements and greasy, stinking rivers. In the age-old debate between
the virtues of town and country life, the country seemed to have gained
a decisive advantage, represented in Jane Austen's novel *Mansfield Park*
(1814) by the 'liberty, freshness, fragrance and verdure' of which the
heroine is deprived when banished to the 'closeness and noise, . . .
confinement, bad air, bad smells' generated by naval and commercial
activity in Portsmouth.[2]

The Urban Labyrinth

Many of the environmental challenges posed by urban development in
this period were associated with the sheer density of settlement that
characterized traditional town centres. The existing pattern of streets,

alleys and 'closes' had evolved in an age when wheeled vehicles were rare, and they seldom provided thoroughfares straight or wide enough to cater for eighteenth-century traffic. Nottingham's Hollow-stone, for example, the main entrance to the town from the south, was until the 1740s so narrow that carriages and waggons had to travel in single file, unable to overtake or to pass another vehicle travelling in the opposite direction. Having penetrated further into the centre, vehicles and pedestrians alike entered an essentially claustrophobic streetscape, a shadowy and sometimes oppressive maze in which both sunlight and fresh air were in short supply; it was reportedly so dark at ground level in Birmingham's Moor Street that the inhabitants needed to use candles at noon on a bright summer's day.

Moreover, even though walking was indisputably the most common means of urban transport as well as a fashionable leisure activity, there was rarely any special provision made for pedestrians.[3] 'Foot-passengers' using the principal streets were sometimes protected from the worst of the traffic by rows of posts erected along the edges of the roadway, as for instance at Colchester; while in Covent Garden in London and at Chester, Nottingham and Tunbridge Wells, pedestrians could shelter from both the traffic and the weather under arcades that ran along the main shopping streets. Elsewhere, particularly in the side-streets, walkers had to have their wits about them to stay both safe and dry. Crossing the street meant not only dodging the traffic and risking a soaking but getting your shoes dirty. Few roadways had been surfaced in the early years of the Georgian period and some towns were notoriously muddy, particularly where the lie of the land did not provide any natural drainage. The streets between St Peter's church and the river Leen in Nottingham, for example, were described in the 1740s as 'one continued Swamp', while the site of one of the town's markets, though 'in the Heart of the Town, was a meer Sink . . . and dangerous to pass especially in the Night'; it had to be spanned by a plank bridge.[4] In some towns the problems were exacerbated by streams or brooks running along the middle of the street, as they did in Bath's Horse Street and along both the Sandgate and the Side in Newcastle upon Tyne. How-ever, even the best urban roads degenerated into a sea of mud in bad weather as their soft surfaces were churned up by passing traffic.

Pedestrians tried to protect themselves from the filth that stained their clothing and encrusted their feet by wearing thick overcoats and stout boots; women often wore wooden overshoes, called pattens, while gentlemen relied on roadside shoe cleaners to ensure that they arrived

at their destinations respectably shod. Householders struggled heroic-
ally to keep the dirt from crossing the threshold, installing iron scrap-
ers outside their doors and mats at every entrance, but were still forced
to sweep out and scrub down their halls and floors every morning. Nor
did dry summers bring them much relief, merely replacing the mud
with choking dust that lay thickest on the busiest thoroughfares, swirling in at the windows and into the eyes of passers-by. The care with
which so many townspeople cultivated 'a Board before their Chamber-
Windows, crowded with a Number of Flower-Pots' reflected these
conditions; sweet-smelling plants – pinks, roses, oranges, myrtle,
angelica, southernwood and mignonette – acted as a barrier against the
smells and dust rising from the street below.[5]

Contemporary wisdom, reflected in the many satires that portrayed
the sufferings of urban pedestrians in graphic detail, suggested that it
was better to stay relatively close to the buildings, thus avoiding the
worst of the traffic and the mud, not to mention the dirty water and
refuse that collected in the gutters. On rainy days it was also possible to
gain some protection from the water spouts that poured down from the
roofs high above by walking in the shelter of overhanging buildings. On
the other hand, keeping to the wall multiplied the risk of falling down
unguarded cellars or tripping over projecting flights of steps. Since
there was no agreed building line, houses jutted out into the roadway
at odd angles, as did the lean-to stalls and sheds often used as shops
by traders and craftsmen; in 1698, for instance, an Edinburgh vintner
complained that a shoemaker's stall had blocked the entrance to
Collintoun's close, 'which did greatly obstruct the repair of persons
going down and coming up the said close and prejudiced the
complainer who keeps a public inn'.[6]

Nightfall exacerbated these problems, turning the streets into dangerous obstacle courses, where hapless pedestrians were at the mercy
of thieves and muggers, as well as of more mundane hazards such as
stinking piles of refuse. Although some urban authorities had begun to
introduce a little light into the gloom by ordering householders to burn
candle lanterns outside their houses on moonless winter evenings, the
illumination that they provided was both too feeble and too infrequent
to open up the streets after dark.[7] Night-time entertainment had
certainly developed rapidly in seventeenth-century London, particularly from the 1680s, but business and social life still came to an abrupt
halt in most provincial towns as darkness fell. The bustle of the streets
during the day was succeeded after nine o'clock by an effective curfew;

'night-walkers' were regarded with suspicion and were liable to sum-
mary arrest.

The Impact of Growth

As urban development gathered pace in Georgian Britain, a rising tide
of people, vehicles and goods began to swamp the already congested
streets of fast-growing provincial towns, subjecting their inhabitants to
the dangers and discomforts that were already commonplace in Edinburgh and London.[8] It was, for example, extraordinarily difficult to find
your way about the larger towns without detailed local knowledge,
something which could no longer be guaranteed in the new world of
large-scale trade and increased personal mobility. The traditional town
had had no need for road signs, house-numbers and street maps. In a
basically oral culture, streets rarely had fixed, official names and buildings were identified by pictorial signs; in any case businesses had tended
to cluster together so that it was relatively easy to locate a particular
workshop or warehouse within a small built-up area. The bewildered
'peasant' who became hopelessly lost in the big city was a well-established comic stereotype, derided for his stupidity. The pace of urban
growth in the eighteenth century, however, meant that it was not only
innocent countrymen who could not find their way. Overhead signs
became a source of confusion rather than guidance in the fast-changing
economies of most Georgian towns and those in London were taken
down in the 1760s for that reason. Businesses moved so frequently that
there was no longer any guarantee that a painted fish marked out a
fishmonger or that a loaf indicated a baker. Even the few street maps
that had begun to appear failed to keep up with the speed of change and
the expansion of the built-up area; William Morgan's survey of London
in 1682, for instance, was not repeated for 60 years, a period in which
the size and shape of the capital changed out of all recognition.

In the most dynamic industrial and commercial towns, as well as in
the capital cities, the sheer inconvenience of moving goods and people
through the streets was beginning to constitute a bottleneck in the way of
further development. Rising populations meant that far greater numbers of people were using the narrow streets, and yet the streets themselves were shrinking as overhanging jetties were filled in with brick to
create fashionably flat façades or modern shop-fronts. Such encroachments in Birmingham, William Hutton complained, 'made those streets

eight or ten feet narrower, that are now used by 50,000 people, than they were, when used by only a tenth part of that number'.[9] It is also likely that, as the built-up area expanded, urban residents needed to undertake more and longer journeys through the streets as they moved between increasingly specialized commercial and residential districts. Evidence of such an increase in personal mobility could be found in towns the length and breadth of the country and with it went an increased demand for both public and private transport. Sedan chairs, private coaches and hired carriages, previously to be found only in the capital cities or the fashionable resorts, began to appear in considerable numbers in provincial towns. In York, for example, the construction of new assembly rooms in the late 1720s necessitated widening several streets in the vicinity to accommodate the expected influx of carriages, and by the 1770s even Birmingham boasted a rank of hackney coaches. In London they clustered so thickly in the principal streets that there appeared to be more carriages than houses; public transport both here and at Bath was already licensed and the fares regulated to protect the travelling public from unscrupulous operators.

The traffic created by passenger transport was nevertheless dwarfed by that generated by trade, especially the vastly increased volume of agricultural produce that was needed to supply the growing urban population. Herds of livestock as well as carts and waggons of all shapes and sizes, loaded with all manner of goods, poured into the towns in ever-increasing numbers, competing for passage through the over-crowded streets and provoking fierce or even violent confrontations as their drivers disputed for precedence in roadways only wide enough for one vehicle at a time. Country visitors were torn between wonder and horror at the pandemonium that appeared to break out at first light and to continue well into the night; they were astonished that their hosts, their senses blunted by long-term exposure, seemed impervious to the uproar.

On market days, in particular, a flood of trade and traffic engulfed town centres; officials found it increasingly difficult to enforce regulations controlling the movement of vehicles and animals, so that shoppers were obstructed and sometimes injured by the waggons, pack-horses, sheep and cattle that jammed the streets. In the faster-growing towns, traditional market-places seemed to have been left behind by the pace of development and they attracted a growing number of complaints. Their cramped central sites were inconvenient for the inhabitants of the newly-developed areas on the periphery of the town.[10]

Moreover, the congestion and clamour associated with market days detracted from the appeal of smart modern shops and houses along the principal streets, especially if the market generated too many unpleasant sights or obnoxious smells. Even in the small town of Ledbury in Herefordshire, the activities of the town's butchers were beginning to generate complaints from an increasingly squeamish public, who by 1800 found the spectacle of cattle being slaughtered and skinned on the spot totally repugnant, especially when the skins were hung out to dry on the rails of the market house.[11]

Unfortunately, this growing fastidiousness coincided with deteriorating conditions as the pressures of urban growth produced a noticeable increase in pollution. Heavy industries had always generated noxious and unsightly waste products. Defoe, for instance, had recognized the environmental impact of the smoke rising from the forges at Sheffield and the salt-works at Tynemouth, and described Aberystwyth as 'a very dirty, black, smoaky place', whose population 'look'd as if they liv'd continually in the coal or lead mines'.[12] The concentration and intensification of industry as the century progressed, however, also intensified its impact. By the 1790s, for example, the Irwell had been poisoned for some miles below Manchester by the chemical discharge from dye-works operating along the banks of the river, while in 1802 Robert Southey vividly characterized the filth swirling around the streets of Birmingham as 'a living principle of mischief, which fills the atmosphere and penetrates everywhere, spotting and staining every thing, and getting into the pores and nostrils'.[13] In many textile towns, as in Glasgow, it was the proliferation of steam-powered machinery after 1792 that made the biggest contribution to urban blight.

It would be a mistake, however, to underestimate the environmental pressures which were building up in towns that were less closely associated with rapid industrialization. Even in small market towns or smart residential centres, the noises and smells generated by open-fronted shops and workshops reverberated in the narrow streets, mingling with the noise, smells and refuse produced by their growing human and animal populations. More coal fires meant that the streets and all who used them became encrusted with the dust which fell from both the carts delivering coal and those carrying away the ashes; smoke from thousands of domestic hearths dimmed the skies and blackened the buildings. In London, plants and people alike were 'Suffocated' by the 'thick and voluminous smoke, which . . . floats over the town', even on the clearest summer days.[14] More people meant more 'night-soil' carts slopping their contents in the street as they made their rounds under cover of darkness to empty cesspits and privies; more horse-drawn vehicles meant more horse manure deposited in the roadway. More often than not, domestic as well as animal refuse was casually disposed of in the streets. As late as 1834, it was reported that the night-soil of Cheapside, one of London's major commercial arteries, was 'kept in poisonous pools, of which the inhabitants pump out the contents into open channels in the streets at night'.[15] Even by the lax standards of the day the state of courts and alleyways behind such principal streets was roundly condemned; it is worth noting that 'respectable' pedestrians were advised to withdraw into such secluded corners to relieve themselves, thus setting themselves above the bulk of the urban population, who had no such inhibitions.

The Contemporary Response

It had long been a commonplace that 'Towns of a considerable Business and a flourishing Trade, seldom give Gentlemen great Encouragement to be fond of settling in them'; indeed the noise, dirt and congestion that were inseparable from industrial and commercial activity were so distasteful that some of the wealthier residents of Colchester were said to have welcomed the decline of its once-flourishing cloth industry in the decades after 1715.[16] Dunghills and defecation, too, would seem hard to reconcile with the much-vaunted 'civility' of urban life. However, there is little evidence of a wholesale flight from the expanding towns. Although some of their inhabitants clearly reacted against the smoke and chaos of urban life, others seemed curiously oblivious to conditions that appear almost intolerable to modern eyes. One formerly desirable residence in the 'garden city' of Nottingham, for instance, was still described in 1815 as 'an enchanting country seat in the heart of the town', although it was now hemmed in by a miscellaneous collection of workshops, warehouses and framework-knitters' cottages, not to mention a Wesleyan chapel whose windows had to be partly boarded up to preserve some measure of privacy for the remarkably resilient house-holder.[17] In Leeds at the turn of the century, people were even prepared to buy newly-built terraced houses with fashionable, classical façades in St Peter's and Park squares, ignoring the mill chimneys and back-to-back housing that predominated in this part of the town.

This apparent indifference to their surroundings stemmed partly from the fact that urban blight was, by its very nature, generally cumulative, the result of a steady concentration of residential and industrial development over many years. The first two or three mills erected on the outskirts of an expanding town were innocuous in themselves and might even attract admiring comments from both residents and visitors for their novelty. The neat cottages of their workforce were even less of a nuisance, especially when fields and gardens lay open on every side beyond the new terraces. It could take a considerable time before such developments grew both in number and in scale to the point where they impinged upon the quality of life of the wealthier residents.[18] Industrial and domestic pollution could seem equally harmless in the early stages, before the insidious effects of fumes and effluent had built up sufficiently to surround town-dwellers with blackened buildings, stunted trees and stinking rivers.

A second factor dulling contemporary reaction to the degradation of the environment was their imperfect understanding of the health dangers posed by the twin evils of uncontrolled industrial development and overcrowding. Noise, dirt and smoke were certainly thought of as unpleasant, but that was a venial sin when weighed against the wealth and activity of which they were an apparently inescapable symptom. The high incidence of chest infections in urban industrial areas, when it was admitted at all, was commonly attributed to unfavourable climatic conditions rather than to the fumes rising from urban chimneys. Medical opinion on the whole agreed with this comforting diagnosis; exposure to smells and smoke was dangerous only when 'excessive'.[19] There was even some surviving attachment to the idea, satirized in Tobias Smollett's novel *The Expedition of Humphrey Clinker* (1771), that strong faecal smells could have beneficial effects, suffocating the dangerous miasma that spread plague and pestilence.

However, a new scientific consensus was emerging that, on the contrary, acute stenches were in fact agents of disease and that the degree of stench corresponded to the degree of danger. Combined with the inexorable rise of death rates in poorer urban areas, this stress on the connection between smell and disease persuaded many doctors working in congested town centres that there was a strong link between urban squalor and poor urban health.[20] It was, significantly, in Manchester in the 1790s that a group of general practitioners founded the first local Board of Health. Lay opinion, on the other hand, was not wholly convinced. Contemporaries argued that, although the air of London might seem unhealthy to strangers, the continued growth of its population proved that 'it must of itself be at least as pure as that of any great city in the world'.[21] In Liverpool, too, local writers chose to ignore the heavy mortality rates recorded for the crowded districts around the port and continued to assert that the town's exposure to brisk sea breezes gave it an unusually healthy climate. Despite frequent and menacing epidemics of infectious diseases in the 1820s and 1830s, particularly of typhus, wealthier residents remained remarkably complacent.

Such residents had compelling reasons not to cut themselves off completely from urban life. The professional and 'industrious' middle classes obviously needed to remain within commuting distance of urban-based businesses, although many had begun to establish 'second homes' in nearby villages. Even the leisured sections of urban society, however, who had little practical incentive to leave the peace and quiet of their country estates, persisted in spending long months amid the noise, dirt and bustle of the towns. In their case the advantages of the clean countryside over the dirty town were balanced by the town's clear pre-eminence as a social and recreational centre, an equation summed up bluntly in 1718 by one young gentleman in response to a summons home: 'Surely you don't think me such a fool as to prefer the Charms of a stupid, dull, Country Life, to the pleasures of the Town?'[22] The traditional attraction of the 'urbane' city centre thus survived the build-up of environmental problems in the Georgian town. Prestigious housing developments which ignored it and offered potential purchasers rural views at the expense of access to shops and assembly rooms tended therefore to fail, as did the ambitious Polygon development begun in 1768 outside Southampton.

Fashion, convenience, habit and ignorance therefore combined to keep both the upper and middle classes in their town houses while the environment deteriorated around them. This in itself, it might be suggested, is sufficient explanation for the growing emphasis during the eighteenth century on the benefits of deliberate intervention in the process of development. It was in the interests of influential residents to slow down the slide into chaos and preserve some of the cherished amenities of urban life; they wished to live in a cleaner, pleasanter environment and they were beginning to realize that dirt was dangerous as well as distasteful. They were also increasingly conscious that human beings had the power to alter their environment; and that towns in particular, being man-made, were inherently adaptable to human needs. Some of them even displayed humanitarian concern for the fate of the poorer members of the community, who had to bear the brunt of the problems of mass living without the comfortable option of escape into the suburbs. The mushroom growth of Birmingham, for example, convinced William Hutton that 'the larger the number of people, the more necessity to watch over their interest with a guardian eye'.[23] The result was growing enthusiasm for stronger planning powers to check the proliferation of the worst sort of urban landscape as well as to promote the best, and to insist on wide streets, efficient drainage and minimum standards of housing.

Revulsion from the chaotic and unpleasant results of the late eighteenth-century building booms is not enough by itself, however, to explain the increasing emphasis on planned development. As Peter Borsay has demonstrated, the planning impulse clearly *preceded* the dramatic deterioration of urban conditions in later Georgian England and encompassed the redesigning of country as well as of urban estates; it reflected a wider cultural enthusiasm for the ordering and improvement of the environment on lines dictated by newly fashionable aesthetic ideas and newly acquired confidence in modern standards.[24] The relics of the past were almost universally condemned, so much so that 'old' became synonymous with 'ugly'. Old streets and old houses were narrow, crooked, dark and inconvenient, jumbled together in a confused mass that not only outraged contemporary assumptions that symmetry and order were the prerequisites of beauty but also contradicted influential assumptions about the social functions of the urban environment. Writers, architects and their wealthy patrons were now inspired by the ideal city of classical antiquity and the renaissance; they believed that conscious manipulation of the urban landscape could produce a civilized, 'urbane' society within the ordered, aesthetically pleasing framework thus created.

This vision of the Georgian town as a social arena on a classical model emphasized the public, rather than the private, significance of development. In contrast with what was presented as the haphazard individualism of the past, when

> every one, probably, built in whatever place and form best suited his own purposes, without consulting the appearance of the town, or so much as imagining that it would afterwards be of any consequence to the public, what situation he chose, or what style of architecture he adopted,

individual taste and convenience should be subordinated to the aesthetic and practical requirements of the wider community.[25] It was assumed that towns of a certain status needed a range of useful and decorative buildings, both public and private, carefully laid out along broad, straight and well-maintained streets that culminated in specially designed architectural or sculptural features to provide residents with impressive 'vistas'. Just as the tree-lined avenues of eighteenth-century formal gardens led the eye towards a distant ornamental temple or fountain, so the streets and squares of Georgian towns were expected to give aesthetic satisfaction, although in the urban context churches rather than temples were the most common visual props. Not for the last time, the absence of such a panorama at the heart of London provoked bitter complaints and demands that Parliament should supply the deficiency by buying up and demolishing the inferior buildings that obscured the view of St Paul's. But this concern for the quality of the urban landscape was not confined to prestigious sites in the capital; thus in the 1730s William Bourne advocated clearing away the buildings around St Nicholas's church in Newcastle upon Tyne so that 'this *Great Ornament* of the Town... would then be wholly expos'd, and strike Beholders with Awe and Wonder', while John Wood wanted to clear away all the obstructions from Bath's High Street to create an appropriate vista of the abbey.[26] Active management of the landscape was clearly imperative if the urban environment was to be successfully remodelled so that it embodied civic and civilized values.

'Useful, Necessary and Elegant Improvements'

It is not surprising, therefore, that the growing number of urban improvement schemes put forward as the Georgian period progressed almost invariably cited the aesthetic advantages that would accrue to the town in question, as well as more practical considerations. On the other hand, it is difficult to avoid the conclusion that the main force behind such schemes was the rapid deterioration in the urban environment brought about by the pressures of economic and demographic growth; only the urgent need for cleaner, safer and above all more efficient communications could have sustained the growing financial commitment involved.[27] As the rising scale of urbanization dramatically multiplied the problems faced by pedestrians and vehicles alike, so the impulse for reform gradually spread from the largest, busiest and wealthiest towns to reach relatively modest communities. In some places the initiative lay with existing executive bodies, such as town corporations or church vestries, but there was no uniform pattern; in both Liverpool and Glasgow, for example, there was a strong tradition of active civic intervention, but in Colchester the corporation itself took no part and improvement depended on the formation of a statutory improvement commission.[28] Nor can a single trigger for such initiatives be identified; some towns responded to the opportunities created by a destructive fire, whereas others embraced 'improvement' more proactively, hoping to attract wealthy visitors by upgrading the urban environment. The results, not surprisingly, were equally uneven, varying from town to town, and even from street to street within the same town. Yet, although improvement schemes were rarely wholly successful, their cumulative impact made a substantial contribution to the distinctive appearance of the Georgian town.[29]

Perhaps the greatest success of all was the achievement of a high degree of visual unity, reinforcing the identity of the street as a coherent architectural unit rather than as a collection of individual buildings. The main agents of change in this respect were the fashionable emphasis on classically plain, relatively flush façades and the social pressures towards conformity. As existing structures were refronted in the restrained and elegant style dictated by urban classicism and newer buildings took their neighbours as a model, street frontages in towns the length and breadth of the country gained architectural coherence with very little intervention from the authorities. This visual effect was strengthened, moreover, by the widespread introduction into principal streets of a range of street furniture designed to mark off a 'foot-way' for pedestrians, with lines of posts on one side to protect them from the traffic and fences or iron railings on the other to keep them at a distance from the doors, steps and basements of roadside properties. The almost universal use of white or 'stone colour' paint for doors, windows and railings alike also helped to draw the street together as a unit.

These minor but significant changes in the urban landscape were naturally most successful where the street concerned was sufficiently wide and straight to allow both pedestrians and vehicles to pass freely. New developments could, of course, lay out wide, airy and convenient street plans wherever the speculators involved believed that they could recover the considerable costs involved in sterilizing so much valuable building land. Some towns were able to follow the example of Restoration London and insist that rebuilding after a fire should take place along wider and straighter roads; a visitor to Shrewsbury in 1717 deplored the fact that 'the irregularity of the buildings can only be cured by a fire'.[30] Other towns had to make their own opportunities and relied more on piecemeal efforts to remove particular bottlenecks, buying up strategically placed properties and either clearing the site completely or rebuilding behind the original fronts. The council in York seem to have operated this policy from the 1720s, making a particular effort to buy up corner sites. By the early nineteenth century the impulse had spread even further; the small Devon town of Chudleigh, whose 1800 inhabitants cannot have experienced the extremes of congestion felt in major centres of population, obtained a rebuilding act in 1808 which specified that the width of its main street was to be increased to 32 feet. In many cases it was possible to achieve quite dramatic results simply by removing the obstructions that had decreased the effective width of traditional streets. In Bath, as in many other towns, the ancient town walls eventually fell victim to the demand for broad streets and easy access. Norwich corporation, for example, which had persisted well into the eighteenth century with the old custom of shutting the city gates on Sundays and at nightfall, voted in the early 1790s to demolish them completely and to allow the remaining medieval walls to crumble and collapse of their own accord.

It would be a mistake, however, to imagine that the self-evident need for wider streets to accommodate the greatly increased traffic always produced prompt and effective action by the local authorities. In all attempts to remodel the urban environment, long-term public interests came into conflict with those of private citizens whose property was threatened by the process of reform; street improvements were no exception. Many townspeople, even those as public-spirited as William Hutton, were not prepared to see their houses and shops demolished without putting up some resistance, and the cost of buying them out was a formidable obstacle to large-scale redevelopment. Although the powers granted to local authorities to raise rates were often considerable in theory, they were tempered in practice by an understandable unwillingness to impose heavy burdens upon themselves and their fellow citizens. New tolls levied to finance the rebuilding of Bristol bridge provoked a riot in 1793 and, while such extreme reactions were rare, few councils or improvement commissions were prepared to force through expensive planning schemes. Oxford, for example, improved its roadways but rejected Hawksmoor's plans for reconstructing a substantial part of the built-up area, just as the council rejected Wood's scheme for rebuilding the centre of Bath on the lines of a major classical city, a 'new Rome' in the west. It was not until Nash's Regent Street development in the 1820s that England saw its first piece of large-scale, publicly supported and architecturally coherent urban planning.

It is important to recognize, too, that even the celebrated grand designs of Georgian town planning were subject to compelling commercial pressures that all too often compromised their original principles.[31] In London in the 1720s, Campbell's ambitious design for Grosvenor Square was abandoned because speculative developers were not prepared to invest in Palladian magnificence. In the case of the New Town in Edinburgh, the city council at first made very little attempt to exert detailed control over development beyond insisting on wide pavements and continuity of the building line; no uniform elevations were prescribed and the integrity of the original plan was compromised by unauthorized building in St Andrew's Square and on the south side of Princes Street. Outraged citizens eventually forced the adoption of a more interventionist policy, pursuing the council for negligence as far as the House of Lords, but no real attempt to impose a substantial degree of architectural uniformity was made until the 1790s, when the imminent development of Charlotte Square threatened to cause a similar public scandal.

Change by way of small-scale improvements, rather than wholesale remodelling, was consequently the general rule. The older areas of most Georgian towns remained almost untouched, their congestion and confusion forming a striking contrast with the 'new towns' of modern houses and streets that grew up around them. In smaller centres it was rare for such new development to extend beyond a few streets, though many more individual buildings were upgraded. Moreover, it was private capital, rather than civic initiative, that transformed the old churchyards, closes and market places of many smaller towns, like Angel Hill in Bury St Edmunds, into 'pseudo squares' surrounded by fashionably refronted houses. Elsewhere the abandoned sites of medieval castles were developed into fashionable residential areas, as in Wisbech where a series of squares and crescents were laid out between 1793 and 1816. In cases like these, it is questionable whether the improvers or developers were involved in 'planning' in its true sense; they were adding a few fashionable elements to the existing landscape rather than attempting to create a new one. Even Bath, the classical Georgian townscape that attracted so much admiration and so many imitators, was largely the result of piecemeal developments. Pulteney's Bathwick estate east of the river was actually the only area of Bath to be planned as a coherent unit; in other parts of town, the appearance of symmetry and order was achieved without any overall direction.

Upgrading the basic infrastructure of the urban environment, in contrast, was increasingly accepted as a vital public service, although one that rarely extended beyond the market-place and other principal streets. Many towns invested heavily in solid, well-drained surfaces for their main thoroughfares, usually by cambering the 'horse road' and laying down a thick bed of pebbles to withstand the constant pounding of the traffic. If a pedestrian pavement was provided this consisted of broad flat flagstones, separated from the road by raised curbstones or posts, an arrangement that attracted favourable comments from foreign visitors unused to the convenience, safety and relative cleanliness which it offered to long-suffering 'foot passengers'.

Improved lighting, too, proved an unalloyed blessing wherever it was introduced. The breakthrough here was achieved by the development and widespread dissemination of oil-burning street lamps, which first began to appear in the streets of London in the 1680s. By the middle of the eighteenth century most large towns and many smaller ones had adopted some form of public lighting, backed by rating schemes, erecting tall wooden or iron lampposts along the main streets and employing contractors to top up the oil, trim the wicks and light the lamps just before sunset. Even a modest provincial town such as Kendal, with a population of no more than 6000, had caught the prevailing enthusiasm and in 1767 the council sent off to London for four dozen globe lamps to keep the darkness at bay. Although the number of public lamps seems modest to modern eyes – 102 were installed in York in the 1720s and 200 in Colchester in the 1760s – their combined effect impressed contemporaries used to staying indoors after nightfall or stumbling about in the gloom. Residents and visitors alike revelled in the opportunities which were opened up to them in this new urban world; fashionable society in particular reorganized its daily routine as theatres, assemblies and shops extended their hours of business. Moreover, the more the streets were used, the lighter they became; the net result of increased evening activity was that the ranks of publicly-funded street lights were supplemented by growing numbers of lamps maintained by individual householders to illuminate their steps and doorways, by the light spilling out onto the pavement from shop windows, by the lanterns of hackney carriages and by the torches carried by link-boys.

As the period progressed, substantial private investment in schemes to supply fresh water to growing urban populations also began to make some contribution to an improved urban environment. The first piped water began to appear in British towns in the 1690s and the Georgian era saw the establishment of a growing number of water companies, not all of them immediately successful; three attempts were made at Sheffield and five at Liverpool before the many technical and commercial problems involved in such enterprises were overcome. Most schemes involved pumping water from a nearby river or spring to a reservoir or water-house higher up the town from where it was distributed in underground pipes made from hollowed-out tree-trunks to communal fire-plugs in the streets or to smaller lead pipes leading into the houses of individual subscribers. By the early nineteenth century the New River Company in London had 400 miles of wooden pipes laid under the city streets; 'such plenty of water', whether piped directly into domestic kitchens or supplied to communal pumps, was regarded by contemporaries as 'undoubtedly . . . one of the principal causes why our capital is the most healthful great city in the world'. The pressure was said to be so good that wealthy householders could install fountains on their balconies or roof gardens.[32] By 1820, the two water companies that had been set up in Glasgow had invested a total of £320,000 in their networks, making piped water an unaffordable luxury for most urban households.

Expense was also a limiting factor when it came to the unending battle to clear the streets of the rising tide of human and animal refuse that threatened to engulf them. Liverpool council were moving in the right direction when in 1719 they signed an eleven-year agreement with two contractors for a twice-weekly collection from pits that were to be constructed at the end of every street and passage. But schemes like this almost invariably broke down in acrimonious disputes about contract compliance, especially about responsibility for the courts and yards off the main streets, while the speed with which rubbish was deposited invariably overwhelmed the uncertain efficiency of the contractors.

The advances introduced by improved technology in dealing with human waste, meanwhile, brought with them new environmental hazards. By the later eighteenth century many of the better residential streets in London and the major provincial towns were equipped with common sewers, paid for by a special rate levied on the properties concerned, which were used in conjunction with the newly available water-closets. The first common sewer in Glasgow, for instance, was not laid down until the 1790s, but the sewerage network expanded rapidly thereafter. However, successful sewage systems merely flushed the problems out of the streets and into the rivers, often with appalling effects.[33] In 1822 the Thames was still rated as the best salmon river in Britain; ten years later there was not a salmon to be seen and the stage was set for the great cholera epidemics of Victorian England. It is symptomatic of contemporary opinion that the first epidemic of 1831–2, which spread rapidly to affect hundreds of towns and villages, killing over 31,000 people, produced only one anonymous pamphlet, published in Edinburgh, suggesting a connection between the spread of disease and the state of the water supply.[34] In Georgian towns, the smell rising from the increasingly murky waters of urban rivers was perceived as a nuisance rather than as a harbinger of disease – particularly in Bristol, where contractors building the great Floating Harbour put a dam across the River Avon, creating a stagnant lagoon in the heart of the city into which every drain and sewer emptied its contents.

A Divided Landscape?

Miscalculations on this scale, however, were rare, and it is clear that towns all over Georgian Britain made considerable progress in combating the worst effects of urban growth and increased trade.[35] The emphasis of urban classicism on street improvements recognized that the streets were at the heart of the urban landscape and that even the most glorious architecture lost its lustre if it was set amid chaos, squalor and overwhelming misery. Important principles about these most public of spaces and about public responsibility for them had been established, and the first steps had been taken towards fulfilling that responsibility through the rating system. Even though expectations were raised much more rapidly than they could be fulfilled, those expectations themselves helped to give the landscape and environment of the Georgian town a new identity and to set standards for future generations.

Yet it is equally clear that the combination of beauty and utility which Georgian townspeople dreamed of achieving in their urban landscape was never fully realized. In particular, an unprecedented gulf opened up during this period between the standards achieved in the more fashionable urban areas and those which prevailed in poorer parts of town. Critics of early nineteenth-century Manchester, for example, claimed that 'there is no town in the world where the distance between rich and poor is so great, or the barrier between them so difficult to be crossed: . . . in one portion, there is space, fresh air, and provision for health; and in the other, everything which poisons and abridges existence'.[36] The principal streets of late Georgian towns were wider, cleaner, better paved and lighted, lined with tall, regular houses or luxury shops, and used by the minimum of heavy traffic. They had in effect been transformed into pseudo-promenades in which wealthy townspeople could idle away their leisure hours without running the risk of dirtying their clothes and shoes, protected from the disorderly sights, sounds and smells that had so offended earlier generations. The only drawback of these broad, open streets so favoured by planners and developers was that they were equally open to the wind and rain, creating a ready market for the umbrellas that began to appear in increasing numbers in the later decades of the eighteenth century.

The main limiting factor which prevented the wholesale adoption of improved conditions was undoubtedly the sizeable capital investment and high maintenance costs involved, which few local authorities would undertake without firm support from the influential ratepayers who ultimately had to foot the bill. Thus improvement schemes were adopted slowly and reluctantly in towns with relatively few wealthy or fashionable residents, notably in the period of rapidly accelerating growth in the later eighteenth and early nineteenth centuries. There was a perceptible difference between the standard of paving in the resort town of Bath, for instance, where 'it is as easy walking . . . , as in a floored room', as an astonished visitor reported in 1766, as opposed to conditions underfoot in industrial Birmingham in 1792, 'a town wherein I should be crippled in a week from a want of flagstones'.[37] It was sometimes difficult even to maintain the width of existing streets against fresh encroachments; one observer noted that modern houses were still being built in Manchester in the 1790s with projecting flights of steps that forced pedestrians off the pavement. Moreover, wealthy rate-payers were naturally most concerned about their own immediate environment and resisted suggestions that they should pay for improvements from which they would derive no obvious personal benefit; in 1810 it required an Act of Parliament to force through plans to spend £6000 on surfacing some of the lesser streets in Bury St Edmunds, for example. As a result, the best conditions were invariably found in new residential developments which were designed from the outset to meet the exacting standards of fashionable townspeople. As a description of Manchester in the 1790s pointed out, the improvements which had taken place there so far were 'very advantageous in themselves; but . . . it is only in the more modern streets that elegance and convenience can be found united.[38] This disjunction between old and new property, and between rich and poor residents, could be as narrow as the width of the carriageway, as was demonstrated in Beverley in Yorkshire, where the south-facing side of Hengate was gradually upgraded while the north-facing side was neglected, falling further and further behind as the value of its houses declined.

It is difficult to avoid the conclusion that, in terms of the urban population as a whole, little had been done to make the landscape of the common streets safer, pleasanter or less congested; the scale and pace of urban growth had simply outstripped the rate of improvement. Few of the reforms penetrated these socially disadvantaged areas of Georgian towns. Their streets naturally remained unpaved and unlit. Their inhabitants had to rely for water on public pumps or even on water carts since they could not afford to have a private supply piped into their houses. Nor were they connected to the new sewerage systems; in such areas refuse collectors called only rarely, especially in the narrow alleys and back lanes, so that waste of all kinds was left to rot for long periods in the street. Indeed conditions almost certainly became a great deal worse as the period progressed, not least because the obnoxious trades which were banished from the principal streets became concentrated in the less socially important areas of town. By 1840, there was growing public recognition that rapid urban growth had created a physically and morally dangerous environment, one in which filth and destitution combined to create a breeding ground for disorder and disease. The widening differentials between rich and poor, and the increasing social exclusivity that was embodied in this divided landscape, clearly threatened traditional conceptions of civic identity and community.

6

IDENTITY AND COMMUNITY

The traditional ideal of urban life portrayed the inhabitants of the Georgian town as a single community, a united and consensual society

> Where decent Chearfulness stood forth confess'd,
> Where social Harmony warm'd every Breast,
> And sober Plenty shew'd that every House was bless'd.[1]

Despite frequent, sometimes acrimonious, disputes over precedence and despite the almost total exclusion of women and wage labourers from their formal structures, for much of the eighteenth century local institutions still commanded the support of the wider urban community. It was accepted without question that every urban ceremony and public event should be organized on the basis of strict rules of hierarchy and status; newly established clubs and societies, as well as centuries-old town corporations and trade guilds, all marched and prayed, feasted and drank in an order that embodied these traditional social and political values.

This widespread acceptance of the established order was based on a recognition that civic institutions played a vital role in providing the infrastructure and services that underpinned urban society.[2] Thus civic support of the poor was recognized as an indispensable safety net, accepted by wealthier citizens as a Christian duty, 'All Men ... [being] justly Entitled to the *common Offices* of Humanity'. It was also recognized, however, that generosity was a necessary condition of social stability. The founder of St John's charity school in Newcastle upon Tyne, for example, acknowledged in 1702 that 'your corporation's eminent charities no doubt have been a means of [the town's] long prosperity and

106

preservation against all the attempts of its enemies'.[3] Philanthropy and pragmatism, therefore, were pulling in the same direction. Generous provision for the poor counteracted the obvious and widening inequalities that divided the urban population, drawing the community together and strengthening social ties.

Poor relief in urban parishes has not been extensively researched, so that generalizations should be treated with caution; attitudes towards the impoverished sections of urban society in Georgian Britain were neither uniform nor consistent. On the whole, however, they appear to have been treated with much more generosity than a strict interpretation of the Old Poor Law, in either England or Scotland, would have required.[4] Parish administrators, who lived in the same crowded streets as their 'clients', appear to have responded sensitively to personal distress. Face-to-face contact often created strong sympathies, encouraging official bodies to adopt welfare policies that reflected the characteristic working patterns and family structures of the urban poor. In Edinburgh, for example, the kirk sessions did their best to help every 'deserving' case who applied to them, even though many of the city's residents, as recent migrants or unemployed adult workers, had no legal right to relief. In the same spirit, many London parishes paid weekly allowances to poor families headed by an able-bodied male 'breadwinner', as well as to individuals who were too old, too young or too sick to earn their own living. The sums involved also grew steadily throughout the period. In St Martin-in-the-Fields, for instance, parish pensions had risen to almost 18 pence a week in 1703, climbing further to around 20 pence by 1720. A century later, the parish of St George, Southwark, was making weekly payments of 3 shillings per person. In addition, grants to supplement wages were being made for an ever-increasing range of everyday necessities, including fuel, rent, medical treatment, school fees, shoes and spectacles. Families in distress could sometimes even receive grants towards buying clothes and furniture.

It is important to recognize that these welfare settlements were not simply handed down to the urban poor by a remote central authority, but were actively negotiated between parish officials and their prospective clients. Both sides in these negotiations, moreover, shared a deep-seated belief that social harmony depended on a close correlation between rights and obligations. The lower levels of urban society expected their 'betters' to feel a sense of communal responsibility towards the poor and needy, just as they were themselves expected to defer to the authority of those above them in the social order. At an almost unconscious level, perhaps, they linked the legitimacy of the wealth and power enjoyed by the civic elite to their own 'entitlement' to relief.

A similar sense of community of interest dictated that the civic authorities should intervene as peacemakers, as well as peacekeepers, when social stability was threatened by popular discontent. Periodic outbreaks of disorder were in fact an accepted part of urban life, invoking a tradition of negotiated settlements 'upon Terms', which invited an equally structured and orderly response from the crowd. The streets and market-places of towns all over Britain had for centuries been the natural venue for a wide variety of riots, protests and demonstrations. However, these protests had tended to express the grievances of a broad spectrum of local society. Angry demonstrations in Lincoln in 1728, for example, incited by rumours that the dean and chapter intended to demolish part of the cathedral, were justified by a former mayor on the grounds that 'the people could rise 20 miles round in defence of their spires, and that the Gentlemen of the County were for preserving their spires'. In this case, leading citizens appear to have identified themselves openly with the 'common good' of the wider community, both inside and outside the city boundaries, in opposition to the narrow sectional interests represented by the cathedral clergy.[5]

In supporting the campaign to save 'their' cathedral, the inhabitants of Lincoln were clearly expressing a well-developed sense of civic identity, based not only on local community of interest, but also on pride in the city's heritage. Jonathan Barry, for example, has argued that Bristol's historic monuments and public buildings were regarded by its inhabitants as physical symbols of its commercial success and independence, making a major contribution to its self-image as a city with an honourable past, as well as a flourishing present.[6] Families with long-established urban roots must have been most susceptible to this close association between the living fabric of the town and a strong sense of the past: men like William Carr, MP for Newcastle upon Tyne, who wrote to a cousin in 1718 that 'I must confess I cann't forbear loving the Place for the sake of your ancestors and mine'. On the other hand, recent migrants to rapidly developing industrial towns could also become fierce local patriots, revelling in the contrast between their dynamic vigour and the 'idle gloom' that allegedly prevailed in many of Britain's historic urban centres.[7]

The extent to which the lower levels of urban society felt that they had a genuine stake in this culture of civic pride remains unclear. Opposition groups within Georgian towns were certainly eager to present themselves as true 'Sons of the City', as well as 'freeborn Britons', seizing on the rhetoric and imagery of civic pride to defend popular rights and traditions. The popularity of ballads, comic songs and doggerel verse addressed to 'sweet Manchester' or 'you good folks of Nottingham' also suggests that a strong sense of civic identity was not confined to a privileged elite. 'Knowing one's place', in an urban context, had much wider implications than a simple endorsement of deference and subordination to the status quo.

The Urban Neighbourhood

Above all, one thought
Baffled my understanding, how men lived
Even next-door neighbours, as we say, yet still
Strangers, nor knowing each the other's name.
William Wordsworth (1805)[8]

Distinct local identities and a strong sense of place explain why so many contemporaries felt 'uneasy and helpless' when they first arrived in a new town. William Hutton, for example, reported on his arrival in Birmingham in 1750 that, 'it seemed singular to see thousands of faces pass, and not one I knew. I had entered a new world, in which I led a melancholy life; a life of silence and tears'.[9] Such comments are often quoted as evidence of the anonymity and alienation of urban society, in contrast with the supposed warmth of community life in the countryside. It is important, however, to recognize that they represent the first impressions of new migrants and first-time visitors, of *strangers* in a strange town, rather than those of established residents. Although they rely for their emotional impact on an implicit contrast with the more familiar world of 'home', that home was just as likely to be in a town as in a village. Hutton, for instance, had lived all his life in Derby and Nottingham, before moving to Birmingham, without experiencing similar feelings of melancholy and isolation.

Caution is also needed when evaluating contemporary reports that the lower levels of urban society, particularly in the capital cities of London and Edinburgh, lived 'in such a fluctuating state, moving from one house to another, that even the oldest inhabitants seldom know one of a hundred of their fellow parishioners'.[10] Most urban property was rented, which undoubtedly encouraged remarkably high levels of mobility.

People traded up to larger premises when wages rose, rents fell or their families expanded; they traded down again just as readily when these conditions were reversed. William Hulme, a Shrewsbury hairdresser, moved house at least five times within the town centre between 1818 and 1841. However, images of the urban poor as an anonymous, shifting mass of humanity reveal more about the anxieties of the rich and powerful than they do about the reality of everyday life in towns all over Georgian Britain. Most of these towns were actually quite small by modern standards, with fewer than 10,000 inhabitants, and extremely compact built-up areas. You could walk right across most eighteenth-century towns, and out into the countryside again, within a quarter of an hour.

Every one of these towns, moreover, was organized into a patchwork of tightly-knit neighbourhoods, 'urban villages' whose inhabitants were so familiar to one another that the presence of strangers was immediately obvious.[11] In 1788, Lord George Gordon, the instigator of the Gordon riots of 1780 and a convert to Judaism, was arrested in a lodging house in Dudley Street, Birmingham, deep within a largely Jewish neighbourhood known as the Froggery. Despite his best efforts to blend into his surroundings – he adopted the appearance, as well as the faith, of an Orthodox Jew – and despite the fact that his new neighbours evidently regarded him with great respect, it had been relatively easy for a Bow Street runner to track him down. Even in the great metropolis of London, as the unfortunate hero of William Godwin's novel *The Adventures of Caleb Williams* (1794) discovered to his cost, an unfamiliar face was bound to attract attention. Each neighbourhood covered a relatively small area, a narrowly defined complex of streets and alleyways, housing about the same number of people as a modest country village. Moreover, even though this population seemed to be constantly on the move, neither families nor individuals moved very far, tending to stay well within the range of local pubs, shops and churches. Francis Place, for example, changed his London address eight times between 1791 and 1833, without moving more than one kilometre away from St Clement Danes church in Fleet Street.[12] This pattern of circular migration suggests a strong sense of attachment to familiar surroundings and familiar faces; very few next-door neighbours were likely to be complete strangers to one another.

Although work-based friendships and loyalties obviously played a significant role in the lives of all those who had to earn their living in the Georgian town, it is clear that the informal social networks of the neighbourhood were equally, if not more, influential in determining the quality of those lives. Neighbourhood loyalties were encouraged by the fact that each area retained a distinct character and identity. In some cases this was determined by clusters of related occupations. Newcastle's butchers were still concentrated in Butcher Bank and the Flesh Market in the early decades of the eighteenth century, while Edinburgh's city council tried to confine the 'offensive' trade of candlemaking to Candle-maker Row. In the later years of the period, newly established textile mills, factories and foundries developed 'colonies' of housing for their workforces, creating new occupational neighbourhoods on the out-skirts of the built-up area. According to the 1841 census, for instance, Spital Row and Scales' Row in Newark were both occupied only by weav-ers, while spinners and weavers also dominated the Glasgow districts of Anderston and Calton. At the same date, 67 glassmakers and their families were crowded together in Glasshouse Row and Scotch Row in Smethwick, streets laid out in the 1830s to house workers displaced by the closure of the Dumbarton Glassworks Company.

Regional and national ties were evident in many urban neighbour-hoods, since recent migrants tended to cluster around coaching inns, public houses or places of worship that represented a link with their point of origin. The London districts of Spitalfields and the Elephant and Castle, for example, were both noted for the number of migrants from Essex who had chosen to settle there, while a high proportion of the population of Greenwich had been born in Kent. London's substan-tial black community created its own social world in the riverside enclaves of Wapping and Limehouse, as well as in Mile End, Stepney and Paddington. Irish immigrants, meanwhile, settled in increasing numbers in and around Covent Garden and Seven Dials. Their impact on the area was already noticeable in the 1730s; a century later the St Giles rookery had earned the nicknames of 'Little Dublin' and 'the Holy Land'. In Manchester, too, the influx of Irish immigrants into the New Town area in the 1820s and 1830s created a distinctive enclave known locally as 'Irish Town'. Glasgow, however, probably had a higher proportion of Irish inhabitants than any other British city, with around one in three of its population in 1841 either first-generation migrants or of Irish descent. Irish pubs have been a feature of British urban life for centuries, as have Roman Catholic chapels, both of them acting as social and cultural centres for the wider Irish community, as well as for their immediate neighbourhoods.[13] Gaelic chapels in Scottish cities provided a similar focus for migrants from the Highlands and islands, while

Welsh-speaking churches flourished in English border towns, as well as in the rapidly-growing cities of London, Birmingham and Manchester. Distinctively Jewish neighbourhoods, including those in Goodmans Fields in London or in central Manchester, were also growing in both size and number in the later years of the period.

Although the advantages of becoming integrated into an established neighbourhood were particularly obvious in the case of ethnic and religious minorities, it could be argued that the evident fragmentation and fluidity of urban society in this period encouraged a much wider recognition of the value of 'good neighbourhood'. According to Jonathan Barry, it was precisely the growing economic, social and political diversity of the urban middle class in this period that encouraged them to join clubs, societies and voluntary organizations in such numbers, in an attempt 'to reconcile (or at least regulate) their differences by means of association'. It would be a mistake, however, to assume that this overwhelming impulse to club together was a phenomenon that was confined to formal associations among the middling sort. On the contrary, as Shani D'Cruze's examination of social relations in Colchester has demonstrated, individual townspeople developed a wide variety of associations and alliances, both formal and informal, which operated simultaneously on different levels and among different types of people.[14] Wealth and status influenced these relationships to the extent that the wealthier sections of urban society had access to a broader range of options and more autonomy in choosing between them. For the vast majority of the urban population, it was the strength and diversity of the social networks operating within their particular neighbourhood that had the biggest impact on their lives.

Neighbourhood networks clearly played a key role in assimilating migrants into working-class communities within the Georgian town. Many immigrants, although probably a minority of the vast numbers who moved into British towns in this period, were eased into urban life by lodging with relatives who were already settled in a neighbourhood and had good local contacts. Others gained a foothold by calling on ties of friendship based on shared origins, culture, faith or occupation. Many examples suggest that 'brother journeymen' felt under an obligation to help out fellow workers, even those outside the formal structures of confraternities, trade clubs and friendly societies. As a penniless, runaway apprentice in Birmingham in 1741, for example, William Hutton was immediately identified as a stranger, but was treated to a meal by two 'men in aprons' – the badge of the industrious lower orders – on the grounds that they knew from personal experience 'what it is...to be a distressed traveller'.[15] They also found him a bed for the night in a nearby lodging house, a vital step in integrating a potential migrant into the neighbourhood. Lodging-house keepers and publicans often acted as 'fictive kin' to their clients, supplying information on job vacancies and extending credit for the purchase of clothes and tools, as well as providing access to neighbourhood social networks and activities.

The readiness of Hutton's chance-met acquaintances to intervene in his life seems to have been typical behaviour within urban neighbourhoods. Privacy was a limited commodity within the tightly packed and poorly built housing that characterized the lower-class areas of Georgian towns. In giving evidence to the New Kirk session in Edinburgh in 1744, for instance, a woman testified that she could identify a neighbour's cough through the thin plank wall between their lodgings. In the alehouse, the workplace or out on the street, where so much of their social and business lives took place, everyone's character and behaviour was on open display. The weight of neighbourhood opinion could bear down on someone who broke the unwritten rules that governed their daily existence. Hostile gossip could escalate into public insult and actual physical injury as a wide spectrum of the local population took an active part in the working out of 'neighbourhood dramas'.

Women seem to have been particularly prominent in such interventions. Their role as 'housekeepers', paradoxically, took them out of the house and into the streets and markets on an almost daily basis, while the nature of 'women's work' outside the home also tended to involve them more closely in neighbourhood networks. Moreover, it is possible that women had a greater personal interest in building up and maintaining the friendships and alliances that sustained both men and women at the lower levels of urban society when times were hard. The main burden of caring for the casualties of urban life, for the sick, for the old and for dependent children, tended to fall disproportionately on women. Moreover, the typical female pattern of low-paid and irregular work meant that they themselves were more likely to become dependent on outside assistance at some point in their lives. In this context, Margaret Hunt suggests that, 'For women, embeddedness in a community of friends, neighbors, relatives, and work-mates was the most effective means to counterbalance the overwhelming power of men both in the family and society'.[16]

It is important to recognize, however, that men were also deeply embedded in these local networks of reciprocal assistance. They were

just as dependent on maintaining a good reputation among their neighbours, without which they would find it difficult to find work, borrow
money or pawn goods. Despite the relative generosity of parish relief
and of private philanthropy within Georgian towns, all the evidence
suggests that the majority of townspeople relied first and foremost on
self-help and on the generosity of their family and friends.[17] Indeed, at
times of acute and widespread distress, as in Glasgow in 1819–20 and
1826–7, official provision for the poor tended to break down completely
under the strain. A good neighbour was someone who could be relied on
in a crisis. A bad neighbour, on the other hand, someone whose selfish
or violent behaviour disrupted the delicate balance of social solidarity,
was a dangerous liability and would be treated accordingly. In a sense,
therefore, the moral and material strength of neighbourhood communities depended as much on their exclusivity as on their readiness to
welcome incomers.

Government and Politics

The diversity and fragmentation of urban societies had a major influence on the formal, as well as the informal, institutions of the Georgian
town. Their inhabitants tended to be more sophisticated, more self-
conscious and more highly organized than those of rural communities;
they could not help generating a lively political world of their own.[18]
Although competing and independent political networks were perhaps
more likely to develop in larger towns, the exercise of authority in
even the smallest urban centres depended on a continual process of
confrontation, consultation and compromise. Maintaining a workable
system of local government in the urban context, therefore, demanded
not merely firm, vigorous leadership, but also a sustained effort to
balance conflicting interests and to draw on lines of political influence
and social solidarity that extended far beyond any narrowly defined
civic elite.

   The public institutions that lay at the heart of this system did not fit
into any single model. Until the passage of the Burgh Reform Act in
Scotland in 1833, and of the Municipal Corporations Act in England and
Wales in 1835, many places that had quite clearly grown into substantial
towns were still officially 'villages' in terms of their institutional
structure. At the other end of the scale were royal burghs and ancient
chartered towns, such as Brackley in Northamptonshire or Conwy in

north Wales, which struggled to register more than 2000 inhabitants in the 1841 census. Many contemporary writers argued that it was precisely the historic character of these towns and the entrenched privileges of their leading citizens that had weakened their ability to adapt to change. 'Charters and Corporations', it was suggested, 'are of eminent Prejudice to a Town, as they exclude Strangers, stop the Growth of Trade, and . . . prevent Ingenuity and Improvements'. However, this apparently unambiguous connection between incorporation and stagnation, whereby all towns subject to 'Corporation-Tyranny' were inevitably doomed to remain 'mean, poor, and ill-inhabited', was not in fact as simple as it appeared. Although many towns without the formal institutions of a borough corporation did indeed 'flourish in People, Riches and Trade', Manchester and Birmingham being the examples most often cited in this context, it was much less easy to explain why the corporate status of Glasgow or Liverpool had not hindered their almost equally rapid growth over the same period.[19]

In the last few decades, research into urban government has revealed that the apparently stark contrast between towns with long traditions of civic culture and control, on the one hand, and dynamic new centres without inherited systems of self-government, on the other, was much greater in theory than in practice. Contemporaries seem to have been remarkably flexible in their response to the challenges facing urban government in this period. Where existing institutions were working effectively, they saw no need to change them. In cases where the accelerating pace of urban development had created new problems, however, or where municipal activity was stifled by factional in-fighting, oligarchy or petty corruption, many of the functions of local government were taken over by a range of statutory commissions, voluntary associations and private enterprise. In both old-established boroughs and upwardly-mobile 'villages', therefore, civic government evolved during the course of the eighteenth century into an improvised, decentralized system that operated far more effectively and responsibly than its unrepresentative structure would suggest.[20] Reformers in the early decades of the nineteenth century certainly uncovered some glaring examples of inefficiency and institutional decay. However, it has to be accepted that many of the problems which had accumulated in British towns by the 1820s had no easy solutions, and that even the most astute, energetic civic leadership could struggle in vain to adapt to changing circumstances. It should also be noted that many 'reformers' were more interested in compiling evidence to discredit their political rivals than in producing a balanced analysis of the strengths and weaknesses of municipal government; the crippling financial problems experienced by Aberdeen and Edinburgh, for instance, were therefore emphasized at the expense of Glasgow town council's continued reputation for fiscal prudence and administrative efficiency. As a result, although the self-perpetuating elites who dominated town councils throughout the eighteenth century were swept away by the reforms of the 1830s, many of the administrative systems over which they had presided survived well into the Victorian age.

The intricate web of parish and civic organizations that actually ran these systems was in some ways an easy target for criticism. Without a strong, unitary authority to exercise overall control, their overlapping jurisdictions and internal rivalries exacerbated the creeping paralysis that overtook many Georgian municipalities in the early nineteenth century. The fact that they relied heavily on the unpaid labour of volunteers was another hostage to fortune; diligent and responsible administration could not be guaranteed in these circumstances. Without it, however, revenues would not be collected and key public services such as the poor relief system, would start to break down. On the other hand, the active participation of so many townspeople in their local institutions, meant that civic administration rested on a broad basis of cooperation and support from the wider urban community. Parish and corporate offices seem to have been popular among the whole spectrum of the 'middling sort'; it is estimated that in Ipswich, for instance, around 160 of the town's freemen held such offices at any one time, whereas the average attendance at the Great Court was no higher than 50. Although the business which they conducted was, for the most part, both time-consuming and routine, it greatly increased the status and influence which these modestly prosperous tradesmen and craftsmen enjoyed within their local community. It also allowed them to express in practice the ideals of solidarity and consensus which underpinned the basic cohesion of urban society.

Women from the wealthier sections of urban society were, of course, officially excluded from active participation in civic government and politics. It is important to recognize, however, that the high levels of office holding among urban businessmen depended on the cooperation of their wives and daughters, since they could not afford to leave their shops unattended to attend council or parish meetings. The recent emphasis on informal political networks as a source of influence and power, rather than on formal office holding, has also tended to focus academic attention on women's political role. 'Husbanding' an electoral interest in an urban constituency, for instance, was a continuous political process which demanded the deployment of a wide range of tactics, including judicious use of the candidates' wives. Aristocratic ladies found themselves 'obliged to be the *Pink of Courtesy* to all the Aldermen & their Wives to the Hundredth Cousin', afraid to alienate the touchy sensibilities of the urban elite by appearing too proud and haughty or, worse still, by refusing to appear at all.[21] Although women who took active, partisan role in public affairs were liable to be criticized for their presumption, the notes left by political canvassers indicate that many male voters were, in practice, 'ruled by their wives'. It seems undeniable, therefore, that the women who were missing from the hustings at election time, and from the grand processions that punctuated the civic year, were much more than passive spectators of the political process.

The same is true of many townspeople, both men and women, who were too poor to be accorded full civil and political rights within their own communities. Their formal exclusion from active citizenship might suggest that the lower levels of urban society were denied any form of genuine participation in civic government. It is undeniable that political activity among 'the meaner sort' was habitually described by the authorities in terms that seem calculated to justify their subordination and defend the existing civic order. Peaceful and well-organized demonstrators were portrayed as anarchic mobs of 'Unthinking Brutes', while it was often suggested that they were literally, as well as figuratively, outsiders. The mayor of Lincoln, for example, claimed that the protest in 1728 was 'not a Lincoln, but a Lincolnshire riot', while the Guildhall riots in Newcastle upon Tyne in 1740 were blamed on 'some turbulent Spirits among those of the Collieries upon the River Wear'.[22] It is clear, however, that the assertive, independent-minded urban workforce felt justified in insisting on their right to be heard; and it is equally clear that they exercised considerable informal influence on the political decisions that were taken on their behalf.

Recent research has stressed, moreover, that the mass of the urban population was just as likely to exert this influence in support of the established social, political and religious order, as it was to champion 'radical' and progressive causes. Political and cultural divisions among the urban poor seem to have mirrored the profound conflicts that split the urban elite into rival, and often bitterly hostile, factions. Despite a long tradition of describing Georgian politics almost exclusively in terms of patronage and self-interest, many historians would now agree with Jeremy Black that 'In much of Britain, hostility, or at least suspicion between different religious groups was a central experience'.[23] In both England and Scotland, the established church was regarded as the ultimate guardian of the moral, social and political order; it was therefore well worth fighting for. The churches were also highly effective in mobilizing their adherents, infusing ideological debates about the exercise of government power with the passionate convictions that were inseparable from religious faith. Given that most Georgian towns contained significant religious minorities, they were bound to become political battlefields.

Urban voters exercised a profound influence on the outcome of eighteenth-century elections, determining the outcome in the counties, as well as in borough constituencies. As a result, their interests were assiduously cultivated by potential candidates as well as by their aristocratic patrons. Thus candidates for the county constituency of Norfolk were obliged to conciliate the citizens of Norwich, Great Yarmouth and King's Lynn, as well as the county's more rural electorate, attending their race meetings, wining and dining their corporations, contributing to local subscriptions and making generous benefactions towards the provision of public buildings and amenities. The enduring legacy of the political and religious divisions that had crystallized during the Civil Wars of the mid-seventeenth century ensured that Georgian towns became an arena for ideological warfare, as much as for social display; indeed in York in the 1720s these two birds were killed with one stone since there were rival Tory and Whig assemblies held on different days.

Peter Borsay has argued that 'fashionable town culture developed an apolitical, even anti-political complexion' in the early decades of the eighteenth century, pointing out that the two York assemblies merged in 1732 with the opening of 'the completest ballroom in England', built at a cost of well over £5000.[24] It seems clear, however, that this genteel consensus represented a temporary truce, rather than a final peace settlement; certainly the 1760s witnessed a resurgence of bitter political hostilities in towns all over Georgian Britain. In Nottingham, for example, where religious dissent exerted a strong influence on party allegiance, the American War of Independence stirred up 'Animosities among the Inhabitants of this Town, which were not settled with that Harmony we would wish to see subsist between Friends and Fellow Citizens'.[25] Fighting broke out in public houses, as Whigs celebrated the victories of the American rebels, to the utter disgust of Tory 'patriots'. The use of social arenas and cultural events to promote political causes was part of a wider phenomenon which made it very difficult to promote any form of non-partisan activity since every initiative was inevitably associated with one or other of the town's competing 'interests'. Charitable subscriptions and improvement societies, for example, were rarely simple expressions of generosity or public spirit; instead they became platforms for the assertion of divisions within the elite, divisions that often reflected underlying political and religious conflicts.[26]

Such was the intensity of these conflicts that contemporaries feared their public expression could bring the elite into disrepute, undermining the very basis of social relations. Rapid population growth among the urban poor at a time when the wealth and well-being of the upper and middle orders of society seemed to be increasing at an unprecedented rate, undoubtedly polarized attitudes towards the intervention of the lower orders in the political process. Even public participation in traditional urban rituals was gradually abandoned as the perceived threat to good order and social discipline posed by the lower orders increased. The changing social climate was clearly demonstrated on Coronation Day in 1821, when the elaborate processions and expensive festivities organized by city authorities throughout the land were greeted with a sullen hostility that occasionally boiled over into boisterous, subversive dissent. In this more abrasive, more divided society, crowds came more and more to represent narrower sectional interests. In one significant example, dating from the 1790s, a popular ballad in praise of 'the brave Dudley boys' employed the rhetoric of civic pride and identity to promote the interests of one section of the local workforce in a labour dispute; this was a long way from traditional ideals of unity and consensus.[27]

As the civic consciousness of poorer townsmen and women became more and more distinct from that of the urban elite, the latter proved increasingly unwilling to sanction any form of protest or demonstration in which 'the mob' played an active role. It did not go unnoticed that the main targets of popular violence in both the Gordon riots of 1780 and the Priestley riots of 1791 were rich Catholics and rich Dissenters respectively, rather than the rank and file of these two religious minorities. The roads out of the capital city on 7 June 1780 were reported to be crowded with 'a prodigious quantity of coaches and four, all leaving London on account of the great disturbances'. 'The streets were swarming with people and uproar, confusion and terror reigned in every part'; 'London offered on every side', recalled another observer, 'the picture of a city sacked and abandoned to a ferocious enemy'.[28] This 'ferocious enemy' was increasingly identified with the urban poor, an identification that was merely strengthened by the 'apocalypse' of the riots in support of the Reform Bill that broke out in Bristol and Nottingham in 1831. The rumbling threat of violence that lay beneath the surface of urban life in the later years of the period should probably be counted, alongside growing environmental degradation, as contributing to the declining appeal of the fastest-growing Georgian towns as places of genteel residence. Living surrounded by 'the dangerous classes', in cities constructed 'upon the infinite abysses' of violence and fear, appeared increasingly undesirable to the wealthier sections of urban society.[29]

Social Differentiation: Gentility

In the case of towns like Nottingham, Preston and Dundee, towns whose character had been transformed within a generation by intensive economic development, the social threat posed by newly rich, but irredeemably vulgar, industrialists seems to have been just as influential as the deteriorating urban environment, or the assertiveness of the urban workforce, in prompting a flight to the country. One well-born resident of Preston is recorded as leaving the town 'in a towering passion', within a few hours of discovering that the fishmonger had sold his finest turbot to a wealthy cotton spinner. 'This', his daughter reported, 'was too much for [his] sense of dignity'.[30] The sudden fracture of 'Proud Preston's' ruling elite seems to indicate that the earlier reconciliation between the rural and urban gentry, between polite and civic culture, so persuasively described by Peter Borsay in *The English Urban Renaissance*, could not survive the demographic and economic stresses which accumulated in nearly every major urban centre in the decades after 1770.

The apparent harmony which reigned in so many of these towns during the 'renaissance' of the later seventeenth and early eighteenth centuries had depended on the willingness of the urban middle classes to offer due deference to their social superiors and to observe the many subtle distinctions of rank and status which pervaded every aspect of social intercourse. A French visitor had observed in 1755 that 'the Englishman constantly holds a pair of scales wherein he exactly weighs the birth, the rank, and especially the fortune of those he is in company with, in order to regulate his behaviour and discourse accordingly'. The definition of 'the genteel Part of the Town of both Sexes' that prevailed in the early eighteenth century, however, included many men and women who were actively engaged in trade or the professions. It remained possible, therefore, as Paul Langford has demonstrated, to combine the values of polite society with the commercial imperatives that dominated the urban economy.[31]

The cut-off point for entry to this privileged social world seems to have fallen between wholesale and retail trade; any occupation which involved serving behind a counter was regarded as unacceptable, while manual labour was completely beyond the pale. In practice, however, many Georgian towns were simply too small to enforce these distinctions, since to do so would have left the few local residents with any pretensions to gentility in lonely isolation. Whereas several hundred people would attend the 'brilliant' assemblies that regularly punctuated the social calendar in major urban centres or fashionable resorts, the wealthier inhabitants of modest country towns had to make do with whatever 'company' they could find. As a result, as Elizabeth Gaskell reminded the readers of *Wives and Daughters*, many urban gentlewomen would 'have to shake hands over the counter tomorrow morning with some of [their] partners of tonight'. Elizabeth Montagu recorded one such assembly in Kent in 1738, where

> to make up the number, [Lady Thanet] is pleased in her humility to call in all the parsons, apprentices, tradesmen, apothecaries, and farmers, milliners, mantua makers, haberdashers of small wares, and chambermaids. It is the oddest mixture you can imagine – here sails a reverent parson, there skips an airy apprentice, here jumps a farmer; and then everyone has an eye on their trade; . . . the shoemaker makes you foot it until you wear out your shoes; the mercer dirties your gown; the apothecary opens the window behind you to make you sick.[32]

Even the notoriously fastidious ladies who ran the assembly rooms in Derby were prepared to admit the family of Mr Francey, the town's principal grocer, although all other shopkeepers were rigorously excluded.

In the 1770s and 1780s, however, the attitudes of townspeople who defined themselves as 'proper company' began to harden, moving from amused condescension to outright hostility towards anyone actively engaged in 'trade'. This was especially noticeable in the most dynamic and expansive urban centres, where growing numbers of people were able to earn the substantial annual incomes that were necessary to support a 'more Polite Way of Living'. By 1803 the *Directory of Kingston-upon-Hull* listed no fewer than 150 prosperous townsmen as 'gentlemen', in addition to the 50 or so bankers, shipowners and richer merchants who were referred to by the more elevated title of 'esquire'. This dilution of the social elite aroused even greater resentment because of the proliferation of commercialized leisure activities within Georgian towns, which had brought many previously exclusive social events within the reach of anyone who could afford the price of a ticket or the cost of a subscription. The entrepreneurs who built or leased assembly rooms, theatres or racecourse grandstands could not afford to turn away potential customers, whatever the origins of their wealth.

Social exclusivity, therefore, became much more desirable in the eyes of traditional urban elites as the eighteenth century drew to a close, although it remained difficult to achieve in practice. Their response was to raise the threshold of what could be classified as true gentility, downgrading sheer wealth in favour of more subtle indicators that emphasized education, refinement and good taste; it was the *quality*, rather than the quantity, of expenditure that distinguished unpretentious good breeding from ostentatious vulgarity.[33] Accent also gained a much greater significance as a social indicator. Whereas it had been acceptable for members of all social classes to share a local or regional accent, the wealthier sections of urban society were now anxious that their children should acquire the cultured, cultivated language and pronunciation that would raise them above the common herd. As a result, more children were sent away to school or educated at home by well-spoken governesses or tutors, well away from the contaminating company of the sons and daughters of the 'Trading parts of the Town'. In a parallel move, the upper levels of urban society also began to desert the public entertainments that had been so characteristic of Georgian towns. Private balls and dinner parties, where entry was controlled by invitation, offered a much less challenging social environment than the more broadly-based company who attended traditional assemblies.

In retaliation, perhaps, against satirical denunciations of their 'mushroom' rise and 'dunghill' origins, the urban middle classes became increasingly hostile towards aristocratic culture and values, portraying the leisured elite as idle 'dispensers . . . and scatterers of money'. As John Brewer has demonstrated, urban businessmen attempted to redefine gentility in ways that stressed the importance of rational knowledge and practical experience, at the expense of rank, fashion and 'mere fortune'.[34] On this reading, polite culture was worthy of respect only to the extent that it could be harnessed to useful ends, encouraging progress, invention and urban improvement. In too many cases, however, it seemed to have encouraged nothing more than vanity, extravagance and corruption; precisely the vices which the prosperous middle classes associated with the older, customary and less orderly patterns of behaviour that ruled the lives of the urban working classes. Bourgeois rationalism and respectability, therefore, distinguished the middling ranks of urban society from the plebeian majority, as well as from the minority of patrician 'drones' who still dominated public life in many corporate towns.

Social Differentiation: Respectability

This changing social climate put an inevitable strain on traditional civic ideals. As the eighteenth century drew to a close, the sheer concentration of urban problems in the poorer districts of the old town centres was beginning to erode the relative tolerance that had characterized Georgian towns in the century before 1780, severing the traditional connection between paternalism and deference. The swelling numbers of the poor now seemed to threaten the very existence of urbane society, overwhelming the resources of local councils and improvement commissions. They were at best expensive and at worst positively dangerous, each one a potential criminal prone to fraud and violent disorder. In Glasgow, for instance, public fears were exacerbated by racist and hysterical images of Irish immigrants, 'these modern Huns', burrowing into the heart of the ancient city and 'nightly issue[ing] to disseminate disease and to pour upon the town every species of abomination and crime'.[35] By the 1840s, fears of 'the dangerous classes' were widespread among property owners in towns throughout Britain, making them all the more anxious to strengthen the boundaries of social demarcation and difference that separated them from this menacing underclass.

One obvious solution for the respectable middle class was to abandon the congested town centres and move to newly-built suburbs on the edge of the built-up area. There are clear signs that by the 1840s social polarization was beginning to be reflected in a more polarized social geography, particularly in the fastest-growing industrial and commercial centres. The desirability of these new housing developments, which offered residents much greater privacy and security, as well as more fashionable accommodation, meant that even smaller, more stable towns acquired one or two streets built specifically for wealthier families, together with a scattering of handsome villas in their immediate vicinity.

In Newark, for example, South Parade was laid out in the 1820s, at the opposite end of the town from the small industrial suburb that grew up in the early years of the nineteenth century. In the rising resort of Aberystwyth, also in the 1820s, a small complex of streets with appropriately fashionable names – Marine Terrace, Laura Place and North Parade – and equally smart accommodation, were developed close to the new assembly rooms, creating an exclusive enclave well away from the distinctly unfashionable neighbourhood around the harbour.

Exclusivity could also be achieved by raising barriers that would exclude 'undesirable' elements from the many clubs, societies and religious organizations which were central to urban sociability in this period. Peter Clark argues that very few English clubs in the years before 1800 had exclusively class-based recruitment policies, although he accepts that Scottish clubs may have been more socially divided throughout the period. On the other hand, given that entry depended on being proposed by an existing member and then standing for election, risking a humiliating rebuff, the social composition of most middle-class societies was more likely to be exclusive than egalitarian. Thomas Carter, for example, a journeyman tailor who moved to London in 1810, succeeded in gaining access to the debates of a literary society on the recommendation of his landlord, but he had to wait 15 years before being elected as a 'poor' member. Snobbery and self-interest were also alleged to have inspired a 'petty aristocracy' within Liverpool's Jewish synagogue in the 1830s to raise the price of entry to the congregation 'in order to keep up a select circle'.[36]

Social exclusion, it is often alleged, went hand in hand with increasing intolerance towards many aspects of popular culture. Blood sports such as bull-baiting were condemned not only because they were barbarous and uncivilized in themselves, but also because they encouraged the urban working classes to drink and gamble away their hard-earned wages, leaving them vulnerable to poverty in sickness or old age. The wakes festivals of industrial Lancashire were similarly condemned by moral reformers; the antithesis of rational improvement, they seemed to represent a deliberate rejection of the key bourgeois values of thrift, sobriety, decency, chastity and self-control. Lower-class 'licentiousness' aroused particular concern because it was all too obvious that many urban neighbourhoods operated a code of morality that took little account of the strict letter of the law, and none at all of middle-class notions of respectability. A good neighbour was someone who offered friendship, sympathy and practical assistance to those around her;

chastity and sobriety, in contrast, were valued much less highly. Women who worked hard for their families and dealt honestly with their friends could therefore be regarded within their own communities as 'decent in their general conduct', despite the fact that they had illegitimate children or drank in public houses.[37] Even the families of shopkeepers and master craftsmen, it was alleged, mixed on equal terms with thieves, fences and prostitutes, while their children played together in the streets.

During the years between 1770 and 1820, however, a determined effort was made to drive a wedge between the respectable working class and the unregenerate poor, an effort that seemed to focus on women's sexual behaviour. Strict standards of propriety were urged on prosperous and socially ambitious tradesmen, who could distinguish themselves from the undisciplined masses by rejecting the free-and-easy morality of the streets and assimilating the idea that their social status depended on the modesty, chastity and refinement of their wives and daughters. The duties of the various constables, beadles and watchmen employed in the later eighteenth century to patrol the streets at night centred on suppressing undesirable behaviour rather than on combating theft or crimes of violence, a preoccupation which was also reflected in the prosecution records of the new police forces of the early nineteenth century. Unruly children were the particular target of middle-class campaigns to banish idleness from the streets on Sundays: in Tiverton, for example, an Association for the Promotion of Order was founded in 1832 to round up 'dissolute' children found playing in the streets and deliver them to Sunday schools. The prostitutes who plied their trade on the streets of every large town aroused even greater moral indignation. They swarmed round the waterfronts of the great ports and the more disreputable areas of the industrial towns, but it was their unmistakable presence in fashionable town centres that caused most contemporary disquiet. A foreign visitor to London in the 1780s, for example, recorded that she was prevented from waiting for a carriage outside the theatre for fear of being mistaken for one of 'the crowd of light women, although they were all better dressed than I, and looked extremely pretty'. The sight of exhausted harlots slumped on the steps of elegant terraced houses was a profound affront to the bourgeois ethos of respectability, as well as to the aesthetic ideals of urban classicism.

The answer, according to the *Nottingham Journal* in December 1781, was to sentence such 'abandoned Girls' to hard labour in a house of correction, so that 'when at Liberty (by Means of honest Industry) they might enjoy the Blessings of this Life in their fullest Extent'.[38] A similar wilful blindness to the harsh realities of life at the lower levels of urban society was evident in more punitive attitudes to the administration of parish-based poor relief. The sharply rising costs of the system in the 1790s, and again in the crisis of the 1820s, encouraged a tendency to blame the 'ignorance and moral errors' of the poor for their all-too-apparent misery; hence the increasing popularity among the elite of measures that were designed both to reduce the cost of relief and to draw a clear distinction between the 'deserving', respectable poor and those who were stigmatized as marginal and 'undeserving'. The moral reformers sincerely believed that it was in the long-term interests of the poor to deny them relief altogether, or to impose such humiliating conditions that potential claimants would be deterred from asserting their traditional 'right' to relief. Even in Bury St Edmunds, an apparently stable and genteel county centre, ratepayers made a determined effort in 1800 to 'badge' the poor, forcing paupers to wear the letter 'P' on their right shoulder, while it was noted in 1809 that subscriptions to public charities had been falling steadily for several years. These harsh and punitive attitudes, however, ran the risk of provoking the violent and disorderly behaviour which they were designed to reform. When a speaker to a vast Chartist rally on Newcastle Town Moor in 1838 urged the crowd of more than 40,000 people to seize weapons and burn the city to the ground if the authorities attempted to implement the new Poor Law, the worst nightmares of respectable society seemed to be coming true.

By the 1830s, therefore, concepts of civic identity and of the urban community had come to reflect the new horizontal, class-based social divisions that had been visible in the capital cities and major regional centres since the 1770s. As relative inequalities of income and status became more pronounced, and rising consumer expectations were frustrated by the uneven and unpredictable nature of 'progress', the balance seemed to have tipped away from 'decent Chearfulness' and 'social Harmony' and towards discord and confrontation. It is important to emphasize, however, that social relations remained ambiguous and dynamic, rather than becoming fixed into a pattern of bitter and violent resentment. Recent research has confirmed Penelope Corfield's assessment that 'In terms of their social order and general viability, [Georgian] towns were ... much less violent, criminal and anarchic than the critics feared. ... Urban growth did not therefore herald a pathological breakdown of society.'[39]

It needs to be recognized, in the first place, that the old social order of paternalism and deference was not a golden age of peace and plenty; that would be to mistake the rhetoric for the reality. In fact, cultural consensus among the broadening social elites during the urban renaissance of 1680 to 1760 was already dependent to a large extent on social polarization, specifically on the eagerness of the middling sort to join with the 'principal Gentlemen' in excluding the bulk of the urban population from their definition of what constituted 'proper company'. It would also be a mistake to be unduly sentimental about the extent of social mixing within the old town centres, since there is unmistakable evidence of sharp segregation at street level, in some cases between different floors of the same building, reflecting the extent of social divisions and disunities even within traditional, relatively stable urban communities.[40]

By the same token, it would be a mistake to exaggerate the extent of social change in the years before 1840. Despite such well-known examples as the building of the New Town in Edinburgh, the pre-industrial pattern of socially mixed neighbourhoods radiating out from a wealthy central district to poorer suburbs, survived well into the nineteenth century in towns all over Georgian Britain. There is equally very little real evidence that there was a sustained effort to suppress popular culture on moral and ideological grounds. Outraged protests dating from the 1790s or 1820s appear very little different in tone and substance from the complaints voiced by sixteenth- and seventeenth-century reformers.[41] The motives for suppressing specific popular customs or activities were often eminently practical, recognizing the fact that racing horses or chasing bulls through crowded urban streets was increasingly dangerous as well as disruptive. It was clearly antisocial for drunken revellers to roam around shooting out the streetlights, as was reported in the *Leeds Mercury* in 1795, while popular support for Birmingham's annual horse-race seems to have fallen sharply in the 1770s after a spectator was killed. Hugh Cunningham's argument that the decay of many traditional forms of popular leisure in this period stemmed from changes within popular culture, rather than pressure from above, has become increasingly persuasive in the last twenty years.[42]

There also remained a powerful lobby within Georgian towns for the maintenance of traditional standards of benevolent paternalism. In Bury St Edmunds, for example, the patrician Court of Governors initially opposed the proposal to badge the poor, although they later gave in to the majority of small traders who urged harsher measures. Parish officials in St George's, Southwark in the early 1830s similarly reported that local magistrates frequently frustrated their efforts to reduce the levels of relief payments; even known prostitutes and Irish families, who clearly did not have any legal right to parish maintenance, were regularly given assistance. Poor relief has always experienced cycles of generosity and meanness, but the urban poor in the early years of the nineteenth century had many influential champions. The Reverend Thomas Dikes, for instance, preaching on the text 'He that is without sin among you, let him first cast a stone', faced his respectable Hull congregation with the uncomfortable question,

> Suppose that, instead of being brought up in a decent and virtuous neighbourhood, you had lived from your infancy in those lanes of moral turpitude, from which are emitted fumes of pollution that might almost corrupt an angel of light – can you say what, under these circumstances, you might have been?[43]

Inclusive definitions of urban identity and community had clearly survived the pressures of urban growth and social differentiation, and were indeed gaining in strength as the Georgian period drew to a close.

7

TOWNS AND CHANGE

Suddenly it occurred to him, that the Age of Ruins was past.... In the minds of men the useful has succeeded to the beautiful.... Yet, rightly understood, Manchester is as great a human exploit as Athens.
Benjamin Disraeli (1844)[1]

The relationship between urban growth and social change in Georgian Britain has inspired a long-running and sometimes heated debate. On the whole, economic historians have tended to endorse the positive images of wealth, progress and civilization promoted by optimistic contemporary observers, arguing that towns played a crucial role in spearheading the growth of the national economy in this period. Given that towns in general are conventionally regarded, in the words of Fernand Braudel, as 'so many electricity transformers. They increase tension, accelerate the rhythm of exchange and ceaselessly stir up men's lives', it seems logical to conclude that urban growth was substantially responsible for the economic and social transformation that accompanied the industrial revolution. Indeed, the energy and enterprise of the urban population has itself been identified as one of the key agents and generators of change. 'I had been among dreamers', reflected William Hutton on his first visit to Birmingham in 1741, 'but now I saw men awake. Their very step along the street shewed alacrity.... They possessed a vivacity I had never beheld.'[2]

Agents of Civilization?

This favourable, even flattering, portrayal of the Georgian town as the powerhouse of both economic and social change was challenged,

129

however, by an equally strong tradition which associated urban life with physical and moral corruption, and with destruction and despair, rather than with prosperity and progress. These pessimistic interpretations initially focused on London, following classical models in portraying 'this great, wicked, unwieldy, over-grown Town' as a squalid and dangerous labyrinth, whose inhabitants were 'almost under the necessity of carrying pistols instead of prayer-books to their parish churches'.[3] As urban development gathered pace, the targets of this moral criticism were extended to include the expanding health and leisure resorts, condemned in conventional terms as hotbeds of gluttony, gambling and illicit sex. To critics of urban culture, as David Eastwood has argued, 'the visible sewerage of the city became a metaphor of the deeper pollution of the mind'.[4]

The headlong expansion of Britain's leading commercial and industrial centres in the later years of the eighteenth century, on the other hand, prompted a radical change in perspective among anti-urbanists, one that emphasized the structural problems of the town rather than the vice and improvidence of its inhabitants. The notorious degeneration of the environment in Nottingham, for instance, which had been described by a visitor in 1780 as 'the loveliest and neatest . . . of all the towns I have seen outside London', made it a byword for dirt, disease and overwhelming misery. 'Here is a *resurrection* of buildings', wrote a disgusted observer in 1810, 'seated like mushrooms in a field cast by chance', and so tightly-packed with impoverished stocking-makers that 'maggots in carrion flesh, or mites in cheese, could not be huddled more closely together'.[5] Notions of progress and improvement were difficult to reconcile with the terrors of cholera and revolution that stalked the slums of the inner city in the early years of the nineteenth century. 'What a place! The entrance to hell realized!', was the reaction of more than one visitor to 'sooty' Manchester, ' the chimney of the world'.[6]

Defenders of urban culture, however, continued to claim that the creative energy of cities like Manchester, when 'rightly understood', was inherently and inevitably progressive. These optimistic urbanists contrasted the economic dynamism, social attraction and cultural diversity of the towns with the life of brutish and monotonous stagnation produced by unquestioning adherence to traditional customs and to irrational, narrow-minded prejudices. The obvious opportunities presented by the expansion of trade and industry, they argued, had naturally tended to attract the brightest and the best young people into the towns, where talented and ambitious workers could command much higher earnings than were available in the countryside. Given that the challenging, competitive climate of city life gave the urban workforce a clear incentive to experiment and innovate, it followed that they would not only accumulate wealth, but would also embrace the superior moral and cultural values of civil society.

The power of the urban environment as a force for change, according to the concluding paragraph of a history of Worksop published in 1826, lay in 'the circulation medium of free and universal intercourse', which eroded 'the relative distinctions of personal or family importance' and created in their place a sense of 'mutual independence'.[7] Worksop in the 1820s may seem a world away from the vitality and awe-inspiring immensity of the great cities of Georgian Britain – its population had barely crept above 5000 by the time of the 1841 census – but this provincial definition of civil society comes straight from the philosophy of the Scottish Enlightenment. So does its author's conviction that the cultivation of social virtues was closely linked to the development of 'modern', liberal values and thence to moral improvement. The more celebrated writers who championed urban virtues in the 1830s and 1840s, men like Peter Gaskell and Robert Vaughan of Manchester and Edward Baines of Leeds, all stressed the importance of the open discussion and debate fostered by urban society, particularly in challenging complacency and spreading progressive ideas. 'Each man stimulates his fellow, and the result is a greater general intelligence. The shop, the factory, or the market place; the local association, the news-room, or the religious meeting, all facilitate this invigorating contact of mind with mind.'[8]

As a result, towns all over Georgian Britain became centres of intellectual activity and social innovation. It seems clear, for instance, that the rising manufacturing and commercial towns played a major part in disseminating the new scientific, technical and financial ideas throughout their localities, and even in setting new educational, artistic and intellectual standards. In Newcastle upon Tyne, to take only one example of many, the Reverend William Turner started two of the first Sunday schools in the north of England at his Hanover Square chapel in 1784, extending his activities in the early decades of the nineteenth century by setting up Royal Jubilee schools for the children of the poor, a juvenile library, and a Literary, Scientific and Mechanical Institute to cater for the educational needs of working-class adults. By 1825, when the Newcastle Literary and Philosophical society (which he had founded in 1793) moved into a splendid new building, it had over 800 members; it had actually been the first 'Lit and Phil' society to admit women. Five years later, the town could boast of three scientific societies, including a Nat-ural History society, launched the previous year. Even outside the great regional centres, clubs and societies with a similarly progressive agenda could be found in relatively minor provincial towns, such as Whitby in Yorkshire with a population of under 10,000. Debating societies, in particular, proved popular in the later years of the eighteenth century, tackling a wide range of political, social, ethical and philosophical ques-tions. In Chesterfield on 12 June 1786, for instance, a hundred men and women spent three hours discussing the question 'Whether luxury is an Advantage or a Disadvantage to the British Nation?', in an atmo-sphere of self-consciously rationalist empiricism.[9]

This new urban world of independent thought and collective endeav-our came to be particularly associated with radical movements for polit-ical reform. In the years after 1780, popular radicalism spread rapidly northwards from London and the southern textile towns to the growing industrial centres of the midlands and the north, which were ideal breeding-grounds for the development and conduct of 'modern' cam-paigns to mobilize public opinion in a political cause. Urban activists led the way in the campaign against the slave-trade, for instance, appealing not only to popular sentiments in favour of 'the universal propagation of liberty and benevolence', but also to a powerful and growing sense that slavery was a relic of an outdated and irrelevant economic system. By the later 1820s and early 1830s, men and women of all classes were flocking in unprecedented numbers to anti-slavery meetings in town halls, assembly rooms, churches, chapels and public houses in towns all over Britain, reading vast quantities of anti-slavery tracts, pamphlets, handbills and newspapers, and signing anti-slavery petitions in greater numbers than for any comparable issue, including Chartism.[10] By the 1830s, it was generally accepted that black slaves, even in the remotest corners of the British Empire, were part of the universal family of man-kind and therefore had a valid claim to share in the 'rights of man'. It was in a similarly radical and idealistic spirit that the Bristol Unitarians invited the Hindu reformer, Raja Rammohan Roy, to preach at their chapel in Lewin's Mead in 1833.

The Limits of 'Progress'

It would be a mistake, however, to discount the continuing strength and appeal of conservative, traditional values within the Georgian town, values that ran counter to what has been termed 'the Enlightenment project'. Many urban radicals saw no contradiction between their support for political reform, for the abolition of slavery or for religious toleration, on the one hand, and their identity as patriotic citizens and subjects, on the other. Speakers at the great abolitionist meetings of the 1830s, for instance, sometimes wrapped themselves literally, as well as figuratively, in the Union Jack to address their audiences. Yet their opponents still tended to portray these liberal, progressive causes as dangerously subversive, threatening the political, cultural and religious cohesion of British society. The passage of the Jewish Naturalisation Act in 1753 was greeted by angry demonstrations in towns all over England, protesting against 'the engrafting into our community [of] these avowed enemies of our Saviour'. Even Protestant nonconformity was suspect, particularly in the 1790s when it became closely associated with political radicalism and with the excesses of the French Revolution. 'Sedition is their Creed', a loyalist ballad warned the inhabitants of Bristol in 1791:

> Feign'd Sheep but *Wolves* indeed
> How can we trust;
> Gunpowder PRIESTLEY wou'd
> Deluge the Throne with Blood
> And lay the Great and Good,
> Low in the dust.[11]

Even in the more liberal climate of the 1820s and 1830s, attitudes to Roman Catholics within the urban community were still shaped by what Linda Colley has characterized as a 'vast superstructure of prejudice'.[12] The bigotry and prejudice that greeted Catholic Irish immigrants to Glasgow and the other growing towns of the western Scottish Lowlands in these years had their counterparts in urban centres throughout Georgian Britain. The radical Sunday school established in Manchester in 1784, with the aim of bringing together the children of Anglicans, Catholics and Dissenters, had been a rare exception to the rule of strict religious segregation. Manchester was in reality notorious for the bitterness of its sectarian divisions, but attempts to encourage ecumenism tended in any case to break down whenever political passions ran high.

Support for the old order in church and state, moreover, could become self-reinforcing. Although the Gordon riots in June 1780, which were provoked by the passage of a Catholic Relief Act, may have reduced the appeal of anti-Catholic bigotry in elite political circles, the conservative press was quick to link this devastating outbreak of civil unrest to 'the false language of patriotism', claiming that campaigns for political reform would lead inevitably to 'such another convulsion as that which reddened the metropolis with fire and blood', or even to 'such another rebellion, as seated Oliver Cromwell in the dictatorial chair'.[13] The political and religious divisions of the seventeenth century cast a long shadow into the Age of Enlightenment, a shadow which is apparent in the contemporary association, quoted earlier, between Joseph Priestley, the radical Unitarian scientist and intellectual, and the Gunpowder Plot of 1605. The violent 'Church and King' mobs who consistently rallied to the defence of the political and religious status quo throughout this period, were as much a product of the urban experience as were the 60,000 peaceful demonstrators who gathered at Peterloo in August 1819 to demand parliamentary reform. Indeed, the reform riots of 1831 in Bristol, Derby, Nottingham and Merthyr Tydfil, the campaign of resistance to the implementation of the Poor Law Amendment Act that raged throughout the northern industrial towns between 1836 and 1838, and the Newport rising of 1839 all attest to the uncomfortable fact that the forces of reaction did not have a monopoly on violence.

In all too many cases, foreign observers noted, both 'the rampant spirit of liberty, and the wild impatience of a genuine English mob' were fuelled by their seemingly unquenchable thirst. Writers from the time of Henry Fielding to that of Charles Dickens went out of their way to deplore 'the insatiable lust for spirits, especially among the common people', linking their habitual drunkenness with the poverty and wretchedness of the urban environment. Fielding, however, was honest enough to acknowledge that hard drinking was also commonplace among the urban elite. 'Polite' sociability almost invariably involved the consumption of large quantities of alcohol, since 'pushing the bottle' in an endless round of toasts and pledges was a common feature of club meetings and private dinner parties, as well as of more informal gatherings in inns and taverns.[14] In Enlightenment Edinburgh, for example, even socially select groups like the Honourable Company of Edinburgh Golfers held their meetings in a common alehouse until 1767. Drunken arguments and brawls punctuated race meetings, balls and assemblies, as well as the proceedings of trade clubs and debating societies. In January 1763, for instance, a 'little sort of riot' took place at the Queen's birthday ball in Wiltshire's assembly rooms at Bath, the epitome of polite culture. When the dancing was abruptly curtailed before midnight, 'the gentlemen' threatened to break the mirrors and chandeliers unless fresh bowls of negus, a mixture of hot sweetened wine and water, were produced immediately – but then smashed the bowls and threw the wine all over the room.[15] Six years later, the mayor was forced to read the Riot Act in the rooms to regain control after a pitched battle provoked by the election of a new master of ceremonies.

Gambling, too, was endemic at all levels of urban society. Labourers and small traders wagered their weekly earnings on games of whist, cribbage, skittles and chuck-farthing, while aristocrats such as Georgiana, Duchess of Devonshire threw away fortunes on the turn of a card or the outcome of a cricket match. Cockfighting, in particular, although it was increasingly condemned as both cruel and brutalizing, continued to appeal to men from a wide range of social groups until it was eventually criminalized in 1849. As Peter Borsay confirms, 'For many the aggression and competitiveness of animal contests, which was heightened by the stakes and heavy betting involved, proved a compulsive pleasure'.[16]

In the light of these examples, it is hard to disagree with Fanny Trollope's admission in the mid-1830s that 'the improvement in English delicacy has been gradual'. Many traditional attitudes and customs had clearly survived into the new urban world, adapting slowly and reluctantly to their changed environment. The *Sheffield Advertiser*, for example, found it necessary in 1790 to remind its readers that wife sales, although frequent, 'particularly among the lower class of people', were actually illegal.[17] Many social functions, both formal and informal, were still associated with traditional seasonal festivals, or with traditional civic ceremonies and rituals. Even the new-style entertainments and cultural activities of the 'urban renaissance' sometimes incorporated more traditional elements, as can be seen in the ritualistic behaviour of 'the company' at fashionable spa and seaside resorts. Despite the strident claims and counter-claims of their promoters, the appeal of hydrotherapy as a medical treatment in this period owed as much to traditional beliefs in the healing properties of sacred springs as it did to the advances of 'modern' science.

Irrationality, therefore, retained a strong appeal at all social levels in this supposed Age of Reason. Although both national and provincial newspapers consistently condemned the 'superstitions' of the rural poor, urban-based witches, wizards and magicians of every description seem to have operated from the towns of Georgian Britain, supplying their hinterland populations with a professional service that continued to command respect among a wide range of potential clients. A north-eastern farmer in the early 1840s, for example, who suspected that the wife of one of his farm-workers was putting the evil eye on his stock, turned for advice to Black Jack of Newcastle upon Tyne, a celebrated 'cunning man', who instructed him to fry the heart of a healthy heifer at midnight if he wished to identify the culprit. 'I was informed . . . that fearful noises were heard at intervals', reported a future Labour MP in his memoirs; 'Let that be accounted for as it may, it is a fact that the cattle plague was stayed.'[18] Recent research has also tended to demonstrate the enduring power of orthodox religion, as well as of magical beliefs, leading historians to question conventional associations between urban growth and increasing secularization. Religious zeal, rather than religious indifference, inspired many of the key figures in the urban enlightenment, and many of the most influential intellectual, moral and political reform movements had a religious basis.[19]

It is also important to take into account significant local and regional variations in the pace of cultural development in the towns of Georgian Britain. Even in county towns or cathedral cities, where you might expect to find a concentration of educated and intellectually curious people living within the town itself, or in its immediate neighbourhood, 'modern' ideas sometimes struggled to make an impact. In early eighteenth-century Stamford, for instance, the antiquarian William Stukeley could find 'not one person, clergy or lay, that had any taste or love of learning & ingenuity, so that I was actually as much dead in converse as if in a coffin'. Even in Lichfield, which Samuel Johnson hailed as 'a city of philosophers', the town's intellectual and cultural community was so restricted that the number of members attending meetings of Erasmus Darwin's botanical society in the 1770s rarely exceeded two or three.[20]

Gender and social differences both contributed to the relatively limited role played by smaller urban communities in generating and sustaining change. Women were often excluded totally from the proceedings of intellectual and cultural societies, for example, while female literacy levels rose only very slowly over time, consistently lagging behind those of men. The rapid expansion of many industrial and commercial towns from the later years of the eighteenth century, on the other hand, meant that the forces of 'progress' had to struggle hard in these dynamic centres to overcome the obstacles created by the sheer pace and scale of urbanization. Although there is firm evidence from the first half of the period that towns were strongholds of popular literacy, for example – indeed that urban life in general encouraged greater literacy among all sections of the population – the rate of development in the later eighteenth and early nineteenth centuries was painfully slow. While older market and county towns retained their lead over rural communities, literacy rates stagnated or even declined in fast-growing towns such as Glasgow, Edinburgh, Bolton, Bury and Halifax, swamped by the influx of illiterate migrants from the countryside, and by their daily struggle to survive in a hostile environment. In Ashton-under-Lyne, for instance, whose population trebled in the early decades of the nineteenth century, the proportion of that population who could sign their own names plummeted from 48 per cent in 1823 to 9 per cent in 1843. In contrast, rates of literacy in London continued to exceed those achieved anywhere else in Georgian Britain, sustaining the capital city's unique metropolitan identity into the new century.[21]

Cultural Transmission: the Influence of London

This evidence of the shallow roots and uneven distribution of cultural and intellectual activity outside the immediate orbit of London, has convinced some historians that the influence of Britain's provincial towns actually declined during this period. Rather than acting as autonomous pioneers of social and economic change within their own hinterlands, they dwindled into mere satellites of the nation's capital, slavishly following metropolitan fashions and diffusing metropolitan values down through the urban hierarchy. On this reading, the highest ambition of provincial towns throughout the length and breadth of the country was to achieve recognition as 'the little *Londons* of the part of the kingdom wherein they are situated', distinguishable only in scale from the wealth and sophistication of the greatest city in Europe.[22]

It would certainly be difficult to deny the immense influence which London exerted over the rest of Britain. Although the impact of its vast markets and myriad producers became perceptibly weaker at greater distances from its immediate south-eastern hinterland, it remained sufficiently strong to justify the inclusion of London on a milestone erected in 1827 on the Mid Steeple in Dumfries, reminding Galloway cattle drovers that the Smithfield meat market lay at the end of a 330-mile journey south. London was also pre-eminent as both a cultural centre and a generator of information and comment, by virtue of the fact that it housed a substantial proportion of the nation's social and political elite, at least during certain parts of the year. Almost all the major innovations in art, literature and music originated there, while new patterns of consumption, new fashions in architecture, and new standards of 'civil-ized' behaviour first found their way into widespread use. Although Edinburgh retained a considerable degree of cultural independence in the eighteenth century, it was already noticeable that the wealthier elements of Scottish society were adopting 'London taste' and were travelling to London, rather than Edinburgh, for the winter season.

A note of caution is sounded, however, in Paul Langford's observation that 'London was the hub of polite transformation, not its motive power. It was visible in every revolution of fashion and taste; it did not deter-mine it'.[23] National culture was becoming sufficiently integrated to make the search for the precise origins of this self-styled 'London taste' par-ticularly elusive. Admittedly, many of the contemporary writers whose works feature heavily in histories of Georgian Britain seemed to accept the cultural dominance of the metropolis without question. It should be remembered, however, that these writers were predominantly based in London themselves, and so had a London-centred view of the world. As John Brewer points out, 'Seen from London, provincial culture looked marginal, most useful for its provision of talent best recognized in the big city. . . . Culture travelled only one way, out from London rather than in from the provinces'.[24] It was clearly possible, however, for ideas and innovations to flow in both directions, rather than simply streaming out of London to an essentially passive provincial audience. Migrants to London could not realistically be dismissed as raw talent, unmarked by their provincial education and experience. Lichfield, for instance, had played a vital part in the intellectual development of both David Garrick and Samuel Johnson, long before they moved to London to develop their careers. It is also important to recognize that the 'Ingenuity, Talents, and Industry' of provincial manufacturers had an aesthetic as well as a mechanical dimension, exemplified by the activities of 'the black artists of the Birmingham forge' as well as by the constant stream of innovations that marked the hosiery and textile industries.[25]

Emulation is in any case an unsatisfactory model for explaining the dynamic and ambiguous process of social change. Many contemporary commentators seem to have assumed without question that the bulk of the population, from presumptuous domestic servants to aspiring pro-vincial merchants, were consumed not only with a fierce competitive desire to outshine their neighbours, but also with a burning ambition to be assimilated into the essentially metropolitan world of the nobility and gentry. Historians need to remember, however, that these commenta-tors were rarely disinterested observers; and that their emphasis on the eagerness of provincial townsmen and women to embrace London's 'superior' cultural and material standards probably reveals more about their own sense of social insecurity than it does about the motives and desires of the majority of the urban population. Many of the new consumer goods and leisure activities seem likely to have appealed to a wide spectrum of this population for their own sakes, irrespective of any metropolitan associations. Curtains and window-blinds, for instance, were a welcome innovation in an increasingly crowded urban environment, valued for their evident utility rather than for the social prestige conveyed by possessing the latest style or fabric, as seen in the best London houses. There may even have been some degree of cultural resistance to trends that were too closely associated with the notorious luxury and extravagance of the 'wicked city'. Stana Nenadic has demonstrated, for instance, that middle-rank consumers in Edinburgh and Glasgow tended to buy locally made consumer goods, many of them acquired second-hand, rather than chasing after the latest London fashions. Echoing the quotation from Disraeli that opened this chapter, her research suggests 'a strongly pragmatic approach to the ownership and use of many household objects', one that emphasized usefulness at the expense of status or beauty.[26]

London, moreover, was not the only paradigm of fashionable modernization that was on offer in Georgian Britain. The aspiring resort of Aberystwyth was certainly hoping to borrow the capital's prestige when renaming some of its principal streets in the early decades of the nineteenth century. Thus Back Lane became Grays Inn Road, and Barkers Lane was transformed into Queen Street. A similar process was at work in the Staffordshire pottery town of Hanley, which chose to 'improve' the image of two of its principal streets by renaming them Piccadilly and Pall Mall. Marsh Lane in Aberystwyth, however, preferred to adopt the name of Bath's North Parade, a frame of reference that was also reflected in a contemporary description of Marine Terrace as 'a promenade that may vie with those of Bath and Cheltenham'.[27] Spa towns and seaside resorts, in fact, often led the way in architectural fashion, partly because it was recognized that innovative design reinforced their all-important reputation for glamour and style. Bath, in particular, became the architectural showcase of the Georgian age, impressing visitors with the scale, as well as the quality, of the speculative developments that nevertheless created a landscape of unique visual distinction. It set the standards which other resorts desired to emulate and, if possible, to surpass. Buxton, Clifton and Brighton, for instance, competed with each other to develop the widest and most grandiose crescent in Britain, a contest which was eventually won by Lewes Crescent in Brighton, planned in the 1820s to stretch for 840 feet along the sea front, a quarter the width again of Bath's original Royal Crescent.

Comparison and competition between Georgian towns was, therefore, much more pervasive and far more complex than advocates of the dominance model of London's social and cultural hegemony are prepared to accept. Aberystwyth had no real ambition to become a miniature version of imperial London; such a comparison would have been wildly unrealistic for a small port and resort town on the west coast of Wales, whose resident population at the time of the 1841 census still fell just short of 5000. At best, as the quotation above demonstrates, it hoped to emulate larger, more fashionable watering-places, portraying itself as 'the Brighton of Wales'. Even its most enthusiastic local promoters, however, must have been aware that its real competitors were to be found among minor, albeit exclusive, resorts such as Tenby and Lynton.[28] Aspiring ports modelled themselves on Liverpool; aspiring metalworking centres emulated the achievements of Sheffield and Birmingham; and aspiring textile towns emulated Manchester, Glasgow and Leeds. Each of these growing regional centres, moreover, presided over a hinterland where intense local rivalries were increasingly expressed through investment in cultural capital, as well as through competition in the commercial and industrial market-place. Although Manchester cotton-spinners had a reputation for cultural philistinism, it was the Manchester Literary and Philosophical Society, rather than the London-based Royal Society, Society of Antiquaries or Society of Arts, that provided a model for the provincial Enlightenment.

The pre-eminent position of Manchester within industrial north–west England makes it abundantly clear that neither the opening up of a national market, nor the creation of a national society, were incompatible with the emergence of strong regional identities, based on dynamic urban centres. In parts of the English midlands and north, as well as in lowland Scotland, both these new patterns of national and regional interdependence seem to have developed side by side.[29] As a direct result, London's traditional hegemony over the provincial towns seemed to many contemporaries to be facing its first serious challenge in the early decades of the nineteenth century, a challenge that perhaps reached its greatest intensity in the 1840s. As Dror Wahrman has suggested, 'For the first time in their collective experience, the "middling sorts" – urban and rural – had a choice'; between embracing a London-centred and London-orientated 'genteel' culture, and asserting their independent, locally focused standards and values in opposition to 'this alien intrusion'.[30]

There is, in fact, a great deal of evidence that demonstrates the enduring vitality and attractiveness of civic – as opposed to metropolitan – culture in Britain's leading provincial centres.[31] Far from exhibiting any symptoms of what might be termed 'cultural cringe' towards the aristocratic culture of the metropolis, urban histories produced in Georgian Britain tended to stress the long traditions of independent thought and action enjoyed by provincial towns. Readers were clearly intended to draw the conclusion that their current prosperity was based on the maintenance of these traditions and on the strength of their indigenous culture. The inhabitants of Newcastle upon Tyne, for example, lived on the northern frontier of the Roman empire, surrounded by what Defoe termed 'abundant business for an antiquary', yet they felt perfectly equal to the comparison. The wooden railways constructed in the early decades of the eighteenth century to carry coal down to the Tyne were hailed as the equivalent of imperial Rome's Appian Way. Indeed, it was argued that the contemporary achievements of the citizens of 'great Nova' exceeded those of their Roman predecessors, since these elaborate and expensive waggon-ways were merely 'a small part of the whole Coal Works'.[32]

This enthusiastic local patriotism was not always compatible with deference to metropolitan ideas of civility. An aristocratic visitor to Bristol, for instance, piqued that its citizens refused to defer to his evident status by doffing their hats to him in the street, complained that they were as proud as Roman senators. To provincial eyes, genteel culture was all too often associated with the luxury, idleness and dissipation of the 'wicked city'; whereas their own traditions promoted 'the spirit of industry and close application to business', as well as the more general Christian virtues of piety, philanthropy and self-restraint. Influential elements among the civic elite of Nottingham, for example, objected to the building of a permanent theatre in the town in the early 1760s, 'either for religious, or commercial Reasons, as prejudicial to the Morals of Mankind, or contradictory to the Manufacture of the Town, by claiming too much Attention from the Populace'.[33] Some months later, one of the leading actors appearing in the St Mary's Gate theatre was arrested under the Vagrancy Act at the conclusion of a performance of Addison's patriotic tragedy *Cato*. The city fathers of Nottingham were eager to embrace change, but only on their own terms.

Cultural Transmission: Town and Country

most people love a Country Prospect, and are even pleased with the most narrow View of it.

Thomas Fairchild (1722)[34]

The emphasis placed on the resilience of civic culture in recent historiography has clearly posed a challenge to the conventional image of provincial townspeople as eager recipients of each and every fashionable innovation emanating from the metropolis. However, it would be equally mistaken to exaggerate the influence that provincial towns were able to exercise over the populations of their own, narrower hinterlands. The inhabitants of Rochdale in the early nineteenth century may well have regarded their expansive and prosperous community as 'the hub of the Universe', but this self-confident assertion of local pride tells us little about how far their 'universe' actually extended into the surrounding network of smaller settlements that linked the town with the agricultural economy of rural Lancashire.[35]

Carl Estabrook's research into the cultural influence of Bristol in the years between 1660 and 1780 suggests that Somerset villagers were just as resistant to the penetration of civic culture into the countryside, as the citizens of Bristol were to 'the infection of the metropolis'. 'The size, relative density, and general commotion of cities made them conspicuous', he argues, 'but we should not assume that these qualities placed them at the centre of rural experience'.[36] On the contrary, he identifies among both villagers and recent migrants to the town a strong attachment to the physical environment, social structures and cultural practices of village life, an attachment which made them actively hostile to the intrusion of urban ideas. In this context, the changes associated with the 'urban renaissance' may actually have exacerbated the gulf between urban and rural mentalities, intensifying the visible and invisible boundaries that separated the two world views. These barriers only began to break down at the very end of the eighteenth century, as parochialism was eroded and suburban development spread out into the countryside. On this reading, claims that provincial towns acted as engines of social and cultural change in the countryside should be treated with a great deal of scepticism.

This challenging view of rural–urban relationships is a salutary reminder that neither the leading role of the town, nor the intrinsic superiority of urban culture, can be taken for granted in this period. On the other hand, Estabrook's findings need to be supported by further local studies before they can be accepted in their entirety. It is by no means certain, for example, that the barriers between Bristol and its neighbouring villages were qualitatively different from those that separated Bristol from Gloucester, or Stanton Drew from Pensford; local identities, like regional identities, continued to flourish in Georgian Britain. It is equally possible that Bristol's relationship with its hinterland may have been exceptional, rather than typical of the connections between urbane (or civic) and rustic society elsewhere in England, Scotland and Wales. Eighteenth-century Bristol was a great commercial and colonial entrepôt, a city facing outwards towards the Atlantic and a 'metropolis of the west' in international, as well as national, terms.[37] In contrast, David Hey's earlier study of Sheffield and its neighbourhood between 1660 and 1740 emphasized the development of 'a local social system' uniting the interests of the urban and rural populations. Jon Stobart, too, has found evidence from north-west England of strong interpersonal networks linking townspeople to family and friends living in other towns and villages across a wide geographical area.[38]

It seems inherently unlikely, therefore, that the mass of smaller towns, with populations of only a few thousand, were as cut off from their surroundings as Bristol appears to have been. As Anthony Wrigley has pointed out, urban settlements are ultimately dependent on the strength of their relationships with the countryside; the more isolated the urban sector, the less successful it will be in attracting the suppliers, customers and migrant labour needed to sustain its economy.[39] A marked cultural and social gap between village and town would, therefore, tend to depress the rate of urban population growth, as well as limiting the influence of towns as agents of change. This is hard to reconcile with the evidence of urban expansion in Georgian Britain, largely as a result of migration from the countryside.

This does not mean, however, that historians can fall back on a simple model of social and cultural change, one that characterizes towns as 'pace-setters for rural England', exporting ideas of rational and secular modernization to an unenlightened, deeply reluctant peasantry.[40] As the complex relationship between urbane and civic culture demonstrates, cultural transmission need not be a one-way process, and there is ample evidence that rural landscapes and rural traditions continued to exercise considerable influence over large sections of the urban population in this period.

It is clear, for instance, that the image of the countryside improved out of all recognition in the course of the eighteenth century.[41] Remote, mountainous areas such as the Lake District, the Peaks and the Highlands of Scotland, which contemporaries of Celia Fiennes and Daniel Defoe had dismissed as savage, bleak and profoundly unattractive, were transformed by a newly discovered appreciation of the natural world into popular tourist destinations. Their wild and romantic scenery appealed to the newly discovered cult of the picturesque, a cult that is often associated with the increasing congestion of busy town centres in the later years of the century. However, the enthusiasm of the urban elite for country prospects and country pleasures almost certainly predates the worst excesses of environmental degradation to be found in Britain's fastest-growing industrial and commercial cities. Manchester and Birmingham, for instance, both maintained packs of municipal fox-hounds, funded by subscription, in the middle years of the century, while the fashion for traditional country sports and pastimes was associated with the fishing, gardening and archery contests that sprang up in towns all over the country.

Fashionable appreciation of the urban environment was profoundly affected by this rediscovery of nature. The regularity and uniformity of classical Georgian architecture, exemplified by the orderly squares and terraces of the West End of London and the elegant 'New Town' of Edinburgh, was already beginning to attract critical comment in the 1760s, when the architect John Gwynne complained that recent developments in St Marylebone conveyed 'no better idea to the spectator than that of a plain brick wall of prodigious length'. Although new towns such as Ashton-under-Lyne, Milford Haven and Pembroke Dock, as well as the Earl of Renfrew's little cotton-spinning enterprise at Eaglesham, were still being laid out in a traditional style, 'charming irregularity' was now the preferred ideal in urban planning. Indeed, in the early years of the nineteenth century, Sir John Soane roundly condemned the 'disgusting insipidity and tiresome monotony' of most modern developments, arguing that Edinburgh's cramped, irregular and notoriously filthy Old Town was in reality 'more beautiful, and possibly not less convenient, than the New Town, with all its regularity and polish'.[42]

It is important to recognize that the aim of most urban residents, however wealthy and fashionable, was to create a more 'natural' landscape within the town, rather than to abandon the town for the countryside. The desirable ideal was encapsulated in the expression *rus in urbe* (country in city); selected elements of the countryside were to be incorporated into the landscape of the Georgian town. Tree-lined walks and both public and private gardens proliferated in the later seventeenth and early eighteenth centuries, striking testimony to the efforts being made to reconcile the pursuit of an essentially urban ideal of civilized society with an appreciation of the natural world. Town squares, it was argued, should be laid out in a 'Rural Manner' in order to 'give our Thoughts an Opportunity of Country Amusements'.[43] A small flock of frightened sheep, with 'sooty faces and meagre carcasses', was therefore imported into Cavendish Square in London to introduce the right note of pastoral tranquillity, while both sheep and cattle were induced to graze the slope below Bath's Royal Crescent.

The Royal Crescent, like several other Bath developments, represented the paradigm of *rus in urbe*, in that its residents could enjoy fine views of the surrounding countryside while remaining within easy reach of the sophisticated social, commercial and medical services provided by Britain's leading health resort. It was the prospect of nature that was so attractive to townsmen and women in the eighteenth century, rather than the muddy and often austere realities of rural life. Indeed, a contemporary observer, sympathetic to the plight of the Cavendish Square sheep, somewhat cynically suggested that 'the next designer of country-in-town, [should] let all his sheep be painted', and that 'if a paste-board mill, and tin cascade, were to be added it would compleat the rural scene'.[44]

Suburbanization merely pushed this sort of hybrid development a little further out from the city centre, as the upper levels of urban society built themselves 'country boxes' along the main roads leading out of – and into – town. What these affluent townspeople appear to have wanted was an affordable version of the carefully-crafted beauty of the great landed estates, not the wild isolation of a romantic and picturesque landscape. The development of St John's Wood in London between 1794 and 1834 led the way, creating an apparently artless arrangement of detached and semi-detached villas set in their own gardens, a style which Nash incorporated into his much more elaborate plans for Regent's Park, but which also undoubtedly influenced the rapid expansion of Cheltenham in the 1820s and the development of the Edgbaston estate on the south-west edge of Birmingham.[45]

Suburban development, therefore, represented a move away from the urban core, rather than a flight from the town itself. 'Embellished villas' and 'cottages orné' were neither wholly urban nor wholly rural. Instead, they were the result of a prolonged negotiation between urban and rural cultures, emphasizing their mutual dependence rather than their supposed incompatibility. It would be just as unrealistic to draw a sharp distinction between rural beauty and urban squalor, as it would be to suggest that the Georgian town was a shining beacon of enlightenment, existing in perpetual opposition to rural ignorance and superstition.

Conclusion

The ambiguity of the urban world's response to nature and the countryside is typical of the flexibility and resilience of urban society as a whole in the years between 1680 and 1840. Although there was no clear-cut triumph for the 'progressive' values of rationality, secularization and modernization, neither was there any pathological breakdown of society in the face of the inevitable pressures of rapid urbanization. Despite Estabrook's contention that 'from the rustic point of view, cities undergoing [such] dramatic changes were a visible object lesson in what to avoid', urban society maintained its attractions.[46] There was no inevitable slide from harmony and order to discord and chaos. Moreover, although the British tradition of anti-urbanism was clearly well-established, it had not yet become so pervasive as to cancel out the influence of the fast-growing and increasingly influential urban minority.

Alongside the hostile portrayals of urban life that had always been the stock-in-trade of clerics, moral reformers and intellectuals reared in the classical tradition, there was an equally strong popular tradition that associated towns with freedom and opportunity. Towns were attractive to their inhabitants, and worrying to moralists, precisely because the urban market-place offered these residents a much greater chance of building viable and independent lives for themselves than they could possibly have enjoyed in an isolated country village. The concentration of employment opportunities and the wide variety of goods and services available in towns all over Georgian Britain allowed both men and women to exercise the ultimate in consumer choice, between industry and idleness, vice and virtue, success and failure.

Gin Lane, one of William Hogarth's most famous images, is all too often reproduced in isolation as a definitive representation of urban decay. Hogarth, however, intended it to be seen together with its companion piece, *Beer Street*. In the first engraving, starving beggars and ragged tradesmen scrabble to survive in a world of poverty, misery and ruin; an 'abandoned' woman, too fuddled with drink to prevent her baby falling to its death, dominates the centre of the picture. In *Beer Street*, in contrast, a plump and pretty servant girl flirts with a group of prosperous trademen, while two well-dressed fishwives are eagerly reading a ballad in praise of the fishing industry. One of them has a foaming tankard in her hand, but there is no suggestion that she is a 'naughty town-woman', leading 'a wicked town-life'.[47] Of course, neither of these images claims to represent the elusive 'reality' of the urban experience; they are both satirical portrayals of contrasting stereotypes of life in the capital city. However, they are clearly grounded in a moral world where both male and female citizens have the power to make choices, in this case between good British beer and deadly foreign gin, in the knowledge that they will have to live with the consequences. Down Beer Street lay peace, plenty and social harmony; down Gin Lane lay both personal and public disaster.

It is important to recognize, however, that such choices were rarely as clear-cut in real life as they were in the minds of moral reformers. The individual men and women who inhabited the Georgian town probably developed a flexible, open-minded attitude to the profound social and cultural changes that were taking place around them, recognizing that the competing claims of civic, urbane and rustic culture were rarely mutually exclusive. As Wahrman suggests, 'It may be that for every person . . . who made a clear choice, there were two who never made up their minds', reconciling their apparently contradictory national, local and neighbourhood identities within a pluralist model in which different choices were appropriate in different contexts.[48]

Urban societies in this period were, therefore, both ambivalent and dynamic, shaped by economic change and by the frictions that were generated in the process. Their vitality came from the conjunction of many different traditions, and that vitality was central to the complex processes of social and cultural change in Georgian Britain.

APPENDICES

Appendix 1   The Largest British Towns, 1680–1841*

Late 17th century†		c.1700		1801		1841‡	
London	311,000	London	575,000	London	959,000	London	1,948,000
Edinburgh	50,000	Edinburgh	50,000	Manchester	95,000	*Manchester*	311,000
Glasgow	18,000	Norwich	29,000	Liverpool	82,000	*Liverpool*	286,000
Newcastle upon Tyne	15,000	Bristol	20,000	Edinburgh	81,000	Glasgow	261,000
Norwich	14,000	Glasgow	18,000	Glasgow	77,000	*Birmingham*	183,000
York	14,000	Newcastle upon Tyne[a]	18,000	Birmingham	71,000	Edinburgh	164,000
Bristol	13,000	Exeter	14,000	Bristol	61,000	*Leeds*	152,000
Aberdeen	12,000	Aberdeen	13,000	Leeds	53,000	Bristol	125,000
Cambridge	11,000	York	12,000	Sheffield	46,000	*Sheffield*	111,000
Oxford	11,000	Cambridge	11,000	Newcastle upon Tyne	42,000	*Wolverhampton*	93,000
Exeter	10,000	Great Yarmouth	10,000	Plymouth	40,000	Newcastle upon Tyne	90,000
Ipswich	10,000	Colchester	9,000	Norwich	36,000	*Plymouth*	70,000

Town		Town		Town		Town	
Great Yarmouth	9,000	Plymouth[b]	9,000	Bath	33,000	Hull	67,000
Canterbury	8,000	Birmingham	8,000	Portsmouth	33,000	*Bradford*	67,000
Dundee	8,000	Chester	8,000	Wolverhampton	31,000	Dundee	65,000
Colchester	7,000	Dundee	8,000	Hull	30,000	Aberdeen	63,000
Hull	7,000	Ipswich	8,000	Nottingham	29,000	Norwich	62,000
Salisbury	7,000	Manchester[c]	8,000	Aberdeen	27,000	*Sunderland*	55,000
Shrewsbury	7,000	Oxford	8,000	Dundee	27,000	*Bath*	53,000
Worcester	7,000	Portsmouth	8,000	Sunderland	26,000	Portsmouth	53,000
Chester	6,000	Shrewsbury	8,000	Paisley	25,000	*Nottingham*	52,000
Coventry	6,000	Worcester	8,000	Bolton	18,000	*Bolton*	51,000
Kendal	6,000	Canterbury	7,000	Exeter	17,000	*Leicester*	51,000
Bradford-on-Avon	5,000	Coventry	7,000	Great Yarmouth	17,000	*Preston*	51,000
King's Lynn	5,000	Hull	7,000	Greenock	17,000	Stockport	50,000
Portsmouth	5,000	Leeds	7,000	Leicester	17,000	*Brighton*	49,000
Rochester	5,000	Salisbury	7,000	York	17,000	Oldham	48,000
				Coventry	16,000	*Paisley*	48,000
				Perth	16,000	*Merthyr Tydfil*	43,000

*Population totals have been rounded to emphasize the approximate nature of the figures, even for 1801 and 1841.

†Towns in *italics* in the later seventeenth century do not appear in the 1841 list.

‡Towns in *italics* in 1841 do not appear in the later seventeenth-century list.

a Figures for Newcastle upon Tyne include Gateshead.

b Figures for Plymouth include Devonport.

c Figures for Manchester include Salford.

Sources: P. Corfield, 'Urban development in England and Wales in the sixteenth and seventeenth centuries', in J. Barry (ed.), *The Tudor and Stuart Town: A Reader in English Urban History, 1530–1688* (1990), pp. 35–62; J. Langton, 'Urban growth', in *CUHB*, ch. 14.

Appendix 2 Trades and professions in five major towns

Manchester 1772	Edinburgh 1774	Birmingham 1777	Newcastle 1778	Sheffield 1787
140 Innkeepers	217 Merchants	248 Innkeepers	175 Innkeepers	206 Cutlers
75 Fustian manufacturers	188 Advocates	129 Buttonmakers	55 Butchers	174 Victuallers
58 Warehousemen	171 Writers	99 Shoemakers	50 Tailors	58 Scissorsmiths
49 Check manufacturers	169 Grocers	77 Merchants	36 Grocers/tea sellers	55 Grocers
46 Hucksters	141 Clerks to H. M. Signet	74 Tailors	35 Peruke makers	31 Dealers
44 Smallware manufacturers	110 Vintners	64 Bakers	32 Attorneys at law	28 Filesmiths
27 Shoemakers	94 Lords/advocates clerks	56 Toymakers	32 Cabinet makers	27 Butchers
26 Barbers	86 Baxters (i.e. bakers)	52 Platers	31 Shoemakers	27 Factors
25 Tailors	80 Shipmasters	49 Butchers	27 Schoolmasters	20 Merchants
24 Clergy	79 Shoemakers	48 Carpenters	22 Linen drapers	19 Bakers
24 Grocers	64 Wrights	46 Barbers	21 Cheesemongers	16 Carpenters/joiners

23 Carpenters/joiners	61 Brewers	46 Brassfounders	21 Flour shops	16 Silver/plated goods
23 Hatters	56 Schoolmasters	39 Bucklemasters	20 Coal fitters	14 Schoolmasters
21 Lawyers	52 Tailors	39 Shopkeepers	18 Flax dressers	14 Shoemakers
17 Yarn manufacturers	46 Barbers	36 Gunmakers	18 Gardeners	14 Surgeons
15 Butchers	45 Milliners	35 Jewellers	18 Woollen drapers	13 Buttonmakers
15 Linen drapers	45 Smiths	26 Maltsters	17 Pilots	13 Clergymen
14 Corn factors	45 Stablers	24 Drapers	16 Bakers	13 Edgetool makers
14 Fustian dyers	39 Physicians	23 Gardeners	16 Coopers	13 Hairdressers
13 Fustian calenderers (i.e. cloth pressers)	35 Clergy	21 Ironmongers	16 Hatters	13 Linen drapers
13 Toy/hardware shops	33 Surgeons	21 Plumbers/glaziers	15 Hackney horsekeepers	11 Tailors
12 Bakers	30 Bankers		15 Whitesmiths	10 Maltsters
11 Cabinet makers	24 Painters		15 Surgeons	10 Silver cutlers
11 Gardeners	21 Booksellers		13 Clergymen	10 Vigo button makers
	21 Goldsmiths/jewellers		13 Hardwaremen	

Sources: *Manchester Directory* (1772); *Williamson's Directory of Edinburgh* (1774); Peason and Rollason, *The Birmingham Directory* (1777); *Whitehead's Newcastle Directory for 1778*; Gales and Martin, *A Directory of Sheffield* (1787). On the use of commercial directories, see P. J. Corfield and S. Kelly, 'Giving directions to the town: the early town directories', *Urban History Yearbook*, (1984), pp. 22–35; E. P. Duggan, 'Industrialization and the development of urban business communities', *Local Historian*, **11** (1975), pp. 457–65.

NOTES

Place of publication is London unless otherwise specified.

Introduction

1. G. Chalmers, *An Estimate of the Comparative Strength of Great Britain* (1794 edn), p. xiii.
2. *The Journeys of Celia Fiennes*, ed. C. Morris (1947), pp. 1–2.
3. P. Benedict, 'Late medieval and early modern urban history *à l'Anglaise*: a review article', *Comparative Studies in Society and History*, **28** (1986), p. 169.
4. Shropshire Record Office, Notebooks and journals of Joshua Gilpin, book 45, f. 98.
5. P. J. Corfield, *The Impact of English Town, 1700–1800* (Oxford, 1982).
6. This research is reflected in the recent survey by R. Sweet, *The English Town, 1680–1840: Government, Society and Culture* (1999) but above all in the monumental *Cambridge Urban History of Britain*, vol. ii: *c.1540–c.1840*, ed. Peter Clark (Cambridge, 2000) [hereafter abbreviated as *CUHB*].
7. See, for example, B. Lepetit, 'In search of the small town in early nineteenth-century France', in P. Clark (ed.), *Small Towns in Early Modern Europe* (Cambridge, 1995), pp. 166–83.
8. J. M. Ellis, 'Consumption and wealth', in L. K. J. Glassey (ed.), *The Reigns of Charles II and James VII and II* (1997), pp. 191–210.
9. P. Jenkins, 'Wales', in *CUHB*, pp. 140–9.
10. T. Devine, 'Scotland', in *CUHB*, pp. 158–64.
11. J. Addison, *The Spectator*, no. 69, 19 May 1711; D. Defoe, *The Complete English Tradesman in Familiar Letters* (2nd edn, 1727), vol. i, p. 381.
12. J. Austen, *Lady Susan, the Watsons, Sanditon*, ed. M. Drabble (1974), pp. 206,180.
13. T. Wilkinson, *Memoirs of His Own Life* (York, 1790), vol. iv, p. 50.
14. E. A. Wrigley, '"The great commerce of every civilised society": urban growth in early modern Europe', *Scottish Economic and Social History*, **12** (1992), pp. 5–23.
15. W. Hutton, *A History of Birmingham to the End of the Year 1780* (Birmingham, 1783 edn), p. 62.
16. P. J. Corfield, 'The new Babylons', in L. M. Smith (ed.), *The Age of Revolution* (1987), pp. 49–62.

1 The Urban Prospect

1. *Is this the Truth? A Poem* (Newcastle, 1741), p. 4.
2. P. Glennie and I. D. Whyte, 'Towns in an agrarian economy, 1540–1700', in *CUHB*, p. 169. For the national populations, see E. A. Wrigley and R. S. Schofield, *The Population History of England, 1541–1871: A Reconstruction* (1989), pp. 208–9; R. E. Tyson, 'Contrasting regimes: population growth in Ireland and Scotland during the eighteenth century', in S. J. Connolly, R. A. Houston and R. J. Morris (eds), *Conflict, Identity and Economic Development: Ireland and Scotland, 1600–1939* (Preston, 1995), pp. 64–6.
3. J. M. Ellis, 'Consumption and wealth', in L. K. J. Glassey (ed.), *The Reigns of Charles II and James VII and II* (1997), pp. 202–3.
4. R. Hyde, *Gilded Scenes and Shining Prospects: Panoramic Views of British Towns, 1575–1900* (New Haven, CT, 1985); D. Smith, 'The enduring image of early British townscapes', *Cartographic Journal*, **28** (1991), pp. 163–75.
5. See M. Reed, 'The urban landscape, 1540–1700', in *CUHB*, ch. 9.
6. T. Fuller, *The Worthies of England*, ed. J. Freeman (1952), p. 419.
7. Quoted in D. Macniven, 'Merchant and trader in early seventeenth-century Aberdeen' (M.Litt thesis, University of Aberdeen, 1977), p. 105.
8. E. A. Wrigley, 'A simple model of London's importance in changing English society and economy, 1650–1750', in his *People, Cities and Wealth* (Oxford, 1987), pp. 135–8.
9. J. Boulton, 'London, 1540–1700', in *CUHB*, p. 316.
10. D. Defoe, *A Tour Through the Whole Island of Great Britain* (1962 edn), vol. i, p. 316.
11. *The Journeys of Celia Finnes*, ed. C. Morris (1947), pp. 184, 247.
12. P. Corfield, 'Urban development in England and Wales in the sixteenth and seventeenth centuries', in J. Barry (ed.), *The Tudor and Stuart Town: A Reader in English Urban History, 1530–1688* (1990), pp. 47–9.
13. A. Dyer, 'Small market towns, 1540–1700', in *CUHB*, pp. 440–4.
14. Defoe, *Tour*, vol. i, pp. 132, 142.
15. P. Jenkins, 'Wales', in *CUHB*, pp. 144–9; R. Hyde, *A Prospect of Britain: The Town Panoramas of Samuel and Nathaniel Buck* (1994), plate 30; Defoe, *Tour*, vol. ii, p. 57.
16. I. D. Whyte, 'Urbanisation in early modern Scotland: a preliminary analysis', *Scottish Economic and Social History*, **9** (1989), pp. 21–38.
17. R. A. Houston, *Social Change in the Age of Enlightenment: Edinburgh 1660–1760* (Oxford, 1994), p. 4.
18. J. de Vries, *European Urbanization, 1500–1800* (Harvard, 1984), pp. 274–5.
19. P. Slack, 'Great and good towns: regional centres', in *CUHB*, pp. 347–8.
20. W. E. Minchinton, 'Bristol: metropolis of the west in the eighteenth century', in P. Clark (ed.), *The Early Modern Town* (1976), pp. 297–313.
21. T. Cox, *Magna Britania et Hibernia, Antiqua et Nova* (1720), vol. i, p. 608.
22. Defoe, *Tour*, vol. ii, pp. 75–7.
23. A. Everitt, 'Country, county and town: patterns of regional evolution in England', in P. Borsay (ed.), *The Eighteenth-Century Town: A Reader in English Urban History, 1688–1820* (1990), pp. 83–115.
24. For a survey of the crisis debate, see A. Dyer, *Decline and Growth in English Towns, 1400–1640* (Cambridge, 1995).

25. See P. Borsay, 'The Restoration town', in Glassey (ed.), *The Reigns of Charles II*, pp. 171–90.

26. E. A. Wrigley, 'Urban growth and agricultural change: England and the continent in the early modern period', in Borsay (ed.), *Eighteenth-Century Town*, esp. pp. 60–6.

27. Corfield, 'Urban development', p. 58.

28. R. Thoroton, *The Antiquities of Nottingham* (1677), p. 499; 'Thomas Baskerville's Journeys in England, *temp.* Car.II', Historical Manuscripts Commission, *Portland MSS* (1893), vol. ii, p. 308.

29. M. Lynch, 'Urbanisation and urban networks in seventeenth-century Scotland: some further thoughts', *Scottish Economic and Social History*, **12** (1992), pp. 24–41.

30. P. Clark, 'Small towns in England, 1550–1850: national and regional population trends', in his *Small Towns in Early Modern Europe* (Cambridge, 1995), pp. 98–100.

31. S. M. Jack, *Towns in Tudor and Stuart Britain* (1996), pp. 159–64.

32. J. Elliott, *The City in Maps: Urban Mapping to 1900* (1987).

33. See R. Sweet, *The Writing of Urban Histories in Eighteenth-Century England* (Oxford, 1997).

34. W. Hutton, *A History of Birmingham to the End of the Year 1780* (Birmingham, 1783 edn), p. 23.

35. See Chapter 5, below.

36. E. L. Jones, S. Porter and M. Turner, *A Gazeteer of English Urban Fire Disasters, 1500–1900*, Historical Geography Research Series, no. 13 (Norwich, 1984).

37. P. Borsay, 'Culture, status, and the English urban landscape', *History*, **67** (1982), pp. 1–12.

38. Thoroton, *Antiquities*, p. 499; G. C. Deering, *Nottinghamia Vetus et Nova* (Nottingham, 1751), p. 6.

39. Fiennes, *Journeys*, pp. 146–8.

40. See, for example, M. Laithwaite, 'Totnes houses, 1500–1800', in P. Clark (ed.), *The Transformation of English Provincial Towns, 1600–1800* (1984), pp. 86–92.

41. A. Cox, 'Bricks to build a capital', in H. Hobhouse and A. Saunders (eds), *Good and Proper Materials: The Fabric of London since the Great Fire*, London Topographical Society, no. 140 (1989), pp. 10–13; T. Porter, *Colour Outside* (1982), pp. 37–8.

2 Urban Growth

1. Quoted in E. Pawson, *The Early Industrial Revolution: Britain in the Eighteenth Century* (1979), p. 213.

2. E. A. Wrigley, 'Urban growth and agricultural change: England and the continent in the early modern period', in P. Borsay (ed.), *The Eighteenth-Century Town (1990)*, pp. 63–8; J. de Vries, *European Urbanization, 1500–1800* (Harvard, 1984), pp. 36–7.

3. J. Langton, 'Urban growth', in *CUHB*, p. 468.

4. *Aris's Birmingham Gazette*, 27 January 1783.

5. L. D. Schwarz, *London in the Age of Industrialisation: Entrepreneurs, Labour Force and Living Conditions, 1700–1850* (Cambridge, 1992), pp. 125–8.
6. E. Mackenzie, *A Descriptive and Historical Account of the Town and County of Newcastle upon Tyne, Including Gateshead* (Newcastle, 1827), vol. i, p. 197.
7. These issues are discussed in Langton, 'Urban growth', in *CUHB*, pp. 457–62.
8. See P. Sharpe, 'Population and society, 1700–1840', in *CUHB*, esp. pp. 502–4.
9. D. Souden, 'Migrants and the population structure of later seventeenth-century provincial cities and market towns', in P. Clark (ed.), *The Transformation of English Provincial Towns, 1600–1800* (1984), pp. 133–68.
10. For migration generally in this period, see I. D. Whyte, *Migration and Society in Britain, 1550–1830* (Basingstoke, 2000).
11. T. Short, *New Observations on City, Town and Country Bills of Mortality* (1750), pp. 1, 65, 73–4. The 'urban graveyard' thesis is controversial: see Sharpe, 'Population and society', in *CUHB*, pp. 504–6.
12. Souden, 'Migrants', in Clark (ed.), *Transformation*, pp. 150–61; H. M. Dingwall, *Late Seventeenth-Century Edinburgh: A Demographic Study* (Aldershot, 1994), pp. 28–9.
13. W. Hutton, *A History of Birmingham to the End of the Year 1780* (Birmingham, 1783 edn), p. 41.
14. D. Defoe, *A Plan of the English Commerce* (1730 edn), p. 268.
15. J. G. Williamson, *Coping with City Growth during the British Industrial Revolution* (Cambridge, 1990), pp. 28–34, 46.
16. For the shortcomings of the available evidence, see R. Woods, 'What would one need to know to solve the "natural decrease" problem in early modern cities?', in R. Lawton (ed.), *The Rise and Fall of Modern Cities: Aspects of Urbanization in the Western World* (1989), pp. 80–95.
17. T. Hitchcock, 'Demography and the culture of sex in the long eighteenth century', in J. Black (ed.), *Culture and Society in Britain, 1660–1800* (Manchester, 1997), pp. 69–73.
18. Defoe, *Plan*, p. 268.
19. R. Adair, *Courtship, Illegitimacy and Marriage in Early Modern England* (Manchester, 1996), pp. 188–223; T. R. Malthus, *An Essay on the Principle of Population* (7th edn, repr. 1973), p. 242. See, however, T. Hitchcock, *English Sexualities, 1700–1800* (Basingstoke, 1997), pp. 38–41.
20. M. Flinn (ed.), *Scottish Population History from the Seventeenth Century to the 1930s* (Cambridge, 1977), pp. 390–5.
21. J. Aikin, *A Description of the Country from Thirty to Forty Miles around Manchester* (1795), p. 392.
22. Key texts on urban consumption include L. Weatherill, *Consumer Behaviour and Material Culture in Britain, 1660–1760* (1996 edn); and J. Brewer and R. Porter (eds), *Consumption and the World of Goods in the Seventeenth and Eighteenth Centuries* (1993).
23. J. Ellis, 'Regional and county centres, 1700–1840', in *CUHB*, pp. 678–82; Wrigley, 'Urban growth and agricultural change', in Borsay (ed.), *Eighteenth-Century Town*, pp. 42–3, 47–50.
24. See below, pp. 114–16.
25. 'Account of Myrther-tedvel', *Monthly Magazine*, **7** (1799), p. 356; B. H. Malkin, *The Scenery, Antiquities and Biography of South Wales* (1804), p. 170.

26. Langton, 'Urban growth', in *CUHB*, pp. 478–9.
27. P. Clark, 'Area surveys: introduction', in *CUHB*, p. 28.
28. Ellis, 'Regional and county centres', in *CUHB*, pp. 682–3.
29. J. Butterworth, *A Complete History of the Cotton Trade* (Manchester, 1823), p. 23.
30. G. Turnbull, 'Canals, coal and regional growth during the industrial revolution', *Economic History Review*, **40** (1987), pp. 537–60.
31. See E. A. Wrigley, *Continuity, Chance and Change: The Character of the Industrial Revolution in England* (Cambridge, 1988).
32. J. V. Stobart, 'An eighteenth-century urban revolution? Investigating urban growth in north-west England, 1664–1801', *Urban History*, **23** (1996), pp. 26–47.
33. For the 'de-urbanization' of shopping in the later eighteenth century, see H. C. Mui and L. H. Mui, *Shops and Shopkeeping in Eighteenth-Century England* (1989).
34. P. Clark, 'Small towns *c*.1700–*c*.1840', in *CUHB*, p. 734.
35. See above, pp. 39–40.
36. E. Pawson, *Transport and Economy* (1977), pp. 324–6; J. Barry, 'The South-west', in *CUHB*, p. 78.
37. D. Garrick, *The Trip to Scarborough* (1777), prologue.
38. *Edinburgh Evening Courant*, 6 April 1767, quoted in J. Lindsay, *The Canals of Scotland* (Newton Abbot, 1968), p. 18.
39. L. Schwarz, 'London 1700–1840', in *CUHB*, ch. 19; R. Porter, *London: A Social History* (1994), p. 131.
40. E. M. Thompson (ed.), *Letters of Humphrey Prideaux to John Ellis, 1674–1722* (Camden Society, new series, 15, 1875), p. 146.
41. J. Addison, *The Spectator*, no. 69, 19 May 1711.
42. J. Boswell, *Life of Johnson*, ed. R. W. Chapman (Oxford, 1970) p. 859.
43. L. Simond, *An American in Regency England: The Journal of a Tour in 1810–1811*, ed. C. Hibbert (1968), pp. 127, 30–1.
44. *St James's Chronicle*, 6 August 1761.
45. Simond, *American in Regency England*, p. 59.

3   Making a Living

1. J. Thomson, *Summer: A Poem*, from *The Seasons* (1746), lines 1457–9.
2. Quoted in P. J. Corfield, 'Defining urban work', in Corfield and D. Keene (eds), *Work in Towns, 850–1850* (Leicester, 1990), p. 211.
3. D. Defoe, *A Tour Through the Whole Island of Great Britain* (1962 edn), vol. ii, p. 75; G. C. Deering, *Nottinghamia Vetus et Nova* (Nottingham, 1751), p. 6.
4. *Whitehead's Newcastle and Gateshead Directory* (Newcastle, 1790); P. J. Corfield and S. Kelly, '"Giving directions to the town"; the early town directories', *Urban History Yearbook*, **11** (1984), pp. 22–35.
5. Good examples of this approach include P. Earle, *A City Full of People: Men and Women of London, 1650–1750* (1994) and E. C. Sanderson, *Women and Work in Eighteenth-Century Edinburgh* (Basingstoke, 1996).
6. J. Gales and D. Martin, *A Directory of Sheffield; Including the Manufacturers of the Adjacent Villages* (Sheffield, 1787), pp. 2, 24, 45, 59, 61, 71.

7. A. Smith, *An Enquiry into the Nature and Causes of the Wealth of Nations*, ed. R. H. Campbell and A. J. Skinner (1976), vol. i, pp. 13–14.

8. M. Berg, 'Technological change in Birmingham and Sheffield', in P. Clark and P. Corfield, (eds), *Industry and Urbanisation in Eighteenth-Century England* (Leicester, 1994), pp. 20–32; *Four Topographical Letters, Written in July 1755* (Newcastle, 1757), pp. 62–3.

9. R. Southey, *Letters from England*, ed. J. Simmons (1951), p. 198.

10. C. Harvey, E. M. Green and P. J. Corfield, 'Continuity, change, and specialization within metropolitan London: the economy of Westminster, 1750–1820', *Economic History Review*, **52** (1999), pp. 469–93.

11. Defoe, *Tour*, vol. i, p. 63.

12. B. Trinder, 'Industrialising towns, 1700–1840', in *CUHB*, pp. 808–15.

13. L. Simond, *An American in Regency England: The Journal of a Tour in 1818–1811*, ed. C. Hibbert, p. 112.

14. R. Warner, *A Tour Through the Northern Counties of England, and the Borders of Scotland* (1802), vol. i, p. 310.

15. G. Jackson, 'The ports *c*.1700–1840', in *CUHB*, p. 727.

16. H. Bourne, *The History of Newcastle on Tyne* (Newcastle, 1736), p. 133.

17. *Elizabeth Montagu: Her Correspondence, 1720–61*, ed. E. J. Climenson (1906), vol. i, p. 35.

18. Hertfordshire Archives, Delmé-Radcliffe MSS, D/ER C311, 11 June. 1759.

19. P. Borsay, 'Health and leisure towns, 1700–1840', in *CUHB*, p. 796.

20. E. Hopkins, 'The trading and service sectors of the Birmingham economy, 1750–1800', *Business History*, **28** (1986), pp. 77–97.

21. I. D. Whyte, 'The occupational structure of Scottish burghs in the late seventeenth century', in M. Lynch (ed.), *The Early Modern Town in Scotland* (1987), pp. 219–44.

22. J. Stobart, 'In search of a leisure hierarchy: English spa towns and their place in the urban system', in P. Borsay, G. Hirschfelder and R. Mohrmann (eds), *New Directions in Urban History* (Munster and New York, 2000), pp. 19–40.

23. Quoted in J. M. Ellis, '"The Black Indies"; the economic development of Newcastle upon Tyne *c*.1700–1840', in W. Lancaster and R. Colls (eds), *Newcastle upon Tyne: A Modern History* (forthcoming).

24. Gateshead Public Library, Cotesworth Manuscripts, CP/4/45, 31 May 1720. See also J. Hoppitt, *Risk and Failure in English Business, 1700–1800* (Cambridge, 1987).

25. J. A. Phillips, 'Working and moving in early-nineteenth-century provincial towns', in Corfield and Keene (eds), *Work in Towns*, pp. 182–206.

26. On this issue see P. H. Lindert, 'English occupations, 1670–1811', *Journal of Economic History*, **40** (1980), pp. 685–712.

27. J. Fiske (ed.), *The Oakes Diaries: Business, Politics and the Family in Bury St Edmunds, 1778–1827* (Suffolk Records Society, 32, 1990), p. 53.

28. Quoted in R. A. Houston, *Social Change in the Age of Enlightenment: Edinburgh, 1660–1760* (Oxford, 1994) , p. 238.

29. O. Hufton, 'Women without men: widows and spinsters in Britain and France in the eighteenth century', *Journal of Family History*, **9** (1984), p. 363.

30. Quoted in Earle, *A City Full of People*, p. 199.

31. For more recent work see P. Sharpe, 'Continuity and change: women's history and economic history in Britain', *Economic History Review*, **48** (1995), pp. 353–69.

32. R. B. Shoemaker, *Gender in English Society, 1650–1850: The Emergence of Separate Spheres?* (1998) reviews much of this literature.

33. E. Haywood, *A Present for a Servant-maid* (1743), p. 45.

34. D. Simonton, 'Gendering work in eighteenth-century towns', in M. Walsh (ed.), *Working Out Gender: Perspectives from Labour History* (Aldershot, 2000), pp. 29–47.

35. A. Vickery, 'Golden age to separate spheres? A review of the categories and chronology of English women's history', *Historical Journal*, **36** (1993), p. 404.

36. P. Sharpe, 'De-industrialization and re-industrialization: women's employment and the changing character of Colchester, 1700–1850', *Urban History*, **21** (1994), pp. 87–8.

37. Quoted in Sanderson, *Women and Work*, p. 107. On this issue see P. Sharpe, 'Dealing with love: the ambiguous independence of the single woman in early modern England', *Gender and History*, **11** (1999), pp. 209–32.

38. M. Berg, 'What difference did women's work make to the industrial revolution?', *History Workshop*, **35** (1993), pp. 22–44.

39. M. R. Hunt, *The Middling Sort: Commerce, Gender and the Family in England, 1680–1780* (Berkeley, 1996); M. Berg, 'Women's consumption and the industrial classes of eighteenth-century England', *Journal of Social History*, **30** (1996), pp. 415–34.

40. For a crisp discussion of the problems involved, see L. D. Schwarz, *London in the Age of Industrialisation: Entrepreneurs, Labour Force and Living Conditions, 1700–1850* (Cambridge, 1992), pp. 157–78; also D. Woodward, *Men at Work: Labourers and Building Craftsmen in the Towns of Northern England, 1450–1750* (Cambridge, 1995).

41. Quoted in M. D. George, *London Life in the Eighteenth Century* (1966), pp. 180–1.

42. A. Young, 'A month's tour to Northamptonshire, Leicestershire, &c. ', *Annals of Agriculture*, **16** (1791), pp. 534–5.

43. Quoted in P. Sharpe, 'Population and society', 1700–1840', in *CUHB*, p. 495.

44. P. Earle, *The Making of the English Middle Class: Business, Society and Family Life in London, 1660–1730* (1989), p. 108; Cotesworth MSS CP/4/96, 25 May 1723.

45. Scottish Record Office, Bill Chamber Process, I. 43,777, John Robinson v. Ralph Ashworth, 1778.

46. R. Campbell, *The London Tradesman* (1747), p. 193.

47. T. V. Jackson, 'British incomes circa 1800', *Economic History Review*, **52** (1999), pp. 257–83.

4   Urban Society

1. J. Holland, *The History, Antiquities, and Description of the Town and Parish of Workshop, in the County of Nottinghamshire* (Sheffield, 1826), p. 156.

2. W. Hutton, *The Life of William Hutton* (1817 edn), p. 115.

3. *Low-life: or One Half of the World, Knows not how the Other Half Lives* (1752), p. i.

4. P. Langford, *A Polite and Commercial People: England 1727–1783* (Oxford, 1989), pp. 1–7; quoted in R. S. Fitton and A. P. Wadsworth, *The Strutts and the Arkwrights, 1758–1830* (Manchester, 1958), pp. 109–10.

5. P. Borsay, 'The English urban renaissance: the development of provincial urban culture, *c.*1680–1760', in his *Eighteenth-Century Town*, pp. 180–1.

6. *Boswell's London Journal, 1762–1763*, ed. F. A. Pottle (1950), p. 309.

7. P. J. Corfield, 'Class by name and number in eighteenth-century Britain', in her *Language, History and Class* (1991), pp. 101–30.

8. K. P. Moritz, *Journeys of a German in England: A Walking Tour of England in 1782* (1983 edn), pp. 33–4. On the significance attached to clothing in this period, see B. Lemire, *Fashion's Favourites: The Cotton Trade and the Consumer, 1660–1800* (Oxford, 1991).

9. *London Magazine*, 1780, p. 197.

10. *The Female Tatler*, no. 17, 12–15 August 1709.

11. Tyne and Wear Archive, Keelmen's Papers, 394/9, 9 May 1738; P. J. Corfield, 'Dress for deference and dissent: hats and the decline of hat honour', *Costume*, **23** (1989), pp. 64–79.

12. Quoted in B. Hill, *Servants: English Domestics in the Eighteenth Century* (Oxford, 1996), p. 217.

13. *Macclesfield Courier*, 29 July 1826, quoted in G. Malmgreen, *Silk Town: Industry and Culture in Macclesfield, 1750–1835* (Hull, 1985), p. 69.

14. W. Hutton, *A History of Birmingham to the End of the Year 1780* (Birmingham, 1783 edn), pp. 27, 25–6; J. Aikin, *A Description of the Country from Thirty to Forty Miles around Manchester* (1795), pp. 388, 392.

15. Quoted in S. Nenadic, 'The rise of the urban middle class', in T. M. Devine and R. Mitchison (eds), *People and Society in Scotland*, vol. I: *1760–1830* (Edinburgh, 1989), p. 115.

16. D. Defoe, *A Plan of the English Commerce* (1730 edn), p. 100.

17. *A Foreign View of England in 1725–1727: The Letters of Monsieur de Saussure to his Family*, ed. M. van Muyden (1995 edn), p. 129; Elizabeth Montagu, *Her Correspondence, 1720–61*, ed. E. J. Climenson (1906), vol. 2, pp. 149, 202.

18. This issue is discussed at length in P. J. Corfield, 'The rivals: landed and other gentlemen', in N. B. Harte and R. Quinault (eds), *Land and Society in Britain, 1700–1914* (Manchester, 1996), pp. 8–12.

19. Langford, *Polite and Commercial People*, p. 121; P. Earle, *The Making of the English Middle Class* (1989), pp. 269–301; S. Nenadic, 'Middle-rank consumers and domestic culture in Edinburgh and Glasgow, 1720–1840', *Past and Present*, **145** (1994), pp. 122–56.

20. S. D'Cruze, 'The middling sort in eighteenth-century Colchester: independence, social relations and the community broker', in J. Barry and C. Brooks (eds), *The Middling Sort of People: Culture, Society and Politics in England, 1550–1800* (1994), pp. 186–7.

21. D. Defoe, *A Review of the State of the British Nation*, vol. 6, no. 36, 25 June 1709; no. 41, 7 July 1709.

22. G. C. Deering, *Nottinghamia Vetus et Nova* (Nottingham, 1751), p. 72. The debate on consumption is briefly summarized by Ellis, 'Consumption and wealth', in L. K. J. Glassey (ed.), *The Reigns of Charles II* (1997), pp. 199–210.

23. Quoted in T. M. Devine, 'The urban crisis', in Devine and G. Jackson (eds), *Glasgow*, vol. i: *Beginnings to 1830* (Manchester, 1994), p. 406.
24. 'Reminiscences of a septuagenarian', *Newark Advertiser*, 20 June 1894; C. Smith, 'Image and reality: two Nottinghamshire market towns in late Georgian England', *Midland History*, **17** (1992), pp. 59–74.
25. *The Diary of Thomas Turner, 1754–65*, ed. D. Vaisey (Oxford, 1984), pp. 3, 106.
26. J. Brewer, *The Pleasures of the Imagination: English Culture in the Eighteenth Century* (1997), pp. 550–7; R. Elbourne, *Music and Tradition in Early Industrial Lancashire, 1780–1840* (Woodbridge, 1980).
27. *Gloucester Journal*, 29 September 1794, 28 September 1818.
28. Quoted in G. Jackson, *Hull in the Eighteenth Century* (Oxford, 1972), p. 267; see also D. Neave, '"Violent idleness": the eighteenth-century East Riding gentleman at leisure', *Journal of Regional and Local Studies*, **11** (1991), pp. 3–15.
29. *Nottingham Journal*, 16 November 1781, 8 December 1781.
30. P. Clark, 'Small town, 1700–1840', in *CUHB*, p. 768.
31. P. Borsay, *The English Urban Renaissance* (Oxford, 1989), is the key text here, but these developments are also explored in P. Clark and R. Houston, 'Culture and leisure, 1700–1840', in *CUHB*, pp. 575–99; R. Sweet, *The English Town, 1680–1840: Government, Society and Culture* (1999), pp. 219–55.
32. For English examples, see M. Reed, 'The cultural role of small towns in England, 1600–1800', in Clark (ed.), *Small Towns in Early Modern Europe*, pp. 121–47.
33. T. Henry, 'On the advantages of literature and philosophy in general', *Memoirs of the Manchester Literary and Philosophical Society*, **1** (1785), pp. 7–29; C. W. Chalklin, 'Capital expenditure on building for cultural purposes in provincial England, 1730–1830', *Business History*, **22** (1980), pp. 51–70.
34. D. Defoe, *A Tour Through the Whole Island of Great Britain* (1962 edn), vol. 1, p. 186; M. Girouard, *The English Town* (1980), pp. 127–44.
35. M. Elwin, *The Noels and the Milbankes: Their Letters for Twenty-Five Years, 1767–92* (1967), p. 108; J. Austen, *Pride and Prejudice*, ed. F. W. Bradbrook (Oxford, 1970), pp. 7–8.
36. Quoted in A. Vickery, *The Gentleman's Daughter: Women's Lives in Georgian England* (Yale, 1998), p. 67; see also J. Ellis, '"On the town": women in Augustan England', *History Today* (December 1995), pp. 20–7.
37. *The Female Tatler*, no. 9, 25–29 July 1709.
38. P. Clark, *British Clubs and Societies, 1580–1800: The Origins of an Associational World* (Oxford, 2000); *Letters from Lady Jane Coke to her Friend Mrs Eyre at Derby, 1747–58*, ed. A. Rathbone (1899), p. 10.
39. See the arguments put forward in A. McInnes, 'The emergence of a leisure town: Shrewsbury, 1660–1760', *Past and Present*, 120 (1998), pp. 53–87; and Sweet, *English Town*, pp. 251–5.
40. Hutton, *History of Birmingham*, p. 128.
41. G. Chalmers, *An Estimate of the Comparative Strength of Great Britain* (1804 edn), pp. 303–4; J. Houghton, *A Collection of Letters for the Improvement of Husbandry and Trade* (1681–3), vol. 4, p. 177.
42. M. Harrison, *Crowds and History: Mass Phenomena in English Towns, 1790–1835* (Cambridge, 1988), pp. 102–39; D. A. Reid, 'Weddings, weekdays,

work and leisure in urban England, 1791–1911', *Past and Present*, **153** (1996), pp. 135–63.

43. Hutton, *Life*, pp. 100–1; T. S. Hendricks, 'The democratization of sport in eighteenth-century England', *Journal of Popular Culture*, **18** (1984), pp. 3–20.

44. *Report of the Select Committee on Children in Factories*, Parliamentary Papers 1818, vol. 3, p. 217.

45. The role of the public house in urban life is discussed in P. Clark, *The English Alehouse: A Social History, 1200–1800* (1983).

46. See M. Smith, *Religion in Industrial Society: Oldham and Saddleworth, 1740–1865* (Oxford, 1994), p. 98; Malmgreen, *Silk Town*, pp. 159–69.

47. *Report of the Select Committee on Public Walks*, Parliamentary Papers 1833, vol. 15, p. 405.

48. *Select Committee on Public Walks*, pp. 354, 66; H. Conway, *People's Parks: The Design and Development of Victorian Parks in Britain* (Cambridge, 1991), pp. 21–38.

5   Landscape and Environment

1. A. Phillip, *The Voyage of Governor Phillip to Botany Bay* (1789), p. v.

2. J. Austen, *Mansfield Park*, ed. J. Lucas (1970), p. 393; J. Thomas, *The East India Company and the Provinces in the Eighteenth Century*, vol. i: *Portsmouth and the East India Company, 1700–1815* (1999).

3. P. J. Corfield, 'Walking the city streets: the urban odyssey in eighteenth-century England', *Journal of Urban History*, **16** (1990), pp. 132–74.

4. G. C. Deering, *Nottinghamia Vetus et Nova* (Nottingham, 1751), pp. 9, 17.

5. *Low-Life* (1764 edn), p. 32; J. Ellis, 'Georgian town gardens', *History Today*, **50** (January 2000), pp. 38–45.

6. Quoted in R. A. Houston, *Social Change in the Age of Enlightenment: Edinburgh, 1660–1760* (Oxford, 1994), p. 125.

7. M. E. Falkus, 'Lighting in the dark ages of English economic history: town streets before the industrial revolution', in D. C. Coleman and A. H. John (eds), *Trade, Government and Economy in Pre-Industrial England* (1976), pp. 248–73.

8. R. Houston, 'Fire and filth: Edinburgh's environment, 1660–1760', *Book of the Old Edinburgh Club*, **3** (1994), pp. 25–36; M. Jenner, 'The politics of London air: John Evelyn's *Fumifugium* and the Restoration', *Historical Journal*, **38** (1995), pp. 535–51.

9. W. Hutton, *History of Birmingham to the End of the Year 1780* (Birmingham, 1783 edn), p. 100.

10. On this issue see R. Scola, *Feeding the Victorian City: The Food Supply of Manchester, 1770–1870* (1992), pp. 150–61.

11. K. Thomas, *Man and the Natural World: Changing Attitudes in England, 1500–1800* (Oxford, 1983), pp. 294–5.

12. D. Defoe, *A Tour Through the Whole Island of Great Britain* (1962 edn), vol. ii, p. 59.

13. R. Southey, *Letters from England*, ed. J. Simmons, p. 198.

14. T. Fairchild, *The City Gardener* (1722), pp. 6–7, 11, 48–9; *Kalm's Account of his Visit to England on his way to America in 1748*, ed. J. Lucas (1892), pp. 88–9.

15. J. Fletcher, 'History and statistics of the present system of sewerage in the metropolis', *Journal of the Statistical Society of London*, **7** (1844), pp. 156–7.

16. Deering, *Nottinghamia*, p. 6.

17. J. Blackner, *The History of Nottingham* (Nottingham, 1815), p. 66.

18. R. Sweet, *The Writing of Urban Histories in Eighteenth-Century England* (Oxford, 1997), pp. 124,131–4.

19. For a contrasting view, see M. Pelling, 'Population and disease, estrangement and belonging', in *CUHB*, p. 219.

20. R. Porter, 'Cleaning up the Great Wen: public health in eighteenth-century London', in W. F. Bynum and R. Porter (eds,) *Living and Dying in London, Medical History*, supplement no. 11 (1991), pp. 68–71.

21. *Gentleman's Magazine*, **17** (1747), pp. 63–4.

22. British Library, Bowes MSS, Add. MSS 40747, ff. 164–5, 20 March. 1718.

23. Hutton, *History of Birmingham*, p. 101.

24. P. Borsay, *The English Urban Renaissance: Culture as Society in the Provincial Town, 1660–1770* (Oxford, 1989), chs 2–4, is essential reading on this topic.

25. W. Enfield, *An Essay towards the History of Leverpool* (Warrington, 1773), p. 21.

26. H. Bourne, *The History of Newcastle* (Newcastle, 1736), p. 109.

27. E. L. Jones and M. E. Falkus, 'Urban improvement and the English economy in the seventeenth and eighteenth centuries', in Borsay (ed.), *Eighteenth-century Town*, pp. 145–6.

28. J. Innes and N. Rogers, 'Politics and government', in *CUHB*, pp. 536–8, 540–3; D. Eastwood, *Government and Community in the English Provinces, 1700–1870* (1997), pp. 64–73; Sweet, *English Town*, pp. 42–56.

29. D. Cruickshank and N. Burton, *Life in the Georgian City* (1990), pp. 3–22; Sweet, *English Town*, pp. 76–89.

30. Hertfordshire Record Office, Panshanger MSS, DE/P F. 58, 12 September 1717.

31. Cruikshank and Burton, *Life in the Georgian City*, pp. 99–133.

32. C. Lucas, *An Essay on Waters* (1756), vol. 1, p. 127; *Kalm's Account of his Visit*, p. 64.

33. A. Hardy, 'Water and the search for public health in London in the eighteenth and nineteenth centuries', *Medical History*, **28** (1984), pp. 262–4.

34. M. Durey, *The Return of the Plague: British Society and the Cholera, 1831–2* (Dublin, 1979), pp. 27–49; D. E. Lipschutz, 'The water question in London, 1827–31', *Bulletin of the History of Medicine*, **42** (1968), pp. 524–5.

35. For a more detailed account, see M. Reed, 'The transformation of urban space, 1700–1840', in *CUHB*, ch. 18.

36. R. Parkinson, *The Present Condition of the Labouring Poor in Manchester* (1841), pp. 12–13; L. Faucher, *Manchester in 1844: Its Present Condition and Future Prospects* (rep. 1969), pp. 69–70.

37. *Letters from Bath 1766–67 by the Revd John Penrose*, ed. B. Mitchell and H. Penrose (Gloucester, 1983), p. 42; *Byng's Tours: The Journals of the Hon. John Byng, 1781–92*, ed. D. Souden (1991), p. 211.

38. J. Aikin, *A Description of the Country from Thirty to Forty Miles around Manchester* (1795), p. 202.

6 Identity and Community

1. *Is This the Truth? A Poem* (Newcastle), 1741, p. 4.
2. These issues are discussed in greater detail in R. Sweet, *The English Town, 1680–1840* (1999), pp. 75–114; I. Maver, 'The guardianship of the community: civic authority prior to 1833', in Devine and Jackson (eds), *Glasgow*, pp. 239–77.
3. N. Ellison, *The Obligations and Opportunities of doing Good to the Poor* (1710), p. 13; quoted in J. Ellis, 'A dynamic society: social relations in Newcastle upon Tyne, 1660–1760', in Clark (ed.), *Transformation of English Provincial Towns*, p. 82.
4. T. Hitchcock et al. (eds), *Chronicling Poverty: The Voices and Strategies of the English Poor, 1640–1840* (Basingstoke, 1997); R. A. Houston, *Social Change in the Age of Enlightenment: Edinburgh 1660–1760* (Oxford, 1994), pp. 234–83.
5. Quoted in J. W. H. Hill, *Georgian Lincoln* (Cambridge, 1966), p. 40; see also A. Randall and A. Charlesworth (eds), *Markets, Market Culture and Popular Protest in Eighteenth-century Britain and Ireland* (Liverpool, 1996).
6. J. Barry, 'Bristol pride: civic identity in Bristol *c.*1640–1775', in M. Dresser and P. Ollerenshaw (eds), *The Making of Modern Bristol* (Tiverton, 1996), pp. 25–47. These issues are discussed more fully in R. Sweet, *The Writing of Urban Histories in Eighteenth-Century England* (Oxford, 1997).
7. Cotesworth MSS CN/9/147, 18 September 1718; W. Hutton, *The Life of William Hutton* (1817 edn), p. 112.
8. W. Wordsworth, *The Prelude*, (1805), ed. E. de Selincourt (Oxford, 1970), lines 117–20.
9. L. Simond, *An American in Regency England*, ed. C. Hibber (1968) p. 26; Hutton, *Life*, p. 154.
10. Quoted in Houston, *Social Change in the Age of Enlightenment*, p. 162.
11. C. Lis and H. Solly, 'Neighbourhood social change in west European cities: sixteenth to nineteenth centuries', *International Review of Social History*, **38** (1993), pp. 1–30; P. Earle, *A City Full of People: Men and Women of London, 1650–1750* (1994), pp. 171–6, 210–6.
12. D. R. Green, *From Artisans to Paupers: Economic Change and Poverty in London, 1790–1870* (Aldershot, 1995), pp. 93–4; Phillips, 'Working and moving', in P. Corfield and D. Keene, *Work in Towns, 850–1850* (Leicester, 1990), pp. 193–7.
13. L. H. Lees, *Exiles of Erin: Irish Migrants in Victorian London* (Manchester, 1979), pp. 55–87; W. Sloan, 'Religious affiliation and the immigrant experience: Catholic Irish and Protestant Highlanders in Glasgow, 1830–50', in T. M. Devine (ed.), *Irish Immigrants and Scottish Society in the Nineteenth and Twentieth Centuries* (Edinburgh, 1991), pp. 67–90.
14. J. Barry, 'Bourgeois collectivism? Urban association and the middling sort', in J. Barry and C. Brooks (eds), *The Middling Sort of People: Culture, Society and Politics in England, 1550–1800* (1994), p. 89; S. D'Cruze, 'The middling sort', ibid., pp. 181–207.
15. Hutton, *Life*, pp. 114–15; P. Clark, 'Migrants in the city: the process of social adaptation in English towns, 1500–1800', in P. Clark and D. Souden (eds), *Migration and Society in Early Modern England* (1987), pp. 280–6.

16. M. Hunt, 'Wife beating, domesticity and women's independence in eighteenth-Century London', *Gender and History*, **4** (1992), p. 23.

17. See P. Thane, 'Old people and their families in the English past', in M. Daunton (ed.), *Charity, Self Interest and Welfare in the English Past* (1996), p. 113–38.

18. For a more detailed discussion of urban government, see J. Innes and N. Rogers, 'Politics and government', in *CUHB*, ch. 16; Sweet, *English Town*, chs 2, 4 and 5.

19. T. Short, *New Observations on City, Town and Country Bills of Mortality* (1750), p. 79; D. Defoe, *A Tour Through the Whole Island of Great Britain* (1962 edn), vol. ii, p. 37; W. Richards, *The History of Lynn* (1812), pp. 783, 972.

20. P. Langford, *Public Life and the Propertied Englishman* (Oxford, 1990), pp. 437–509.

21. M. Elwin, *The Noels and the Milbankes: Their Letters for Twenty-Five Years, 1767–92* (1967), p. 216; Elizabeth Montagu, *Correspondence*, vol. 2, p. 207.

22. Quoted in Hill, *Georgian Lincoln*, p. 40; J. M. Ellis, 'Urban conflict and popular violence: the Guildhall riots of 1740 in Newcastle on Tyne', *International Review of Social History*, **25** (1980), p. 341.

23. J. Black, 'Eighteenth-century English political history: the local dimension', *Local Historian*, **23** (1993), p. 105; see below, pp. 133–4.

24. P. Borsay, *The English Urban Renaissance* (Oxford, 1989), pp. 280–1; *Passages from the Diaries of Mrs Lybbe Powys*, ed. E. J. Climenson (1899), p. 17.

25. *Nottingham Journal*, 1 December 1781.

26. See Sweet, *Writing of Urban Histories*, pp. 187–235; S. Nenadic, 'The middle ranks and modernisation', in Devine and Jackson (eds), *Glasgow*, pp. 292–301.

27. S. Poole, '"Till our liberties be secure": popular sovereignty and public space in Bristol, 1750–1850', *Urban History*, **26** (1999), pp. 40–54.

28. A. Henstock (ed.), *The Diary of Abigail Gawthern of Nottingham, 1751–1810* (Thoroton Society, 33, 1980), p. 36; N. W. Wraxall, *Historical Memoirs of My Own Time: 1772–84* (1904), p. 199.

29. Quoted in G. S. Messinger, *Manchester in the Victorian Age: The Half-Known City* (Manchester, 1985), p. 90.

30. *The Diary of Frances, Lady Shelley, 1787–1817*, ed. R. Edgcumbe (1912), vol. i, p. 3.

31. J. A. Rouquet, *The Present State of the Arts in England* (1755), p. 17; G. C. Deering, *Nottinghamia Vetus et nova* (Nottingham, 1751), pp. 75–6; P. Langford, *Polite and Commercial People* (Oxford 1989), pp. 1–7.

32. E. Gaskell, *Wives and Daughters*, ed. F. G. Smith (1969), p. 329; *Montagu Correspondence*, vol. i, p. 29.

33. These themes are explored in J. Raven, *Judging New Wealth: Popular Publishing and Responses to Commerce in England, 1750–1800* (Oxford, 1992); E. Copeland, *Women Writing about Money: Women's Fiction in England, 1790–1820* (Cambridge, 1995).

34. Gateshead Public Library, Ellison Manuscripts, A/36a/35, 9 May 1716; J. Brewer, *The Pleasures of the Imagination* (1997), pp. 510–13.

35. Quoted in Devine, 'Urban crisis', in *Glasgow*, vol. i, p. 406; J. Pagan (ed.), *Glasgow: Past and Present* (Glasgow, 1884), p. 32.

36. P. Sharpe, 'Population and society, 1700–1840', in *CUHB*, pp. 492–3; B. Joseph, *Address to the Seatholders of the Liverpool Congregation* (Liverpool, 1838), p. 4.

37. Quoted in A. Clark, 'Whores and gossips: sexual reputation in London, 1770–1825', in A. Angerman et al. (eds), *Current Issues in Women's History* (1989), p. 236.

38. *Sophie in London, 1786*, ed. C. Williams (1933), p. 112; *Nottingham Journal*, 1 December 1781.

39. P. J. Corfield, *The Impact of English Towns, 1700–1800* (Oxford, 1982), pp. 144–5.

40. See Houston, *Social Change in the Age of Enlightenment*, pp. 8, 132–46.

41. R. Hutton, *The Rise and Fall of Merry England: The Ritual Year, 1400–1700* (Oxford, 1996), pp. 111–12, 227.

42. H. Cunningham, *Leisure in the Industrial Revolution: c.1780–c.1880* (1980), pp. 15, 51; see above, pp. 82–6.

43. Quoted in Jackson, 'The ports', in *CUHB*, p. 729. See also W. H. Fraser, 'From civic gospel to municipal socialism', in D. Fraser (ed.), *Cities, Class and Communication* (Hemel Hempstead, 1990), p. 64.

7   Towns and Change

1. B. Disraeli, *Coningsby* (1927 edn), pp. 160–1.

2. F. Braudel, *Civilization and Capitalism: The Structures of Everyday Life* (1981), p. 479; W. Hutton, *The Life of William Hutton* (1817 edn), p. 111. For a more sceptical approach, see M. J. Daunton, 'Towns and economic growth in eighteenth-century England', in P. Abrams and E. A. Wrigley, *Towns in Societies: Essays in Economic History and Historical Sociology* (Cambridge, 1979), pp. 245–72.

3. Anon., *Hell upon Earth: Or the Town in an Uproar* (1729), p. 1; W. A. Speck, *Literature and Society in Eighteenth-Century England, 1680–1820: Ideology, Politics and Culture* (1998).

4. D. Eastwood, *Government and Community in the English Provinces, 1700–1870* (1997), p. 62.

5. K. P. Moritz, *Journeys of a German in England* (1983 edn), p. 176; F. C. Laird, *The Beauties of England and Wales*, vol. 12 (1810), p. 102; *Nottingham Review*, 17 April 1829.

6. Quoted in A. Briggs, *Victorian Cities* (reprinted 1990), p. 134; *Byng's Tours*, p. 183.

7. J. Holland, *The History, Antiquities and Description of the Town and Parish of Worksop* (Sheffield, 1826), p. 156.

8. R. Vaughan, *The Age of Great Cities: or, Modern Society Viewed in its Relation to Intelligence, Morals and Religion* (1843), p. 152; R. J. Morris, 'Civil society and the nature of urbanism: Britain, 1750–1850', *Urban History*, **25** (1998), pp. 289–301.

9. J. Golinski, *Science as Public Culture: Chemistry and Enlightenment in Britain, 1760–1820* (Cambridge, 1992), pp. 56–63; T. Kelly, *A History of Adult Education in Great Britain* (Liverpool, 1992), chs 6–8.

10. Quoted in J. Money, *Experience and Identity: Birmingham and the West Mid-lands, 1760–1800* (Manchester, 1977), p. 219; S. Drescher, 'Public opinion and the destruction of British colonial slavery', in J. Walvin (ed.), *Slavery and British Society, 1776–1848* (1982), pp. 22–48.
11. Quoted in M. Dresser, 'Protestants, Catholics and Jews: religious difference and political status in Bristol, 1750–1850', in Dresser and Ollerenshaw (eds), *Making of Modern Bristol*, pp. 100,106.
12. L. Colley, *Britons: Forging the Nation, 1707–1837* (1992), p. 36; C. Haydon, *Anti-Catholicism in Eighteenth-Century England, c.1714–80: A political and social study* (Manchester, 1993).
13. *Morning Post*, 12 July 1780; *Morning Herald*, 12 March 1781, quoted in H. Barker, *Newspapers, Politics and Public Opinion in Late Eighteenth-Century England* (Oxford, 1998), pp. 89–90.
14. Moritz, *Journeys of a German in England*, pp. 64, 33; R. A. Houston, *Social Change in the Age of Enlightenment: Edinburgh, 1660–1760* (Oxford, 1994), p. 222.
15. Northumberland Record Office, Carr-Ellison (Hedgeley) MSS 855/5: A. Hollier to I. Carr, 31 January 1763.
16. P. Borsay, *The English Urban Renaissance,* (Oxford, 1989), pp. 177–8; K. Thomas, *Man and the Natural World* (Oxford, 1983), pp. 143–91.
17. F. M. Trollope, *Paris and the Parisians in 1835* (1836), vol. i, p. 229; *Sheffield Advertiser*, 19 February 1790. For a general introduction to these issues, see P. Clark and R. Houston, 'Culture and leisure', in *CUHB*, pp. 599–604.
18. J. Wilson, *Memories of a Labour Leader* (1910), p. 64; B. Bushaway, '"Tacit, unsuspected, but still implicit faith": alternative belief in nineteenth-century rural England', in T. Harris (ed.), *Popular Culture in England, c.1500–1850* (Basingstoke, 1995), pp. 189–215.
19. J. E. Bradley, *Religion, Revolution, and English Radicalism: Nonconformity in Eighteenth-Century Politics and Society* (Cambridge, 1990); R. Sweet, *The English Town, 1680–1840* (1999), pp. 207–18.
20. W. C. Lukis (ed.), *The Family Memoirs of the Rev. William Stukeley, MD* (Surtees Society, 73, 1880), vol. i, p. 109; J. Boswell, *Life of Johnson*, ed. R. W. Chapman (Oxford, 1970), p. 708.
21. M. Sanderson, *Education, Economic Change and Society in England, 1780–1870* (Cambridge, 1995 edn), pp. 1–10; R. A. Houston, *Scottish Literacy and Scottish Identity: Illiteracy and Society in Scotland and Northern England, 1600–1800* (Cambridge, 1985), pp. 42–70.
22. *Annual Register* (1761), p. 207. The debate is neatly summarized in P. Borsay, 'The London connection: cultural diffusion and the eighteenth-century provincial town', *London Journal*, **19** (1994), pp. 21–35; R. Sweet, *Writing of Urban Histories* (Oxford, 1997), ch. 6.
23. P. Langford, *A Polite and Commercial People* (Oxford, 1989), p. 71.
24. J. Brewer, *The Pleasures of the Imagination* (1997), p. 494.
25. J. Blackner, *The History of Nottingham* (Nottingham, 1815), p. 231; W. Hutton, *A History of Birmingham to the end of the year 1780* (Birmingham,1783 edn), p. 18.
26. L. Weatherill, *Consumer Behaviour* (1996 edn), p. 83; Nenadic, 'Middle-rank consumers', pp. 132–3. See also D. Levine, 'Consumer goods and capitalist modernization', *Journal of Interdisciplinary History*, **22** (1991), pp. 66–77.

27. T. O. Morgan, *New Guide to Aberystwyth and its Environs* (Aberystwyth, 1851 edn), pp. 88–9.

28. W. J. Lewis, 'Some aspects of the history of Aberystwyth: ii. "The Brighton of Wales"', *Ceredigion*, **4** (1960), pp. 19–35; J. K. Walton, *The English Seaside Resort: A Social History 1750–1914* (Leicester, 1983), pp. 45–59.

29. J. Langton, 'The industrial revolution and regional geography of England', *Transactions of the Institute of British Geographers*, **9** (1984), pp. 145–67.

30. D. Wahrman, 'National society, communal culture: an argument about the recent historiography of eighteenth-century Britain', *Social History*, **17** (1992), p. 45.

31. J. Barry, 'Provincial town culture, 1640–1780: urbane or civic?', in J. H. Pittock and A. Wear (eds), *Interpretation and Cultural History* (Basingstoke, 1991), pp. 198–234.

32. Defoe, *Tour*, vol. ii, p. 252; British Library, Bowes MSS, Add. MSS 40747, ff. 184–5, 22 April 1721; Bourne, *History of Newcastle*, p. 159.

33. *The Letters of the Rev. John Wesley*, ed. J. Telford (1931), vol. iv, pp. 279–80; *The Nottingham Journal; or, Cresswell's Weekly Advertiser*, 15 May 1762.

34. T. Fairchild, *The City Gardener* (1722), p. 43.

35. I. Mills, *From Tinder-box to the Larger Light: Threads from the Life of John Mills, Banker* (Manchester, 1899), p. 103.

36. C. B. Estabrook, *Urbane and Rustic England: Cultural Ties and Social Spheres in Provinces, 1660–1780* (Manchester, 1998), p. 13.

37. K. Morgan, *Bristol and the Atlantic Trade in the Eighteenth Century* (Cambridge, 1993); see above, p. 14.

38. D. Hey, *The Fiery Blades of Hallamshire: Sheffield and its Neighbourhood, 1660–1740* (Leicester, 1991), ch. 6; J. Stobart, 'Social and geographical contexts of property transmission in the eighteenth century', in Stobart and A. Owens (eds), *Property and Inheritance, 1700–1900* (Aldershot, 2000), ch. 5.

39. E. A. Wrigley, 'City and country in the past: a sharp divide or a continuum?', *Historical Research*, **64** (1991), pp. 107–20; see above, pp. 7–10.

40. P. J. Corfield, *The Impact of English Towns, 1700–1800* (Oxford, 1982), p. 186.

41. The shift in attitudes is summarized in Thomas, *Man and the Natural World*, pp. 243–54; A. Hemingway, *Landscape, Imagery and Urban Culture in Early Nineteenth-Century Britain* (Cambridge, 1992), pp. 72–5.

42. Quoted in D. Cruickshank and N. Burton, *Life in the Georgian City* (1990), p. 3; J. Soane, *Lectures on Architecture, 1809–36*, ed. A. T. Bolton (1929), pp. 156–7.

43. Fairchild, *City Gardener*, p. 12; J. Archer, '*Rus in urbe*: classical ideas of country and city in British town planning', *Studies in Eighteenth-Century Culture*, **12** (1983), pp.159–86.

44. J. Stuart, *Critical Observations on the Buildings and Improvements of London* (1771), pp. 10–12.

45. L. Davidoff and C. Hall, *Family Fortunes: Men and Women of the English Middle Class, 1780–1850* (1987), pp. 368–9; C. B. Estabrook, *Urbane and Rustic England* (Manchester, 1998), pp. 253–75

46. Estabrook, *Urbane and Rustic England*, p. 279.

47. R. Paulson, *Hogarth*, vol. iii: *Art and Politics, 1750–64* (Cambridge, 1993), pp. 17–26, plates 2–3; W. Wycherley, *The Country Wife* (1675), Act 2, Scene 1.

48. Wahrman, 'National society, communal culture', p. 71.

FURTHER READING

Given the vast amount of material published on the development of towns in the 'long' eighteenth century, it is difficult to keep a guide to further reading within manageable proportions. What is offered here is therefore neither a comprehensive bibliography nor a definitive selection but a guide to some of the most influential and useful works for those coming new to the subject.

General surveys of eighteenth-century society

M. J. Daunton, *Progress and Poverty: An Economic and Social History of Britain, 1700–1850* (Oxford, 1995).

J. Gregory and J. Stevenson, *The Longman Companion to Britain in the Eighteenth Century, 1688–1820* (2000).

K. Morgan, *The Brith of Industrial Britain: Social Change, 1750–1850* (2000)

R. Price, *British Society, 1680–1880: Dynamism, Containment and Change* (Cambridge, 1999).

J. Rule, *Albion's People: English Society, 1714–1815* (1992).

Studies of urban development

P. Borsay (ed.), *The Eighteenth-century Town: A Reader in English Urban History, 1688–1820* (1990).

P. Borsay, *The English Urban Renaissance: Culture and Society in the Provincial Town, 1660–1770* (Oxford, 1989).

P. Clark (ed.), *The Cambridge Urban History of Britain*, vol. ii. *c.1540–c.1840* (Cambridge, 2000).

P. J. Corfield, *The Impact of English Towns, 1700–1800* (Oxford, 1982).

M. Girouard, *The English Town* (Yale, 1990).

T. Hitchcock and R. Shoemaker, *Economic Growth and Social Change in the Eighteenth-Century Town* (TLTP History Consortium Courseware, 1995).

R. Sweet, *The English Town, 1680–1840: Government, Society and Culture* (1999).

J. Walvin, *English Urban Life, 1776–1851* (1984).

Recently published specialist works

J. Barry and C. Brooks (eds), *The Middling Sort of People: Culture, Society and Politics in England, 1550–1800* (1994).

J. Brewer, *The Pleasures of the Imagination: English Culture in the Eighteenth Century* (1997).

P. Clark, *British Clubs and Societies, 1580–1800: The Origins of an Associational World* (Oxford, 2000).

P. Clark (ed.), *Small Towns in Early Modern Europe* (Cambridge, 1995).

P. J. Corfield, *Power and the Professions in Britain, 1700–1850* (1995).

D. Cruickshank and N. Burton, *Life in the Georgian City* (1990).

L. Davison et al. (eds), *Stilling the Grumbling Hive: The Response to Social and Economic Problems in England, 1689–1750* (Stroud, 1992).

T. M. Devine and G. Jackson (eds), *Glasgow*, vol. i: *Beginnings to 1830* (Manchester, 1994).

H. T. Dickinson, *The Politics of the People in Eighteenth-Century Britain* (1994).

P. Earle, *A City Full of People: Men and Women of London, 1650–1750* (1994).

P. Earle, *The Making of the English Middle Class: Business, Society and Family Life in London, 1660–1730* (London, 1989).

D. Eastwood, *Government and Community in the English Provinces, 1700–1870* (1997).

C. B. Estabrook, *Urbane and Rustic England: Cultural Ties and Social Spheres in the Provinces, 1660–1780* (Manchester, 1998).

P. D. Halliday, *Dismembering the Body Politic: Partisan Politics in England's Towns, 1650–1730* (Cambridge, 1998).

P. Hembry, *The English Spa, 1560–1815: A Social History* (1990).

T. Henderson, *Disorderly Women in Eighteenth-Century London: Prostitution and Control in the Metropolis, 1730–1830* (1999).

D. Hey, *The Fiery Blades of Hallamshire: Sheffield and its Neighbourhood, 1660–1740* (Leicester, 1991).

T. Hitchcock et al. (eds), *Chronicling Poverty: The Voices and Strategies of the English Poor, 1640–1840* (Basingstoke, 1997).

K. Honeyman, *Women, Gender and Industrialization in England, 1700–1870* (Basingstoke, 2000).

E. Hopkins, *The Rise of the Manufacturing Town: Birmingham and the Industrial Revolution* (Stroud, 1998).

R. A. Houston, *Social Change in an Age of Enlightenment: Edinburgh, 1660–1800* (Oxford, 1994).

M. Hunt, *The Middling Sort: Commerce, Gender, and the Family in England, 1680–1780* (Berkeley, 1996).

J. Landers, *Death and the Metropolis: Studies in the Demographic History of London, 1670–1830* (Cambridge, 1993).

P. Langford, *Public Life and the Propertied Englishman, 1689–1798* (Oxford, 1991).

T. Meldrum, *Domestic Service and Gender, 1660–1750: Life and Work in the London Household* (2000).

R. J. Morris, *Class, Sect and Party: The Making of the British Middle Class: Leeds, 1820–1850* (1990).

R. Porter, *London: A Social History* (1994).

A. Randall and A. Charlesworth (eds), *Markets, Market Culture and Popular Protest in Eighteenth-Century Britain and Ireland* (Liverpool, 1996).

N. Rogers, *Crowds, Culture and Politics in Georgian Britain* (Oxford, 1998).

L. D. Schwarz, *London in the Age of Industrialisation: Entrepreneurs, Labour Force and Living Conditions, 1700–1850* (Cambridge, 1992).

P. Sharpe, *Adapting to Capitalism: Working Women in the English Economy, 1700–1850* (1996).

R. Sweet, *The Writing of Urban Histories in Eighteenth-Century England* (Oxford, 1997).

I. D. Whyte, *Migration and Society in Britain, 1550–1830* (Basingstoke, 2000).

J. G. Williamson, *Coping with City Growth During the British Industrial Revolution* (Cambridge, 1990).

K. Wilson, *The Sense of the People: Politics, Culture and Imperialism in England, 1715–85* (Cambridge, 1994).

INDEX

171